WHY
THE BEST MAN
FOR THE JOB IS
A WOMAN

WHY

THE BEST MAN

FOR THE JOB IS

A WOMAN

THE UNIQUE FEMALE QUALITIES OF LEADERSHIP

ESTHER WACHS BOOK

HarperBusiness
An Imprint of HarperCollins*Publishers*

HarperCollins books may be purchased for educational, business, or sales promotional use. For information please write: Special Markets Department, HarperCollins Publishers Inc., 10 East 53rd Street, New York, NY 10022.

FIRST EDITION

Designed by William Ruoto

Printed on acid-free paper

Library of Congress Cataloging-in-Publication Data has been applied for

ISBN 0-06-661986-6

00 01 02 03 04 ❖/RRD 10 9 8 7 6 5 4 3 2 1

To my husband, Leslie,
my children, Sophie and Charles,
and my parents, Peggy and Ellis Wachs

CONTENTS

ACKNOWLEDGMENTS

A book is much more than a solo endeavor, and I would like to thank all the wonderful people who helped me fulfill this dream.

I thank my loyal friend and editor, Laureen Connelly Rowland, for her critical thinking, valuable insights, and thoughtful guidance that helped me navigate the journey of writing a book. She believed in the project, and her strong support never waned. She gave me momentum. I also am deeply indebted to my publisher, Adrian Zackheim, and to Lisa Berkowitz, who had the vision to make this book a reality. And I thank my agent, Jane Dystel, for her support from the outset. Of course, I must thank the women executives in this book for taking the time out of their hectic schedules to participate.

I also thank my friends, colleagues, and family who took the time to read sections of the book and share with me their valuable thoughts that contributed to the writing: Eric Wahlgren, Peggy Wachs, Ellis Wachs, and Leslie Book. Eric, in particular, deserves special kudos for helping me get over the hump. Thanks to Ken Hyatt as well. I thank my sisters, Elizabeth Sahlman and Margie Weingarten, for their moral support as well. A final thanks goes to my aunt Hensy, whose strength and will serve as an inspiration.

INTRODUCTION

Wanted: A topflight executive to rev up a venerable Dow 30 company scrambling to adjust to the Internet era. Ideal candidate must have stellar management experience and cutting-edge ideas for turning the old-line company into a lean, mean, on-line machine without abandoning its tried-and-true strengths. The ability to develop broad goals, the financial know-how to deliver consistently fat profits for share-holders, and the drive to jump-start the company's operations are also a must. No lily-livered types need apply. Oh yeah, salary close to $100 million in cash and stock options.

When Hewlett-Packard Company's board went hunting for a new number one, it cast a wide net to find a suitable candidate—and selected a woman. After screening 100 possible applicants, the board of the Palo Alto–based computer giant made a unanimous choice— Carleton (Carly) Fiorina, the forty-five-year-old former president of the $20 billion global service provider business of Lucent Technologies. HP bet on Fiorina to restore momentum to a company that had been a leader in the personal computer revolution in the 1980s but had missed the Internet boat. HP had cast aside a tradition of hiring leaders from within its own ranks to attract Fiorina, who had become a Lucent star when she oversaw that company's successful IPO and lured big clients to speed its growth. In July 1999, she became the first outsider ever to lead one of the pillars of Silicon Valley industry.

With revolutionary changes in corporate structures, a new breed of leader is emerging, and that breed is female. Women are rising in the ranks of dozens of industries not traditionally welcoming or supportive of females, including telecommunications, computing, e-commerce, advertising, energy, consulting, television, information technology, and hospitality. A growing number of female chief executive officers and presidents have replaced men or excelled over rivals in male-dominated industries because they possess the qualities of leadership that top firms are seeking today. These women are not only driven individuals who are skilled at marketing and sales, but they wield considerable financial skills and have a talent for managing people in a fast-paced economy bent on nonstop innovation. They all display an uncanny ability to identify and hone in on opportunities that others simply do not see.

These female executives who are reaching the pinnacle of their professions represent a new leadership paradigm distinct from anything that's come before. Unlike their male peers, predecessors, or even the women who have succeeded in the past, these women embrace their femininity, using it to their advantage in business, while picking and choosing the most effective tried-and-true techniques regardless of gender origin. In the past, many women business leaders assumed traditionally masculine traits. To run a company, they became domineering, authoritative, and "tough." But the women featured in these pages assert themselves in a different way. Rather than simply issuing orders to achieve strong results, new paradigm leaders create an independent vision that inspires their employees. They rebuild the rules of their businesses to fuel growth. They possess a laser focus on achieving objectives. They use their financial and management savvy to transform their companies. And they foster collegial relationships with employees and clients by relating to these people in a "high-touch" way. They are obsessed with customer preferences, and they have the courage to withstand opposition. Each of these female executives has a wide range of skills in her arsenal that complement teamwork and partnering, hallmarks of the Information Age. Nearly all have achieved revenues well over $100 million. This book examines some of the most powerful women in American business, and reveals the similarities in the way they run their companies as well as the reasons behind their progress.

What makes these fourteen women successful? First, each has a gravity-defying level of self-confidence, which drives her to assume an extraordinarily high level of risk and to disregard precedent to go her own way. These female executives have earned their reputations in businesses in which others failed or discounted, or in uncharted territories others avoided. Even those who inherited senior positions from influential husbands or fathers made key decisions that their renowned and beloved predecessors would have opposed.

Second, these women are gifted with a preternatural sense of exactly what their customers want—an instinct that helps them anticipate change and capitalize on it. Instead of punting this task of handling clients to senior managers, these women own the function themselves. They all spend a lot of time in this area, whether calling customers on the phone, conducting face-to-face meetings, contacting them through e-mail, or coming up with novel ways to assess customer satisfaction instead of simply conducting the occasional focus group. Despite the broad range of fields in which these women work, each maintains a missionary zeal for understanding consumers and a visceral drive to deepen bonds between the companies they run and their clients. These women understand deeply that customer service is a do-or-die hallmark of the Knowledge Era, and make it a top priority.

Third, all of these women display their feminine side when it comes to managing employees and attracting customers. At a time in business when most executives are fixated on bits and bytes, these women foster a more collegial environment in their companies by employing traditionally feminine qualities like nurturing, displaying empathy, engendering loyalty and respect, and playing down their own egos to play up the accomplishments of the team. Their skill in abolishing hierarchies, collaborating with employees, and connecting with customers helps them excel in a highly competitive digital age in which partnering is a vital competitive advantage. They do not use these abilities simply because they are feminine qualities, but to lure customers and keep talented employees.

Why the new approach? Simply copying male leadership styles did not usher women into top jobs at America's leading companies. During the 1980s, the era of power dressing and bulging shoulder pads for female executives, women made scant progress toward entering the boardroom. Even in 1999, women filled just 12 percent of senior executive positions in the Fortune 500—an increase of only 3 percent since 1995, according to Catalyst, a nonprofit research organization that tracks the representation of women in American corporations. And in a recent study of 200 Internet companies, executive-search consultants at Spencer Stuart discovered that women held only 2 percent of board seats.

But if female chief executive officers are rare, many women are now represented at the highest corporate levels, and those who have gained the spotlight hold influential posts. Most of the women in this book believe that gender gives them innate advantages. And most of these women believe that the gender-based differences for which they were once belittled have become distinct advantages in our new economy. Rigid hierarchies and top-down management approaches are as outmoded now as the eight-track tape. With the advent of the Information Age, managers have had to adopt and perform different functions just to stay in a game marked by intense global competition. Whether in information technology or other sophisticated service fields, skilled employees are working more independently, contributing to problem solving, focusing on customers, and laboring to cut costs. Workers are no longer paid simply to do, but to think. What's more, following an era of downsizing, today's knowledge workers chase the best opportunity offering the greatest chance for learning new skills, getting rich, and advancing their careers. Because of this trend, attracting and keeping talent has become a tougher and more essential part of a manager's job. As a result, managers have adopted the new role of coordinating, facilitating, coaching, supporting, and nurturing their employees. They must combine such abilities with the competence to be decisive and strong.

The women who appear in this book understand the new economy and have clearly made significant progress—they lead high-profile firms from Internet pioneers to prominent television networks. The secret of their success lies somewhere in these three lessons—they are extremely self-confident, they possess a keen sense of customer demands, and they tap into their feminine side to lead. The number of females at the top is surely growing—after all, women comprise the majority (51 percent) of the population, and many have only recently amassed the over twenty years of management experience common among prominent business leaders.

Evidence is mounting that the style of leadership women offer is beneficial not only to employees but also to the bottom line. In a 1996 Michigan-based human resource consulting firm study comparing the management skills of male and female managers, women were rated significantly better than their male counterparts by their bosses, themselves, and their employees. In the study, which included 941 managers across seventeen states, women came out ahead with an even greater margin than in a first study conducted in 1994. "Both studies challenged the conventional wisdom that women are only better at communicating, empowering people and being positive," says Lawrence A. Pfaff, who runs the consulting firm that undertook the study. "Female managers were rated significantly better than their male counterparts in areas beyond these softer skills. Women are more decisive, better at planning and better at facilitating change than men."

The explosive growth of women-owned businesses over the past twelve years is another testament to the skills and talents that allow women to succeed in this new world. Between 1987 and 1999, the number of women-owned firms climbed by 103 percent nationwide, employment jumped 320 percent, and sales soared 436 percent. Expansion outpaced these firms' overall business growth by nearly five to one, according to the National Foundation for Women Business Owners. As of 1999, there were 9.1 million women-owned companies in the United States, employing 27.5 million people and generating over $3.6 trillion in sales. These businesses accounted for 38 percent of all firms in the country.

WOMEN AND BUSINESS LEADERSHIP

Although a growing number of CEOs, presidents, managers, and small business owners are women, few are included in management guides on your bookstore shelves. But female business leaders have penetrating insights to offer, and this book details the paths and approaches of some who are among the best and the brightest. While their immediate situations may change, these women were selected because they embody enduring, proven leadership qualities that set them apart from their predecessors and peers.

Whether they run their own businesses or have risen in traditional corporations, the women featured in this book were chosen precisely because they possess the dynamic leadership skills that distinguish them from their male predecessors and the men who dominate their industries. Unlike other books about women in business already on bookstore shelves, this is neither a career tips guide nor an examination of those who have broken the glass ceiling. Instead, these pages focus on several of the leading women in American business, describing what they do differently, and why it works.

Chapter 1 describes the new paradigm of leadership—the seven qualities these women, who have made their way into the boardrooms of some of the country's most prominent businesses, possess, and how their approach differs from women who preceded them.

Though this book is not a how-to guide, the lessons of new paradigm leadership are concise, vital, and applicable to any executive wanting to get ahead. Because there is no formula to follow, one must create his or her own approach. But understanding the common traits among these successful women will provide a solid starting point. Chapters 2 through 8 present the characteristics that capture this new leadership dynamic with profiles of the fourteen top women executives to illustrate these traits in action. And finally, Chapter 9 introduces some up-and-coming female business leaders who share the qualities of the new paradigm, and are rising quickly to the tops of their corporations. Without a doubt, all these women are changing the face of management. As the new millennium dawns, the best man for the job will increasingly be a woman. Both male and female executives rising through the ranks of corporate America can learn from women who guide top firms today. More and more excel to the top of blue-chip companies each day!

1

PIONEERING THE
NEW PARADIGM

Orit Gadiesh has been breaking into boys' clubs and performing under pressure since she was an aide to the deputy chief of staff in the Israeli army at the age of seventeen. In the war room, she helped army strategists draft a plan to overcome opposition from all sides. She served during the late 1960s and early 1970s, a period in Israeli history known as the War of Attrition, when the tiny nation was attacked frequently across all its borders and Egypt was a bitter foe. Back then, the choices her superiors made literally had life and death implications. But today she is the one leading the troops—as chairman of one of the most macho American consulting firms in the industry, Bain & Company. At the age of forty-two, she took on that prominent role after its founder, William Bain, Jr., brought the company to the brink of bankruptcy.

Gadiesh is not alone. Based primarily on her marketing savvy and business acumen, Margaret (Meg) Whitman was recruited to run eBay, Inc., turning the on-line auctioneer into a household name and one of the leading businesses on the Web practically overnight. After building a $20 billion international business for energy giant Enron Corp., Rebecca Mark, a divorced mother of twins, landed the chairman and CEO job at the company's new water arm, Azurix. Darla Moore left her family's South Carolina farm to rise up in New York's male bastion of banking. Then she assumed control of husband Richard Rainwater's stock portfolio and nearly tripled his net worth. Shelly Lazarus became chairman and chief executive officer of advertising giant Ogilvy & Mather after winning the hefty IBM account, the largest in the history of her agency. Ellen Gordon turned her father's Tootsie Roll Industries from a sleepy candy maker into a winner on Wall Street, and one of the strongest performers in the business. Although she started as a secretary at ABC Sports, Patricia Fili-Krushel rose to become the highest-ranking woman in television after assuming the presidency at ABC Television Network. Not only was she given greater responsibilities than her male predecessor, but she helped her network achieve one of its biggest programming successes in years—*Who Wants to Be a Millionaire.*

These women are all "new paradigm" leaders, noted for their abilities to blend feminine qualities of leadership with classic male traits to run their companies successfully, and become some of the most powerful women in American business. Nearly all have reached the president, chairman, or chief executive officer level of thriving companies raking in well over $100 million in revenues. All are active leaders who have not merely kept the companies they head in a successful holding pattern. Instead, they have dramatically boosted profits and revenues. Most have taken over their companies from men and topped their results. They have also launched new initiatives that have significantly added value to their firms. They do not bother trying to run their companies just like their male predecessors, nor do they follow established norms, because they are outsiders to the corporate world. They have taken risks in their careers and developed their leadership skills by working diligently in overlooked, disparaged, or undiscovered areas of business. By excelling in these professional danger zones, they have become confident enough to rely on their own instincts and to exercise their own judgment. They lead in their own new way, and they are part of a new generation of women who chose a different path to excel in the corporate world.

Up until the mid-1990s, women were still conspicuously absent from top positions at almost all the largest companies in the United States. Catalyst reported in 1996 that only 2.4 percent of the chairmen and chief executive officers of Fortune 500 firms were women. So where were the women in business if they weren't storming the boardrooms of America's most important firms? They were beginning to succeed on their own, primarily by building their own small businesses.

"Now, a second wave of women is making its way into top management, not by adopting the style and habits that have proved successful for men, but by drawing on the skills and the attitudes they developed as women," explains Judy B. Rosener, the University of California at Irvine management professor who in 1990 wrote an influential article called "Ways Women Lead" for the *Harvard Business Review*. "They are succeeding because of, not in spite of, certain characteristics generally considered to be 'feminine' and inappropriate in leaders."

SUCCEEDING LIKE A MAN

When the first generation of women entered the workforce in earnest in the 1970s, they succeeded in the only way they could: by imitating the qualities and characteristics associated with their male colleagues. Authoritarian leadership structures were pervasive, and tight control was a hallmark of the businesses men made. America's booming economy of the late 1960s bolstered the common view that traditional male management styles were highly effective. And women were not exactly welcomed into management ranks. It was judicial mandate rather than goodwill that prompted companies to begin opening their doors to women. Title VII of the 1964 Civil Rights Act made discrimination against women in education or employment illegal. But the passage of equal opportunity legislation did not ensure equal treatment.

Developed on assembly lines and factory floors during the Industrial Age, the "traditional" approach to corporate leadership was particularly well suited to huge manufacturing runs of essentially undifferentiated products. Some of the management techniques that were used seem lifted from a military manual: operating through a hierarchical structure, command-and-control system, top-down decision making, domination of employees, and reliance on standardized codes for judgment and evaluation of others.

But as the women's liberation movement helped America's females set their sights on goals apart from getting married and having families, they began to struggle to rise through the ranks of these companies. Although increasing numbers of women graduated from college and went on to professional schools, most landed in low-paying jobs that *Ms.* magazine labeled "the pink-collar ghetto." This professional slum spanned sales, secretarial, and food services, many of which offered only part-time jobs. In 1979, women's incomes represented only 59 percent of male earnings, while unemployment rates exceeded male averages by about 20 percent.[1] The wage gap revealed not just the denial of equal pay for equal work, but more subtly the assumption that certain tasks, traditionally performed by women, were inherently less valuable.

Few females became top managers during the decade, and those who did had virtually nonexistent track records—so to be successful, women abided by the rules of the men's clubs they were joining. Looking the part was essential in establishing credibility. Women adopted a style of dress that resembled that of their male counterparts, replete with neckties and big shoulder pads. Competition was the name of the game, and winning at any cost, whether within or outside the company, was the goal. Rank was the primary source of respect in this milieu, where traditional leaders told underlings what to do, and they, in turn, carried out orders. The tight structure favored by male leaders kept them at a distance from their customers. And the various levels of rigid vertical hierarchy coupled with a high degree of employee specialization distanced senior executives from workers.

Women took on male methods to excel in corporations because of the negative stereotypes associated with their own gender. Conventional wisdom at the time affirmed that women were doomed to fulfill supporting roles, as men took all the leads in a company, because of inherent female weaknesses—it was assumed that women lacked ambition and experience, were just too friendly and helpful, and failed to lead or take charge.

As a result, few women in the 1980s climbed to the top rungs of the corporate ladder. In fact, according to various studies, women's already paltry numbers in senior executive suites in numerous industries, from advertising to retailing, were starting to decline by the conclusion of the decade.[2] The rate of expansion in numbers of women appointed to Fortune 1000 boards slowed by the late eighties, after women's share of the director chairs reached 6.8 percent. Women were hardly moving into chief executive suites—most were just there to take dictation.

For all these reasons, a "feminine style" of management has long made women executives wary. Stereotypes persist that female managers have trouble in the workplace, and yet the women in this book—and many whom you encounter in your daily life—excel because of the very traits that were once deemed weak or inferior.

Regardless of gender, today's CEO can no longer tap his or her company's full potential using a command-and-control style long associated with the masculine mind-set. With buzzwords like "integration," "consensus," "collaboration," and "teamwork" being tossed around, the model for great leadership is undergoing a major overhaul. The next generation of leaders will be those who can build a vision based on awareness of economic transformation, then help their partners and staff fulfill that vision. As Patricia Aburdene, coauthor of *Megatrends for Women*, puts it, "Leaders who spark people today don't just tell others what to do. The struggle is more about how to invest in a well-educated workforce, then develop effective ways to mine its brain power. The key to this is catalyzing your resources."

THE ESSENCE OF NEW PARADIGM LEADERSHIP

New paradigm leaders are redefining stereotypes of how women guide companies, and illustrate every day that they can play with, and beat, the big boys at their own game. In the past, that meant being just as aggressive as, if not more aggressive than, male rivals and colleagues. Now, top women executives, like their male counterparts, have to draw on a wide range of skills to get to the top and stay there.

To grow their businesses, new paradigm leaders combine many of the managerial talents traditionally attributed to men with many of the stereotypically "weaker" female skills. The traditional view of men at work is that they are assertive, seek to take charge and dominate, rely on hierarchy and status as a power base, and use standard codes for judging the performance of others. A common conception of female executives today is that they merely nurture, mentor, promote family-friendly policies, and seek consensus. The women in this book cannot be belittled by such preconceived notions. While management gurus may promote some of these features, most know that these attributes will not assure success in our global economy. Because of their knowledge, these women have styles and business skills that men feel comfortable with—otherwise, they would not be able to hold on to their positions of authority. Yet surpassing male rivals is something they have done throughout their careers. Standard yardsticks such as revenues and profits document their success. In technology, stock price and market capitalization also display their prowess.

Many women fall into this leadership category, making the group limited yet hardly finite. Brilliant top executives who draw on both feminine and masculine styles include media maven Oprah Winfrey, Oxygen Media's Geraldine Laybourne, Elektra Entertainment

Group's Sylvia Rhone, Avon Products' Andrea Jung, Walmart.com's Jeanne Jackson, and Paramount Pictures' Sherry Lansing. A disproportionate number of women in technology are featured here for two reasons. First, the technology sector is the fastest-growing industry in the United States, and the field has been the biggest driver of economic expansion in recent years. Second, men have traditionally dominated this industry.

There are many, many accomplished women out there who were considered for this book. But the fourteen women examined on these pages were selected because they personify the seven characteristics ascribed to new paradigm leadership. They include:

Orit Gadiesh, chairman of Bain & Company

Ann Winblad, partner of Hummer Winblad Venture Partners

Meg Whitman, chief executive officer of eBay, Inc.

Marcy Carsey, cofounder and co-owner of the Carsey-Werner Company and partner of Oxygen Media, Inc.

Darla Moore, president of Rainwater, Inc.

Rebecca Mark, chairman and chief executive officer of Azurix Corp.

Patricia Russo, chief executive officer of Lucent Technologies' Global Service Provider Business

Ellen Gordon, president of Tootsie Roll Industries

Shelly Lazarus, chief executive officer of Ogilvy & Mather Worldwide

Marilyn Carlson Nelson, chairman and chief executive officer of Carlson Companies

Patricia Fili-Krushel, president and chief executive officer of WebMD Health, the consumer division of Healtheon, and former president of ABC Television Network

Kim Polese, cofounder and chief executive officer of Marimba, Inc.

Martha Ingram, chairman of Ingram Industries

Loida Lewis, chairman and chief executive officer of TLC Beatrice International Holdings, Inc.

WHY NEW PARADIGM LEADERS EXCEL

New paradigm leaders achieve for three main reasons:

1:   *Self-assurance compels new paradigm leaders to stay motivated and take risks.*

New paradigm leaders understand that risks are a necessity in business and that self-assurance provides the backbone to take them, but confidence has never been associated with women in business. The female executives in this book defy that stereotype. All of these women are goal-oriented and have extremely driven personalities.

Early in her career, Rebecca Mark saw that taking risks was vital to her success at energy giant Enron Corporation. Rather than feeling intimidated, she took on increasingly difficult challenges and became known for that, going so far as to stake her reputation as a force in the energy industry on her ability to accomplish the near-impossible. As a result, she became a top contender to succeed her boss, Kenneth Lay, as chief executive officer of $31 billion (1998 sales) Enron Corporation, after she persevered to pull off a multibillion-dollar power plant deal in India.

2:   *An obsession with customer service helps them anticipate market changes.*

All these women possess a preternatural sense of customer demands that enables them to anticipate changes in the marketplace early enough to capitalize on them. While it's both easy and understandable for executives who reach the top levels of their companies to get bogged down in the big-picture, long-range strategy and planning, the executives featured in this book make a thorough understanding of customers a number one priority. In most cases, that means working long hours and traveling far more than they'd like. Orit Gadiesh flies over 17,000 miles every month to meet with clients both in the United States and abroad, and spent 100 days traveling outside the country for business in 1999. Shelly Lazarus spends about 250 hours a month with customers.

3: New paradigm leaders use "feminine" traits to their advantage.

The leaders in this book have effectively used traditional "feminine" qualities such as empathy, collaboration, and cooperation in their management styles to achieve better results. Pretending that men and women are the same requires females to keep adapting to the male culture of business. Men and women often bring different approaches to looking at problems, opportunities, and decisions. The more approaches available, the better the outcome for both individuals and companies.

Shelly Lazarus worked her way up the corporate ladder for twenty-seven years before becoming chief executive officer of the $10 billion (1998 billings) Ogilvy & Mather Worldwide. But she did not do it alone. Lazarus realized early on that if she wanted to build the company's advertising business, she would need to invest her colleagues with a sense of ownership in a project, and trust them to execute.

The women who embody new paradigm leadership are more than just trailblazers. They do not merely break stereotypes, but point their companies in new directions to capitalize on changes in the marketplace. As business theorist James Champy wrote, "Free markets need free men and women to invent the future." These female executives are doing just that.

THE SEVEN KEY CHARACTERISTICS OF NEW PARADIGM LEADERSHIP

1: Selling the Vision

With unemployment at an all-time low, today's employees are about as loyal to the company they work for as they are to a brand of paper towel. Never before in corporate America has the "vision thing" mattered so much to anyone outside the executive suite. A leader with a fresh, independent plan for her company's growth and future has a distinct advantage in luring and keeping great talent and eager investors. Vision is not about lofty ideals, but about a concept that is easily understandable to all and will take a business to the next level.

Orit Gadiesh, head of Bain & Company, jump-started the elite consulting firm that stalled in the early nineties amid an exodus of top executives and lagging revenues. The spark plug? A new vision that spelled out how to reinvent the company, redirect its focus, and restore its healthy pride. Employees originally heading for the door were won over by her innovative ideas, energy, and enthusiasm. Over time, clients flocked back to Bain, and revenues swung back into a steady growth mode.

Ann Winblad followed her own instincts, and was one of the first to develop a venture capital firm focused on software start-ups. She had a vision of what her industry and her company could and would become long before anyone else—male or female.

2: *Reinventing the Rules*

Forget what your mama—or your boss—told you. Following the rules can be bad for your career. In these days when a pimply faced high school dropout with a computer powerful enough to run flight operations at Cape Canaveral may be industry's next wunderkind, the old rules of corporate leadership no longer apply. Leaders who fail to rewrite their job descriptions every second on the job in a bid to innovate and break into new markets will find themselves being written off. While women have traditionally been socialized to please others, new paradigm leaders know, through their intuition and experience, that good girls rarely post great returns. The strongest managers today not only anticipate change, they create entirely new organizations that respond effectively to shifts and engage others in the search for innovation.

Meg Whitman, eBay's numero uno, could have stayed at her job at toymaker Hasbro where she had already made a big splash. She turned the Pawtucket, Rhode Island, company's sleepy preschool division into a booming business by selling children's obsessions like Barney, Teletubbies, and Mr. Potato Head. But Whitman decided to move to the on-line auctioneer because she believed she could draw on the intense devotion of its customers to drive tremendous growth at the company. She was taken with the idea that many users had quit their day jobs to sell collectibles on the fledgling site. Now she's made eBay one of the most explosive growth companies on the Internet today. Her novel approach enabled eBay to continue turning a profit, setting it apart from so many other Net upstarts.

Marcy Carsey also went her own way in creating an independent production company with partner Tom Werner. Uninspired by new management at ABC where she was a chief programmer, Carsey felt she could offer better shows and attract wider audiences by producing programs on her own, then selling them to the networks. After she shed her high-level network job, she relied on her own intuition rather than on conventional wisdom in the television industry because she saw herself as a member of the audience. Instead of accommodating requests for sitcoms from studio executives, she produced programs she liked. Her groundbreaking series, such as *The Cosby Show* and *Roseanne,* caught fire with audiences and made television history.

3: *A Laser Focus to Achieve*

Go where others fear to tread! Being aggressive and ambitious, long considered distinctively male traits, are key qualities that old and new paradigm leaders share. But the type of drive new paradigm leaders embody differs from the raw form of motivation to succeed that compelled leaders before them. The women featured in this book have an ability to identify and hone in on opportunities that others simply don't see, then excel in that uncharted territory through their laser focus to achieve.

Darla Moore, now president of Rainwater, Inc., can credit her keen sense of vision for her stellar career trajectory. Handed what most considered a professional lemon of a job assignment at Chemical Bank—lending to bankrupt companies—Moore decided to squeeze out some lemonade. She transformed her area into a thriving business, for the bank and rocketed up the career ladder.

Rebecca Mark also relied on her bold sense of vision and intrepid will to find her niche in the overseas market. When she began working at Enron, primarily a United States–based gas and pipeline company, she led the charge to expand the company internationally into emerging markets in 1991. Rather than waiting for developments to become more pleasant, she stormed into places deemed treacherous for business, from Mozambique to India. Armed with determination and indomitable spirit, she built the business from nothing into a $20 billion powerhouse before launching Enron's water subsidiary, Azurix, in 1999.

4:   *Maximizing High Touch in an Era of High Tech*

In an era when a growing number of people conduct business through e-mail, voice mail, passwords, and PINs, leaders who succeed today—and will continue to do so in the future—are those who guide with a strong, personal "bedside manner." Although these executives are just as technologically savvy as their peers, their skills in working with staffers and relating to customers in a "high-touch" way give them a critical edge and separate them from the pack. New paradigm leaders understand the importance of taking the time to build partnerships whether it is with staff, customers, consumers, suppliers, or other companies within the same or related industries. New paradigm leaders believe that cooperative relationships make them stronger as leaders because they are able to draw on a wider range of input— which makes the company stronger still.

High touch is a key element in Shelly Lazarus's strategy. She wooed key clients to Ogilvy & Mather by forming bonds with them, engendering loyalty in employees and striking a chord with consumers to achieve results. A leader in the travel business, Marilyn Carlson Nelson has a distinct approach in her field—she has shifted her company's focus to customer service at a time when the industry is becoming more automated and impersonal. Nelson recognized early on the growing importance of technology to her business as reservations become increasingly automated, but saw the opportunity for service to become a differentiator. Nelson believes that high-touch service is essential in making travel a fulfilling personal experience.

5: Turning Challenge into Opportunity

As the case of "Chainsaw" Al Dunlap illustrates, swinging the hatchet alone these days does not cut it, so to speak. Dunlap made heads roll when he was hired to revive sputtering Sunbeam Corporation in 1996, but he was pushed out two years later after his slash-and-burn tactics only made matters worse. New paradigm leaders are earning the crown titles of "turnaround queens" because they are able to acheive what the ax-men before them failed to do: Make the bold strokes but also win the cooperation of others in their organization to make any transformation a sustained success.

When Patricia Russo took over the Global Business Systems (Global) unit of phone giant AT&T Corporation, she had to shore up a struggling division and tackle an unprofitable industry to excel. She made her mark not just by cutting costs and downsizing, but by selling a new vision to employees, refocusing company goals, shoring up customer satisfaction, and returning the business to financial health.

When Ellen Gordon became president of Tootsie Roll, she had an outmoded company to revitalize. She understood that to turn the business around she had to successfully manage continuity and change. She employed her keen sense of fiscal discipline and upgraded technology systems at the company to run a more efficient business. Rather than cut workers, she shifted employees into different areas as Tootsie Roll expanded, and spurred long-term growth.

6: An Obsession with Customer Preferences

With the Information Age making it easier for customers to shop around for the best blouse, sitcom, mortgage, or ticket to Bali, company leaders must work harder to give the people what they want before their competitors do. Today, top executives must get to know their customers well enough to think like them. This connection goes beyond standard market research or focus-group findings. There is no substitute for spending time with clients to become expert at their businesses and to ascertain their demands.

A link to customers enlightens new paradigm leaders and improves their results. Former ABC Network president Patricia Fili-Krushel is obsessed with what viewers want, and has drawn on that knowledge to come up with stellar programming successes like *Who Wants to Be a Millionaire.* The show struck a chord with audiences and helped her revitalize the network.

Kim Polese, CEO of technology company Marimba, Inc., which delivers software over networks, has been gearing her company's products toward the needs of business customers. By keeping close tabs on what clients want, she's attracted big-name customers like Charles Schwab & Company, Cisco Systems, and DaimlerChrysler.

7: Courage Under Fire

Although decisiveness has traditionally been viewed as a male characteristic, new paradigm leaders have risen to prominence because they rarely flinch when the situation requires making a tough call. Rooted in a high level of confidence, their decision-making skills come with a twist. These female executives have all made surprising decisions, and had the courage to withstand powerful opposition.

For instance, Martha Ingram and Loida Lewis are two such leaders who stepped in to run their husbands' empires following their deaths. Lewis literally unseated her husband's handpicked successor to take over the billion-dollar food company TLC Beatrice. Ingram also stepped over the chief executive officer her husband had selected, who was a giant in the field, to become chairman of distributor Ingram Industries. Both women had to stand up to their husbands' number twos and boards of directors to make decisions that their very successful and much beloved, but now deceased, husbands would not have made.

THE FEATURES OF THE OLD PARADIGM

The first wave of women who rose to positions of authority in the seventies and eighties adopted the masculine model—the old paradigm—as a means to success. To see why the new paradigm works better, it is important to understand the limitations of the old paradigm. The qualities that lifted female executives to positions of authority in the past have become passé and inefficient in the high-flying Information Age that defines the nineties and the dawn of the new millennium.

The old paradigm is:

- *Masculine*—Men run all but a few of the Fortune 500 companies. Masculine qualities such as being tough, aggressive, taking no prisoners, and winning at all costs have always been prized in American business. Along with many of these positive traits for business, masculinity also includes some negative ones, such as being autocratic, hoarding power, and dominating.
- *Hierarchical*—A strict vertical bureaucratic structure has long been standard practice at companies run by titans of American industry. Rank is the primary means of power in this milieu. Information is filtered as it travels up the chain of command to reach the chairman and chief executive officer, and communication between the boss and junior employees is limited.
- *A command-and-control structure*—As long as there have been CEOs, they have been telling workers what to do. Company chiefs

issue orders and subordinates carry them out. Performance evaluations and bonuses are linked to the employee's ability to complete assignments successfully and efficiently. Instructions come from above, and staff members are not involved in setting goals. Leaders believe they have all the answers and are not interested in gathering information and opinions from colleagues.

- *Opposition to change*—When structures are inflexible and information is filtered on its way to the top, management tends to take on a lumbering quality. Micromanagement is a common result as well. With a rapidly changing marketplace, management must remain nimble and responsive to external challenges. Elaborate structures hinder flexibility.

- *Defined by individual effort*—The vertical structure and command-and-control system value individual effort. It is through outstanding solo work that one can rise in these rigid settings. A focus on teams is absent.

- *Indirect communication trickling down through the company's vertical structure*—A rigid structure where everyone knows his or her place within a hierarchy means information also travels through that pyramid. It gets watered down in the process.

As a result of these factors, old paradigm leadership can often be ineffectual in today's competitive and fast-moving knowledge economy, where many of the old rules and standards no longer hold, the job market is tilted in favor of the employee, a company's vision is just as important as its valuation, and leaders aren't satisfied with winning "at all costs."

OLD PARADIGM LEADERS

Linda Wachner, chairman and chief executive officer of Warnaco Group, Inc., and Jill Barad, former chairman and chief executive officer of Mattel, Inc., are prime examples of old paradigm leadership. Both women declined to be interviewed for this book.

In 1986, Wachner became the first woman to acquire and head a Fortune 500 company. Her ability to muscle her way through a predominantly male-dominated business world using old paradigm methods powered her remarkable career. But some of those old paradigm traits that enabled her to get where she is have become liabilities in today's changing economy.

Wachner was the first female vice president in the 100–year history of Warner's, a women's lingerie manufacturer and retailer. When she began her career in retail, she knew she wanted to be the one in charge, and she doggedly pursued that goal. She personally borrowed $3 million and led a $485 million hostile leveraged buyout of Warner's parent company, Warnaco, in 1986. She made a splash in a year where women held only about 2 percent of senior management jobs, according to Korn/Ferry International.

Warnaco was an ailing underwear maker when Wachner got hold of it, and she brought leadership to the company in a dictatorial, commanding style. She slashed costs—decimating management staff from 200 people in the corporate office to seven. And she wasted no time reducing the portfolio of businesses from about fifteen weaklings to two main cash generators: intimate apparel, as lingerie is known in the retail business, and menswear. Next, she consolidated production, boosted output, and renegotiated contracts with suppliers to extract better terms. She discarded products that were poor sellers and promoted items with higher margins instead. She also added licensed goods with big brand names and cachet, like Calvin Klein, Valentino, Fruit of the Loom, and Chaps by Ralph Lauren. Then she worked to gain market share and expand her retail business within high-end shops like Bergdorf Goodman and Dillard Department Stores, and added specialty retailers such as Victoria's Secret and mass marketers including Kmart and Wal-Mart. She also ventured into hot new products like the Miracle Bra and body slimmers. Soon, running one company was not enough for Wachner. In 1990, she decided to buy a second—the $350 million apparel maker Authentic Fitness, which licenses Speedo swimwear in the United States. She is one of only a handful of executives to command two large public corporations.

At first, the company prospered under Wachner's direction. Warnaco stock climbed 130 percent between 1991 and 1996, compared with 46 percent over the same period for peer companies and 104 percent for the Standard & Poor's 500.[3] But since then, the stock market has been tougher on her companies. The company suffered net losses of $12 million in 1997 and a whopping $32 million in 1998. Those two straight years of earnings disappointments have caused Warnaco's shares to plummet over 76 percent since June 1998. Despite lagging earnings, Wachner remains one of the highest-paid executives in the country, and has been criticized for her lofty salary of $11.5 million in 1997 and 15.6 million in 1998. In April 2000, Warnaco stock was trading close to its 1991 IPO price of $10.

Although Linda Wachner still leads Warnaco, Jill Barad has not been able to keep her job at Mattel, largely because of her old paradigm management style. During her reign at the world's largest toy-maker, Barad's inability to collaborate successfully with top executives at her company, her incapacity to promote open communication with associates (particularly regarding bad news), and her micromanaging approach to business placed her in the old paradigm camp and contributed to her demise.

Barad, forty-eight, conducted business in an assertive, autocratic style typically associated with men. She excelled in an environment at Mattel, where she was constantly pitted against colleagues, and developed skills associated with old paradigm leadership to defeat all her foes as she rose to the top. While she climbed the corporate ladder, the methods she used propelled her career and her company's fortunes to the pinnacle of the toy industry. Under her direction, the Barbie line grew from $200 million in 1982 to an estimated $1.9 billion in sales in 1997.

Since she won the chief executive spot at Mattel in 1997, however, Barad's old paradigm leadership skills became liabilities. Her travails have been widely documented. She proved unable to keep the nearly $5 billion company on its strong growth path, and ineffective at stemming the tide of losses plaguing the business. In 1998, while earnings rose 14.6 percent, sales fell 1 percent, the first revenues decline at the company since 1988. Between March 1998 and February 2000, Mattel stock has lost 74 percent of its value, and stunned shareholders were left to rummage for reasons why $14 billion in market value had disappeared during that period. Diverting blame, she became notorious for pushing out talented managers. Sales of the blond doll she was famous for reviving, Barbie, dropped 14 percent in 1998, presenting big problems for the toymaker that derives an estimated 45 percent of its revenues from the doll. She missed sales targets by more than $500 million that year. Then she reportedly pushed out her number two, Bruce Stein. In April 1999, the company announced it would cut 3,000 jobs—10 percent of its workforce—and close plants. Despite downsizing, her woes deepened as she was bitterly criticized for overpaying for acquisitions, particularly her May 1999 purchase of the Learning Company for $3.8 billion, 4.5 times sales of the software maker with its maturing and lackluster business. With no advance notice, Barad shocked shareholders by announcing losses during 1999 when gains were expected, especially during the latter half of the year. She soon fired the two executives who ran the Learning Company.

While red ink and Barad's "volatile management style" plagued Mattel, profits at rival and number two toymaker Hasbro, Inc., surged as strong sellers like Furbies, Teletubbies, and Pokémon paraphernalia raked in revenues. Soon investors were demanding her removal, and in February 2000, Barad resigned.

Barad's old paradigm flaw of suspiciously guarding her power limited her ability to address some of her most pointed criticisms, including her lack of financial acumen, denial of troubles with the company, and inability to delegate authority to subordinates. Analysts repeatedly cited her unwillingness to share power and work with strong managers as detrimental to the company's future prospects. Many talented executives left. Some of the skilled staffers she lost might have been able to help Mattel break out of its downward spiral.

To be sure, Barad and Wachner have paved the way for the success of other women by rising through the ranks of some of America's leading corporations. Wachner still ranks among the most powerful women in the country. But the manner in which Barad used to run Mattel and that which Wachner employs at Warnaco distinguishes them from the other women who appear in this book. The noncollaborative and dictatorial approach both Barad and Wachner use put them at a disadvantage in today's changing world. Their management styles hampered their progress and their ability to grasp the need for change. While the tactics these women used suited the times and consumer goods industries in which they rose, most of these methods no longer fit the current economic environment defined by intense global competition.

Business in our global economy is teeming with ambiguity and change. Attracting customers with their ever-increasing demands has never been more difficult. Companies merge and break apart constantly. Technology has revolutionized entire industries at a dizzying pace. The Internet and a company's capability to use it effectively has made delivering shareholder value an increasingly complex task.

The glut of dot-com companies seeking new CEOs presents an unparalleled opportunity for leaders who subscribe to the new paradigm theory of management. By October 1999, there were about 450 CEO vacancies at dot-com start-ups and the Internet units of established companies, according to the *Wall Street Journal.*

New paradigm leadership is not about discarding the old paradigm wholesale, because the leading executives featured in the following chapters borrow elements from the old paradigm, such as ambition and courage under fire. Then they add some new elements, to refine and improve on it. In the process, they use traditional feminine traits to their advantage in redefining the rules of business. The female executives rising to the top positions now work to foster a creative and collegial workplace to achieve their goals. New paradigm leadership offers lessons that are universal because all managers can learn from the traits that have helped these effective female executives excel.

"In the new climate," writes James Champy, the author of *Reengineering Management*, "with competitive ships constantly looming up over the horizon . . . what must be abandoned by the new management of our corporate ships . . . is a whole ideology, a whole way of thinking about power. Power no longer belongs in boxes, in titles, in ranks. In the new heavy weather, those . . . count for nothing."[4]

2

SELLING THE VISION

It's not a mission statement or words that are on the wall somewhere. It is a set of principles that everybody in the organization understands that are core to its identity.

— ORIT GADIESH

Bain & Company was in deep trouble. Its reign as one of the hottest management consulting firms in the 1970s and 1980s was over. Long gone were the glory days between 1973 and 1986, when the firm's profits grew at over 50 percent a year as its coveted consultants whipped struggling companies like National Steel and Chrysler Motors into shape. By 1991, Bain teetered on the verge of bankruptcy. Revenues had plummeted 35 percent, and staff had been cut by more than 30 percent after rounds of layoffs, according to an article called "Physician, Heal Thyself" in *Forbes*.[1] The firm's once illustrious founder and president, William (Bill) Bain, Jr., stepped down amid controversy that his efforts to cash out had burdened the company with a crippling debt. And rumors that the firm was up for sale pervaded the industry.

Like many of the key executives who abandoned the company, Bain senior partner Orit Gadiesh got a flood of lucrative and tantalizing offers to jump ship. But the Israeli native who *Fortune* magazine has twice touted as one of the most powerful women in American business turned them all down, and chose to stay. Her decision helped persuade eleven other senior partners to remain, and helped avoid a mass exodus. She then landed several big clients, including Kraft Foods, Inc., Motorola, Inc., and Philip Morris Companies, Inc., which were crucial to keeping the company afloat and helping to win back revenues. But Gadiesh knew a key ingredient to a full comeback was still missing, and it was up to her to deliver it.

The room grew quiet as Gadiesh stood before 600 Bain consultants at the firm's annual meeting in August 1992. She talked with a faint trace of an Israeli accent for forty minutes about restoring confidence in Bain & Company. "We've turned around financially, we've turned around the business—even our competitors are beginning to acknowledge that," she said in a speech that became the subject of a Harvard Business School study on leadership. "Now it's time to turn around what they really fear, what they've always envied us for; it's time to turn around our collective pride in what we do."

An outburst of cheers followed as the data-oriented, buttoned-down crowd of consultants jumped to its feet. "It was electric and extraordinarily uplifting," recalls Bain vice president Mike McKay, who was then a manager at the firm. "Back then, Bain was not a place you felt proud to be at, and I was questioning whether I should stay. All the senior people who had attracted me to the firm had left or were leaving, and a firm like Bain is only as good as the people who are in it. You had to apologize for the place to friends. Her speech marked the end of something old and the beginning of something new because she had never been in charge before. She had never been 'the man.' And this was the first time that it was clear to me that she had picked up the torch from Bill Bain and the company's founders, and would lead us forward. She gave me a reason to stay because she gave me confidence that the organization was sustainable. If she hadn't, I wouldn't be here today."

Gadiesh was not simply touting company policy, she was communicating her vision to her employees. As one would expect, Bain consultants focused primarily on figures until she shifted their attention to restoring pride in their ability to achieve results for clients. Drawing little attention to herself, she inspired those around her by rallying them to a common cause—the reinvention of Bain. And she is in good company. A common characteristic of new paradigm leaders is their ability to create an independent and counterintuitive vision to make their companies successful, as seen also in venture capitalist Ann Winblad. Before it was in vogue, Winblad focused on nurturing software start-ups and foresaw the growth of her industry. Her unconventional approach to getting involved early in the process and pursuing talent distinguished her from rivals. At forty-eight, she has already appeared on lists of the top (mostly male) power brokers of the Information Age in publications like *Time, BusinessWeek, Vanity Fair*, the *New York Times Magazine*, and *Upside*.

When Martha Ingram of distributor Ingram Industries had to fire a key executive, she immediately flew out to explain her strategy and assure dismayed employees that their company would grow even faster without this highly regarded manager. When her power project in India was canceled and most thought the deal was lost, Rebecca Mark of Enron spent six months in the distant land talking with more than thirty officials to get the plant back on track. Although she lacked a background in technology, eBay chief executive Meg Whitman brought her own distinctive vision to the company, resulting in success on Wall Street and prominence in the field.

New paradigm leaders have a tendency to lay out a plan of action that breaks with precedent at the companies they run, but not arbitrarily. Throughout the 1990s, executives have understood that the "vision thing" is critical for motivating their employees and spurring them not merely to meet goals but to fly past them. A clear vision can put employees on the path to innovation, but an independent vision offers a whole new philosophical architecture for building company priorities. New paradigm leaders, because they are mavericks just beginning to populate executive suites, form visions that often buck existing trends and conventions. They inspire colleagues by appealing to their sense of cause. Their conception of the company's future does not rest on tired old mission statements and buzzwords. Instead, they spell out prescriptions for a new company mindset and novel plans of action that help separate their firms from the pack. Through their radical notions, new paradigm leaders can help power a corporate turnaround or takeoff, depending on their intent.

"It would have been very easy at that time to just diversify into other businesses because our core business was so troubled, but Gadiesh said, 'Wait, we are successful for a reason,'" explains Tom Tierney, worldwide managing director of Bain. "She mobilized others to take pride in their own strengths and build on those."

Within one year, Gadiesh not only revived morale, she also helped grow the company's bottom line and dramatically expanded its world-wide client base. Staging an impressive comeback, she and her firm's 204 partners have kept the private Boston-based company profitable ever since. She restored the luster to the Bain & Company name, and in 1998, the firm reeled in $600 million in revenues, an increase of over 18 percent from the prior year, according to industry newsletter *Consultants News*.[2] This revenue figure is more than double the peak of $240 million the firm achieved under Bill Bain's direction. She claims revenues are growing steadily at close to 20 percent a year. *Fortune* magazine labeled her as one of the most charismatic leaders in corporate America,[3] and ranked Bain as the world's eighteenth-largest management consulting firm, falling just below McKinsey and Boston Consulting Group for strategic CEO-level work.[4] The firm now has twenty-six offices with 2,200 employees worldwide, and has advised more than 1,500 businesses, including Motorola, Microsoft, and Dell. Gadiesh herself has counseled hundreds.

Like Whitman, rather than pursuing conformity among her employees or issuing orders, she tries to guide colleagues and to encourage them to experiment. She uses her counterintuitive words to energize and challenge. Because of her pride-turnaround speech in 1992, the industry trade magazine *Consulting* calls her "a spiritual leader" for the industry who has articulated the virtues of the consulting profession in the 1990s better than anyone else in the field.[5]

She has a name for her independent vision—she calls it "True North." She derived the term from her husband of nine years, Grenville Byford, a businessman and adventurer who has sailed the world by himself. "Unlike a traditional compass pointing to magnetic north, which is fickle and unreliable, a gyrocompass works on its own internal mechanical system and always points to True North. The most important thing a leader can do is establish a True North," she explains. "It's not a mission statement or words that are on the wall somewhere. It is a set of principles that everybody in the organization understands that are core to its identity. It serves to unify a global organization like ours in an environment where everything is changing. It builds a level of trust so that we are not just a collection of people each doing their own thing. And it anchors us so we can experiment and take risks. Our True North is getting strong results for clients."

THE VIEW FROM OUTSIDE

New paradigm leaders view their outsider position in corporate America as a distinct advantage and draw on it to devise an independent vision to sell to their employees. They must, in the words of Betty Lahan Harragan, who wrote a popular career advice book for women in 1977, "compete in a world they never made."[6] Rather than trying to emulate male company chiefs who came before or issuing orders to motivate staff like Linda Wachner and other old paradigm leaders do, new paradigm leaders often choose a different path. They are interested in people, and listen and communicate in ways that build rapport and level the learning field rather than distancing themselves from colleagues. The core values they promote help them motivate employees in fields with highly skilled workers. The companies they reshape become less hierarchical as a result. As business theorist Sally Helgesen writes of our knowledge-based economy, "Influence and persuasion take the place of giving orders."[7]

Posing a vision of one's own takes guts when one is coming from that outside vantage point, but defiance is common to these leaders. They rely on their own laser focus to achieve, rather than on a male model, to set their company's core values to empower those around them while also strengthening themselves. They downplay their own egos and unlock the talents of employees by appealing to them on a human level. Once these leaders have clarified their vision, they feel free to take risks because they know that everyone in the company is on the same page. Their employees, who now have a clear idea of the company's direction, are also stimulated to take innovative paths to further it. "I spoke passionately because those were not just words to me," Gadiesh explains. "By and large that is who I am."

The ability to sell an independent vision is not only a key element of solid leadership, it's also crucial in keeping a company strong. Leading executives must also execute that vision by generating results. Without it, a chief executive may lose his or her job. A slew of male and female CEOs have wrestled with this issue. Old paradigm leader Jill Barad is one. A skilled marketer, she made the blunder of using her promotional style, so effective in building the Barbie brand, on Wall Street. She told investors both in 1998 and 1999 that the business was in good shape just before Mattel disclosed steep shortfalls in sales and earnings. The company's stock was decimated during her tenure as a result.

WIELDING POWER AS A WOMAN

Gadiesh has been peddling her vision since she started out in consulting. At forty-eight, she is the only woman to lead a top-ranked firm in the industry. Like Meg Whitman, Rebecca Mark, and all the other new paradigm leaders, she has excelled in a male-dominated field. Few women even become partners in consulting firms, so the fact that Gadiesh is chairman is pretty extraordinary. At the largest management consulting firm, Andersen Consulting, women account for only 13 percent of the firm's partners and associates.[8] At Ernst & Young MCS, just over 15 percent of the top 200 partners and senior managers are women.[9] Many women do not stay in the field long enough to rise because consulting is not a family-friendly field—lengthy hours, intense travel, and inflexible benefits are symptomatic of the industry. Some women also lack the education they need to excel. Most of the men who rise in consulting have advanced degrees in business. The percentage of women enrolled in two-year MBA programs has been flat at 29 percent since 1994.

Orit Gadiesh would be shocking even if she was not chairman of one of the most secretive firms in one of the most staid industries. The first feature one notices is her hair. It's magenta. She wears bright red nail polish on her fingernails. She has never conformed to the standard dress code at the office. When she joined the firm, superiors encouraged her to wear conservative dark suits, short jackets, and bow ties. She chose to ignore them, opting for black instead, and short skirts that end four inches above her knee. For an interview, she's chosen skin-tight black leggings and a black jacket. She sports a bold leopard-patterned gray, black, and white scarf around her neck. Standing nearly six feet tall in her three-inch black heels, she moves confidently with a determined gaze, but clanks when she walks as her large silver bracelets noisily bang into each other. She also wears big silver earrings and a silver brooch cast in modern geometric lines.

To find her Back Bay office, one must walk up two escalators then ride two elevators, but she decides not to meet there. Confidential papers are on her desk, so she's chosen a suite on the forty-first floor of the Westin Copley Plaza Hotel next door—very hush-hush. Until she lets out a deep and lusty laugh.

"I don't have a need to run things," she says. "My office is the same size as every other partner at the firm. Real leadership is not about your title. It's about being good at what you do so that people are willing to follow you. Part of what a leader has to do is project a certain confidence. And leaders have to be willing to initiate change and institute a certain set of values."

Gadiesh was the third female consultant Bain ever hired. In 1977, she was bombarded with a slew of offers after graduating in the top 5 percent of her class at Harvard Business School, and chose Bain. She gained notoriety as a top consultant in an unusual field for a woman, the steel industry. One client, a multibillion-dollar steel giant, presented her with a hard hat imprinted with a saying above the brim: "A little light will lead us." In Hebrew, "Orit" means "light." She was instrumental in assisting National Steel, which hired Bain in 1981, when it was the highest-cost producer of flat rolled steel in the country. With Bain's efforts and Gadiesh's help, National Intergroup, as it was renamed, became one of the lowest-cost steel producers in the country by 1984.

From the start, Bain acted as a high-flying sounding board for chief executive officers of blue-chip companies. As a strategy consultancy, Bain helps clients devise overall plans for growth based on analysis of markets, product cycles, competitors, pricing, and other fundamentals. The biggest corporations in the world pay millions for such advice, which typically is given by high-priced young Ivy League business school graduates equipped with the latest analytical tools.

Bill Bain founded the firm in 1973, after escaping from the Boston Consulting Group with six colleagues and two former clients. While other firms produced massive reports of recommendations, Bain caught fire as one of the first to focus on implementing results for clients. When Bain consultants worked directly with chief executive officers to put the firm's recommendations into practice on long-term projects, fees soared. Bill Bain called it "relationship consulting," in which a consultant became a "quasi-insider" at the client company and was judged by client results. Dun & Bradstreet reportedly paid the company close to $35 million for one year's work. Bain revenues grew close to 40 percent a year, compounded, during its first ten years. The firm also promised not to help competitors of clients—a policy that added to the company's exclusive allure.

But Bill Bain's greed and carelessness nearly bankrupted the company he built as he made the very mistakes he had warned clients to avoid. He and his fellow partners were anxious to cash in on the firm's rapid growth. Between 1985 and 1986, he and the firm's other founders sold 30 percent of the company to develop an employee stock ownership plan (ESOP), and made off with $200 million in what they considered hard-earned profits. The firm had to borrow money to pay off the founders, burdening it with $25 million in annual interest payments. The debt mired the company just as Bain's profits had begun to drop. Its dependence on a handful of clients became a liability when the recession hit and many blue-chip customers cut their consulting budgets. Then, too, new consulting companies entered the fray, intensifying competition. In April 1988, Bain laid off 10 percent of its professionals, and more layoffs followed. Divisions at the firm widened as younger partners wanted a larger piece of the profits, while Bill Bain spent less and less time working. "We all had observed how consultants lose touch when they stop spending time with clients," Gadiesh recalled. "We decided to never let that become an issue again in our company."

With the company's revenues in decline, Bill Bain made another massive miscalculation. In early 1989, he hired Peter Dawkins, a former Heisman Trophy winner and army brigadier general, to act as a rainmaker and to run the firm's North American operations. Despite his high-level contacts, Dawkins lacked a background in consulting, and his presence angered many of Bain's partners, who wanted more of a say in management. Finally, some of the company's top talent left the firm.

A QUICK MIND AND A PASSION FOR CLIENTS

By 1991, Bain was close to bankruptcy, and Gadiesh made the bold decision to remain at the firm, attract new clients, and talk to employees about her vision of restoring pride in the company. Since then, she has been labeled the company's "spiritual backbone," and was elected chairman of the firm in 1993. Bill Bain no longer owned any part of the firm he founded, and Gadiesh, along with a team of partners, transformed the company into a partnership. According to the new structure, seventy-five partners owned 60 percent of the business, and the ESOP owned the remaining 40 percent.

Why did she choose to stay when most people were heading for the exits? Gadiesh showed courage under fire, another trait of new paradigm leadership. "I felt very strongly and passionately that what Bain & Company set out to do—our product, our results-oriented approach, and the way we work with our clients—was unique and worthwhile," Gadiesh says. "While we had a hiccup in there because of some financial issue that had to do with the founders, I thought if we could just get over it with some restructuring then we could get right back to [our clients]."

Gadiesh expressed her independent vision through her words and actions. She signed an agreement to remain at Bain for two years, and served on a policy committee. She also called headhunters and told them she would not speak to them for the next two years. "I always had sort of had an open door so people knew they could talk to me. Some people literally call my office a railroad station. If there's an issue for anybody at any level, I will stop and focus on them," she explains. "Most people don't talk to their peers about job offers, but many talked to me. And I encouraged other people to talk to colleagues as well about their decision to stay. Everyone was talking about who was leaving and why, but nobody heard anyone talking about who was staying and why. Somebody had to start, and I decided to do it. That was actually an important beginning of the reversal."

From the start of her career at Bain, Gadiesh had proved a tough and loyal consultant. When she and a senior partner were coming back to the office in a taxi from her first presentation, a steel spring from a truck shattered her window. Glass sprayed in her face and cut her upper lip. She got stitches before arriving at a dinner meeting with clients that night. Another time, she was mugged while walking down a London street on the way to a dinner meeting with a client. The robbers grabbed the bag in which she was carrying her dress shoes. She filled out a police report, then strolled into the restaurant wearing her sneakers. "This is not about me, ever. It's not about proving you're smart or you're this or you're that," she says. "It's about focusing on the client and what they need. I just got up, did what I needed to do and walked into dinner with the client."

Some clients would not take Gadiesh seriously at first. Even today, she is often mistaken for the chairman's secretary. Sometimes, when she enters a meeting with a male colleague, the client gazes at her associate instead of her while speaking. She asks coworkers in advance just to look at her during meetings so that the client will be viewing her associate's ear unless he turns his attention toward her. "I think being a woman in a business like this is a double-edged sword," she says. "If you walk into a room with six guys wearing blue suits, you are going to stand out. If you say something stupid, they are going to remember it, and if you say something smart, they will remember it, too. Ultimately, being focused on the job at hand and being competent balance out the negative attention you get."

Her sense of vision helped her rise quickly through the ranks at Bain, even though the company was renowned for its macho atmosphere. Colleagues say her uncanny and unparalleled rapport with senior executives of major American companies caused her rapid rise. Many clients ask for her by name, and even invite her to private dinner meetings where they seek career advice from her. Being brutally honest and direct in quickly sizing up the situation for clients was a skill that helped her garner results and attention. Many clients sing her praises, including George Fisher, chairman of Eastman Kodak Company. "Initially, the fact that Orit was so darn smart and opinionated was disarming," says Fisher. "She understands business as a game of strategy in a military sense and is extremely persuasive. She doesn't just show up with a bunch of prepared slides. We come out of a meeting with her holding a different opinion than we had going in. To me, that says a lot."

Rather than shoot for lofty ideals that are impractical for clients, she works with management to come up with a strategy that the client company can actually execute. "Being perfect in an environment where a perfect solution can't be implemented isn't practical," she says. "You have to listen to clients very carefully. By listening to the things people say about why something is hard to implement, you can either learn how to convince them or find another solution. If you don't convince the people who ultimately turn solutions into practice, you get a very small yield."

AN INTREPID CHARACTER

Gadiesh's parents and her upbringing abroad gave her some powerful tools for excelling in a largely man's world. Born in the port city of Haifa, Gadiesh grew up in Israel as the elder of two daughters. Her father was an Israeli army commander who moved the family to that country's center of commerce, Tel Aviv, when she was a year old. Her father, too, was a consultant of sorts, helping to reorganize and professionalize the Israeli military. After leaving the army, he became a prominent businessman who ran Monsanto's Israeli subsidiary. A quiet man who was humble about his accomplishments, her father spoke little about what he did at work. But he taught his daughter skills she would need later—self-confidence and an ability to extend trust to others. He did not lay down expectations for her schoolwork or for boys she would date. "I trust you completely," she recalls her father saying. "You will figure it out." She came home with straight A's.

It was her mother who taught her the valuable lesson of how to speak up and be persistent in achieving her goals. A former nurse who became a homemaker after having children, her mother focused her attentions completely on her children when they were young. And she was anything but shy. In 1978, Gadiesh's cousin was wounded while serving in the army. When he went to the hospital, the doctor said he would lose his eye. Then her mother arrived. She flatly refused, and insisted they keep trying to find a way to save the eye. "I'm sure she got on everyone's nerves, but my cousin can see today," says Gadiesh. "My mother is the kind of person who believes there is no such thing as something that cannot be done."

Gadiesh shares her mother's belief in doing whatever it takes to overcome obstacles, and that spirit helped her excel after joining the Israeli army. Although two years in the army is required for all Israeli teens, she began a year early at the age of seventeen and landed a plum position. She served from 1969 through 1971 as an aide to the deputy chief of staff, Ezer Weizman, who was in charge of all operations, including military intelligence. Enemies were pounding the country across its borders. As a teenager, Gadiesh was in the war room while army brass were mapping a strategy. "You see very quickly they are people, too, and you learn to respect them enormously," she says. "But you also learn not to be intimidated by them. That's my role today with clients."

Following her army service, Gadiesh focused on her education. She earned a bachelor's degree in psychology at Hebrew University, but was unenthused by the prospect of teaching. After a graduation visit to the United States, she applied to the Harvard Business School. With limited knowledge of English, she wrote her application in Hebrew, then worked laboriously to translate it. Despite having to learn English as she went along, she graduated at the top of her class. The same workaholic tendencies that made her a standout at Harvard have paid off at Bain.

Gadiesh's counterintuitive vision has guided her as chairman of the firm. She acts more like an employee than the boss. Unlike Bain's founders, who cut back their work with clients and lost touch with the business, or executives at other service firms, who tend to sell products or handle administrative tasks when they enter management, Gadiesh spends 70 percent of her time with clients. She typically works over seventy hours a week, and is known for staying until midnight with the rest of a case team before an important presentation. By putting in time with clients, she sends a powerful message that senior partners need to stay involved for the firm to continue to grow. "Actually being on the front line forces you to stay current and allows you to shape the things that are being worked on," she says. "And the quality of the work is far superior when senior people are truly involved. If not, they lose touch and bad things happen."

Partners at Bain are also more accountable these days than they were under Bill Bain and the founders. "We have a different compensation approach now," she says. "In our firm, partners get compensated based on the results, including profits, growth, or revenues, that they bring to the client. We really put our money where our mouth is."

Gadiesh also has a distinct collaborative style that has come to the fore since she has assumed the role of chairman. She describes the firm as "very flat." Now she chairs the committee of partners that makes all the strategic and management decisions for Bain. "In a partnership, you never edict things. It's counterproductive because our assets are people," she says. "We wrestle with issues, then a group of leaders votes to make decisions, and then move on. If there's any source of power in this company, it comes from being good at what one does. It doesn't come from seniority or titles."

Like Meg Whitman, Gadiesh is a leader who embraces change and tries to engage colleagues and customers in the process. To facilitate change and bring greater urgency and immediacy to their jobs, she encourages consultants to be practical and clear when explaining recommendations to clients. She firmly believes in expanding Bain's focus on clients beyond the chief executive officer. She encourages the firm's consultants to work with staff at every level of the organization down to the salespeople in the field. "I call it 'Monday morning at eight o'clock,'" she explains. "I tell my colleagues, 'Imagine you are the client and you are starting your day. Now, what are you going to do differently.' If we can't figure out how our plan is going to get implemented, then results won't happen. It's not just about numbers and data. Most [clients] don't want to change because it's scary, but if you engage them and make them part of a team working on it, it becomes theirs as much as ours."

She also tries to introduce her vision to all employees. Inside Bain, Gadiesh has long been regarded as a junior consultant's most generous mentor. The company attracts graduates from topflight business schools, including Harvard, Stanford, and Wharton. "When she started out, women were trying to prove how tough they were," recalls former "Bainie" Dan Quinn, who now runs Rath & Strong, a rival consultancy. "She showed she could hang with the best of them when she was at the steel and auto companies she worked with, but back at the office, she was like a parent to many of the people at Bain. Her office was like a train station on Fridays because so many people would go to her and ask for advice. She would really spend quality time with them, especially with women MBAs who didn't have anyone else at the firm to look up to."

True to her independent vision, Gadiesh has taken unorthodox steps with employees that most leading executives would never dream of to inspire her colleagues. Bain's McKay remembers a time when he was disappointed and frustrated that he did not receive a promotion he expected. "Orit was someone I sort of barely knew, but she took me aside and spent time with me when she saw that I was discouraged," he recalls. "She even set up job interviews for me at different firms so I could consider other options. But she told me, 'I believe in you, and this will take care of itself.' She was right. I am a vice president here now."

Because the pay scale is similar throughout the industry, Gadiesh relies on creating an unconventional and desirable atmosphere to attract good employees. She once dressed up in a red-sequined jacket to sing a parody of "New York, New York" with the Bain Band during an annual meeting. She's been seen playing the popular college drinking game Quarters with young consultants at 2 A.M. She calls Bain an "apprenticeship business," where junior consultants are paired with senior partners so they can learn how to do the job well. To further these efforts, she was part of the policy committee that approved the Bain Virtual University, an on-line training program available throughout the firm to employees. "Beyond the formal training seminars we offer, it continuously updates new skills and new approaches," she explains. "It also tells you who to go to anywhere in the company to find out about any topic. This is the kind of business where you learn all the time, and our focus on implementation makes us different from other firms. It's not stuffy. It's a fun place to be. I'm open and direct and I mean business, but I'm also a great believer in a sense of humor. I'm still learning every day. That's one of the reasons I'm still here."

Rather than being tied down by convention, Gadiesh always pursues her own path. She married nine years ago, and has no children. Her husband is a former Bain consultant and native Englishman who now owns the restaurant chain John Harvard's Brew Houses. The couple lives in upper-crust Brookline, a suburb of Boston. She is a voracious reader who plows through 100 books a year. To relax, she often takes long walks with her husband and their Old English sheepdog. She is devoted to her work, though, and has overcome her fears in the process. Talking before an audience used to terrify her, but her powerful speeches have solidified her reputation as a charismatic leader. "There's a convention that says you're always best at the things you like doing," she says. "But I think you need to push yourself to do things that you haven't done before and you're not comfortable doing to become better at what you do. Eventually you will start enjoying them, too, or you should have somebody else do your job."

THINKING OUT OF THE BOX

Like Orit Gadiesh, prominent venture capitalist Ann Winblad built a career on her fresh and independent vision. Although she hates the word "vision," her unconventional view has driven the explosive growth of her venture capital firm. Today, thousands of venture capitalists crowd Silicon Valley stalking the latest software investment, and women are not as uncommon as she was when she first appeared on the scene back in 1989. When she launched her venture capital fund that year, however, she was among the early players in the industry to understand the power of software. She joined with John Hummer, an investor seeking start-ups to fund who was also a former center for the Seattle Supersonics. She and her partner became known as the odd couple of venture capital: She is five-foot-three, and he towers at six-foot-ten. At that time, few anticipated what the business would become—a more than $50 billion domestic industry and the fastest-growing sector of the U.S. economy.[10] But because she had already started her own software company in 1975, then sold it in 1983 for $15 million, she knew she could be instrumental in helping others do the same. "It's a really different industry and some people don't get it," she says. "But the longer they don't get it, the longer they will be like deer in the digital headlights."

Winblad distinguished her fund from the pack by adopting an unorthodox strategy. While rivals invested broadly in computer hardware, chips, and networking, Winblad and Hummer were the first to invest only in software start-ups. Before the Internet exploded, software was a hard sell in a Silicon Valley that revered hardware makers such as Apple Computer and Silicon Graphics. "John had a proclivity for software and he saw in me independent thinking," she recalls. "It took a real independent thinker to set up a software-only fund in the days when it was undervalued by venture capitalists. Software was the Rodney Dangerfield of the computer industry. It got no respect. But I was a product of the software industry. I lived and breathed it, where [Hummer] had only invested in it."

In 1990, Winblad and her partner began their fund with $35 million in money from institutional investors anxious to participate in the growth of the budding technology sector. The Hummer Winblad Venture Partners fund returned $260 million in four years, yielding a hefty annual return of 50 percent for its investors on the money she initially invested. By comparison, the average venture capital firm historically returned about 20 percent per year at that time, according to Venture One Corporation, a San Francisco–based venture capital research group. Winblad also created two additional funds and collected over $200 million from pension funds and institutional investors that she has invested in software and Internet companies. In June 1999, she launched the company's fourth fund with $300 million, three times more capital than the firm's last fund. Hummer Winblad has invested in more than sixty companies since its founding and currently has more than $520 million in assets under management. Some of the firms she helped launch include PowerSoft, Liquid Audio, HomeGrocer.com, The Knot, Wind River Systems, Arbor Software Corporation, and Net Perceptions. She even appeared on *Fortune*'s list of the fifty most powerful women in American business in 1998.[11] She makes about fifty deals a year, and has distinguished herself in a booming industry. Venture capital investment reached a record $14.3 billion in 1998, an increase over the prior year of 24 percent, according to PriceWaterhouse Coopers LLP's *Money Tree Report*.[12] And there has never been a better time for the software industry, she says. In the early 1990s, venture capitalists invested less than $200 million a year in software companies, but they pumped a record $4.5 billion into those companies in 1998 alone, a 57 percent increase over 1997.

Unlike many other venture capitalists who plow money into a start-up after its launch, she has such a strong sense of vision that she becomes an investor when the newly minted business is little more than an idea. Her firm is the first investor in about 80 percent of the deals it makes. She views her role not simply as a source for funds but as an experienced "coach" who can teach budding entrepreneurs and draw on classic feminine talents to nurture and develop employees in these emerging companies. Her outlook recasts the traditional view of a venture capitalist as a "moneybags" to that of a key player in the start-up itself who can boost that nascent company's chance of being around for the next fiscal year. Her penchant for rolling up her sleeves and getting involved in the nitty-gritty details of the businesses she invests in keeps her plugged into the latest developments in the rapidly changing technology industry. It has also helped her forge connections across Silicon Valley, and leads her to discover new investment opportunities. She constantly builds her contacts, and is a fixture at industry conferences and events. As a new paradigm leader unafraid of breaking the mold of what makes a traditional venture capitalist, she has been able to rack up a sterling track record for her own firm. "I don't see myself as a financier, but a company creator," she explains. "What has changed with the Net is we can now build whole industries."

Like Patricia Russo in telecommunications, Darla Moore in banking, and other new paradigm leaders, Ann Winblad rose in a field where women were virtually nonexistent. But the reputation she earned as Silicon Valley's savviest software investor has assured her respect in her own right. "Ann is in a class by herself," says Larry Buchsbaum, editor of the *Money Tree Report*, which tracks investments by venture capitalists. "She stands out because she is so innovative and proactive in uncovering entrepreneurs."

A typical venture capitalist is a man with a business degree from Harvard or Stanford and a solid background managing successful high-technology firms. There are so few women venture capitalists even today that statistics on their representation in the industry are virtually nonexistent. The reasons for the gap, experts say, lies in the dearth of women entering computer science and engineering during the 1990s. At universities, men outnumber women at least three to one in most courses in these disciplines, according to the American Association of University

Women. While demand for computer scientists has skyrocketed for the past few years, the proportion of women in 1996 who intended to declare computer science as a major was only 1.4 percent, according to the National Center of Education Statistics. Knowing this, Winblad asked, "Does this microphone pick up a female voice?" after arriving at the podium during a recent industry conference.

Like Meg Whitman, Ann Winblad dares to be different. She takes pride in her office, a former plumbing factory in San Francisco's ultra-hip South Park section, because it's more than thirty miles north of "venture capital row" along Sand Hill Road in Silicon Valley's Menlo Park, where the majority of high-tech venture capital firms are located. She says she stays away from the others because she is afraid of alerting rivals to the nature of her deals, and dislikes the herd mentality. "Eagles don't flock," she says.

Hummer Winblad is housed in a loftlike space where wide wood planks cover the floors and exposed industrial pipes run along the ceiling. Light streams through the broad windows into her office and across her industrial-style brown wooden slab desk. And having launched her own software start-up back in the mid-1970s, while she is certainly one of the original "geeks," she does not look the part. After all, she is the former head cheerleader at her high school in Farmington, Minnesota. Her fine blond hair wisps down to her shoulders, and short bangs fall across her forehead. She is classically dressed in a tailored black pantsuit with a beige ribbed turtleneck. A pair of Paloma Picasso sterling silver X earrings is all the jewelry she wears. Petite and animated with piercing blue eyes, she stays on a tight schedule and glances at her gold Rolex watch frequently to check the time. She is out on the road so often that some officemates say they rarely see her. "Most venture capitalists just sift through plans and wait for somebody they already know to call them," she says. "Our approach is more aggressive."

Winblad has a new vision to sell—she enjoys playing a part in recruiting top-level talent and crafting strategy. As a start-up veteran, she aims to help entrepreneurs get past hurdles she has already cleared. "We are usually the first venture capitalists in a deal so our core job is to set up a strong management team," she says. "We look at what's functioning and what isn't before we invest, and make strong suggestions that changes be made. Our only asset is that intellectual capital. In other industries, it's different because the power is in the money, not the people. Dollars make no difference in our industry. There are no barriers to entry—men, women, horses, and dogs can compete."

Her industry connections help her make links that solidify the future of the companies she funds. She paired one of her start-ups, Homegrocer.com, with Internet powerhouse Amazon.com. The linkage virtually assures the new company's success. In November 1999, the burgeoning on-line grocer lured $100 million of new private stock financing, bringing its total to $162.5 million, and attracting IPO interest. She helped link another of her start-ups, the popular bridal registry site The Knot, with home shopping network player QVC. As a result, The Knot received a $15 million investment from QVC. In November 1999, The Knot was the first Internet wedding business to launch its IPO, and shares jumped 50 percent on its first day of trading.

"She is like the third eye," explains David Liu, chief executive officer and cofounder of The Knot. "In Asian cultures, that third eye connotes vision, but it really means wisdom. She's seen all the trials and tribulations of firms going through the start-up phase so she knows what you need to do to get through it. She is not going to set your strategy as a company, but she helps you navigate the challenges of developing your business. And she has instincts that are extremely well honed. She is the consummate networker and the ultimate cheerleader so she can help you reach your goals. Now our company is publicly traded and worth over $100 million."

Winblad's approach to her job is similar to business theorist Sally Helgesen's description of the modern chief executive in *The Female Advantage*: "Given the changing nature both of work and of people who work, there emerges a need for leaders who can stimulate employees to work with zest and spirit. Leaders must . . . devise organizational structures that encourage and nurture human growth."[13]

Winblad employs her counterintuitive vision to help entrepreneurs take their skills to the next level. She helps nurture ideas and give birth to new companies, but defines nurturing as "setting the bar" rather than a soothing, overly feminine activity. "My job is to be the realist, the pragmatist, so I describe market realities," she says. "My assumption is that people want to be the best, so my motivator is to say, 'Okay, if we want to win the Olympic gold medal, then the bar is here.' I always stand at 10,000 feet and look down at the whole team—the chief executive officer, the chief financial officer, and all the managers. Coaching is great for these young companies because it helps them understand their strengths and weaknesses. I am a great recruiter, networker, and architect, and I help move the company toward a position of strength. These CEOs in high-growth companies don't have the time to do that because they are stuck in a tsunami of information. So the coach plays a key role in company formation. I'm really interested in projecting ahead. Other people don't want to do that because they don't want to make future guesses and look silly."

The entrepreneurs she funds benefit from her foresight. In 1998, Liu received over $5 million in backing from Winblad's firm, which now owns over 20 percent of his on-line wedding site, The Knot. Once, Liu selected a CFO for the company, but Winblad encouraged him to hold out for a stronger candidate. "I presented someone who I thought was very bright and capable to Ann, but she said, 'She's smart, but she's not the right person to be CFO when you are pitching your business to America Online or QVC. I thought Ann was crazy. How could I attract a more capable person to an Internet start-up? And I was anxious to unload the financial duties of CFO to someone else because I was so busy with all of my own responsibilities as CEO of a fledgling business. But we wound up getting Rich [Szefe], who was CFO of Random House and turned down a job at

Barnes and Noble to work for us. She thought we should have the best, and she believes in an unrelenting pursuit of excellence. And she's right. She helped me believe, too."

Like Rebecca Mark and other new paradigm leaders, Winblad had big plans for her future. After persuading three computer programmer colleagues from her post-college job at the Federal Reserve Bank of Minnesota to quit and join her, Winblad started her own company building accounting software. In 1975, she borrowed $500 from her brother and launched Open Systems, Inc. The foursome opened offices in Minneapolis above the studio of the musician formerly known as Prince. "This was the riskiest thing I had ever done in my life. But sometimes you just have to take the risk," she said. "I can still recount the joy in the early days of starting a business, when we had to shut down the executive offices once orders began coming in so that we could help pack boxes in the shipping department. It's a real thrill when you can say you built a product that people really want or need."

After reeling in strong earnings growth and expanding the company to 120 employees, Winblad and her partners were successful enough to sell the business in 1983 for $15 million. She claimed that the lack of financial backing for software firms in the Twin Cities area drove her to leave town.

Winblad took her share of the money and headed for Mecca as far as technophiles are concerned: San Francisco. At first she thought she wanted to start another software firm, but found that growth in the PC software industry had flattened. While Microsoft was booming, she noted that other software companies were consolidating. Instead, she began to do some consulting work for clients, including PriceWaterhouse, Apple, and Microsoft. She met Bill Gates at a conference in February 1984, and the two dated for the next three years.

During an assignment for a venture capital firm, she met Hummer. The former first-round draft pick, who played in the NBA for six seasons and earned degrees from Princeton and Stanford, began recruiting her to help him start a venture capital fund dedicated to software.

"John went after me because he saw me start my own company and make the tough decision to sell it with 100 percent growth, so he knew I was an independent thinker," she recalls. "He also wanted to recruit me because I grew up in the software industry, where he had not. And he wanted to attract me because he needed someone who had already made a small transition toward a coaching role rather than a player who was leading a start-up company. The timing could not have been any better for us because the software boom would begin again in 1990."

Apart from the unique focus of Hummer Winblad, the pair distinguished themselves by setting up shop in Emeryville, California, just east of San Francisco. Their location put them at the center of University of California at Berkeley–inspired start-ups, and far afield from the center of venture capitalism in Menlo Park. In 1997, they shifted their offices to San Francisco, but remained distant from the bulk of venture capitalists. Today, she oversees a small staff of thirteen, and offers them a lot of autonomy. "I don't look over anyone's shoulder," she says. "The ability to think out of the box is key to our industry."

Like Meg Whitman and Marcy Carsey, Ann Winblad reinvents the rules and thinks out of the box. For instance, she devised the "Gong Show," another feature of her firm that is unique in the industry. Since 1989, she has set aside one day each quarter to audition entrepreneurs looking for funds, and runs it just like the old television show. More than 4,000 companies have come before her through this open event. She gives each a half hour to make its presentation. "That whole strategy of sitting at your desk, waiting for someone to pitch you an idea didn't make sense to me," she says. "We are much more accessible. With the Gong Show, my idea was to bring in new talent to make sure we are unbiased and don't miss out on important opportunities. We listen to people who are passionate. It's unscreened. I think to be a great leader in this business you must always reevaluate your assumptions."

BEYOND ALLY MCBEAL

Like Marcy Carsey, Winblad's iconoclasm fueled her journey from her hometown to the pinnacle of her industry. She grew up in Red Wing, Minnesota, a tiny town of 2,100 people, with one stop sign and no traffic lights, twenty-five miles south of Minneapolis. She was the eldest of six children—five girls and a boy. Her father was a high school football and basketball coach, and her mother was a home-maker. She lived in a modest household but did not feel deprived. Positive and upbeat was the atmosphere at home. She played a lot with her sisters and brother, and showed an entrepreneurial flair at an early age. While her siblings drew pictures, Ann would peddle their drawings to neighborhood parents. One sister, Patty Jorgensen, told the *San Francisco Chronicle*, "I remember she'd be making Barbie doll clothes and selling them. I would beg for one, but she'd say, 'No, I'm selling these.'"[14]

Winblad's parents passed on their regard for education. Ann stud-ied diligently, and had a knack for math and science. She also loved to read and plowed through most of the books in her local public school library. "My brother turned out to be incredibly soft-spoken and became the underachiever of the family," she says. "He was the only one of us who didn't go to college. I think he was really overwhelmed by all these bright girls. My four sisters have all risen in their chosen professions."

Like Orit Gadiesh, Winblad learned from her father to believe in herself and trust her own instincts. From an early age, he taught her to challenge herself. Every night, while her mother was tucking in the three younger children for the night, her father would take the three bigger girls outside to play. He had his daughters run races in the backyard while building their sense of independence. From these daily activities, she learned not to compare herself to the crowd, but to go her own way and set her own goals—important assets in devel-oping her own sense of vision as a leader. "He would put little stopwatches around our necks, and we would go off to race. But we would try to beat our previous best time, not each other," she said. "The fact that my dad didn't have us race each other was fundamental. We were always taught to improve our own abilities."

Thanks to her father, Winblad developed a strong sense of self that would later give her the confidence to pursue her own vision. While all her friends had curfews, Winblad's father gave her a lot of leeway. "Every time I would ask what time I had to be home, my dad would always say, 'You seem to be sensible and smart, so use your own good judgment,'" she recalls. "The fact that he endowed me with the power to make decisions at an early age helped me learn how to make good choices. For me, that's all you have. You completely fail in the technology industry if you can't make good decisions rapidly. As you get older, no one else sets the rules for you, and judgment is what this is all about."

Her father also believed in Winblad's abilities. She was athletic, and won a letter competing in a regional track event. The valedictorian of her graduating class at Farmington High School, she scored a four-year scholarship at the then all-women College of St. Catherine in St. Paul, Minnesota. She graduated in 1973 with a degree in math and business administration. "My father never said, 'Only boys can do this or only girls can do that,'" she recalls. "He grew up in a family with five boys and one girl, the opposite of ours. And his sister is such a secure, confident woman."

At college, Winblad's entrepreneurial spirit thrived. She fell in love with computers, calling them her "lemonade stand." She would write software programs for male classmates in exchange for their girlfriends' typing her papers. She juggled three jobs to pay her way: She worked as a cocktail waitress at a dive where the bartenders called her Sunshine, a bookkeeper at a hardware store, and a customer service representative for Northwestern Bell. She also made one of her greatest discoveries: Guys from wealthy families "weren't any smarter than me."

Winblad then went on to earn a master's degree in international economics and education from the nearby almost all-male University of St. Thomas in St. Paul, Minnesota. Like Orit Gadiesh, she was deluged with job offers after graduate school. She was looking for a job where she could work with computers, but passed up offers from 3M Company and the FBI to take a position as a systems analyst at the Federal Reserve Bank of Minneapolis because the building was the "coolest she'd ever seen."[15] It would be her last job that involved working for someone else. Thirteen months later, she was bored. A colleague she shared a cubicle with disappeared for an hour each afternoon to watch *I Dream of Jeannie.* Her boss stole credit for a flex-time scheme she proposed. And she felt she was given special treatment because of affirmative action.

"I was highly paid and was moving up quickly—they raised my salary three times in a year—but I hated feeling like I was the chosen girl," she recalls. "And people had absolutely no passion about the work. Their intellectual curiosity was low. They would come in at 9 A.M. sharp, and by 5 P.M. it was a ghost town. Frankly, we all wore skirts hiked up to our asses. I actually saved a couple things I wore. I thought, 'What if I ever bent over?' We were all Ally McBealed, and there were no feminists in Minneapolis. I wanted something else, something better. One day I just decided to quit my job. I had no money and a ton of student loans, but I needed to resign because my future was not there. It was the smartest thing I ever did."

Winblad's software start-up project would give her the insider status needed to maneuver easily in the venture capital world, and she proceeded to rack up a sterling track record. Among more than sixty software and Internet companies Hummer Winblad funded, only one faltered: Slate, a start-up focused on pen-based computing. That company slumped, despite bragging a roster of industry legends, including Dan Bricklin, creator of the Lotus 1–2–3 spreadsheet. Slate was ultimately bought by Compaq Computer, and Hummer Winblad lost almost $1.2 million in the deal, according to *Wired* magazine.[16]

She learned from the mistake: "We knew it was a great team with a great product, but we knew when we invested that the market wasn't quite ready for it. We violated our first rule: Choose large-market real estate. That was stupid. Failure teaches you that you have to be careful. When you look at the glass as being half full, you need to make certain that the variables that fill up the glass are within your reach instead of being controlled by others."

Like Patricia Fili-Krushel, formerly of ABC, and Kim Polese of Marimba, Ann Winblad relies on her passion for pleasing customers when choosing a start-up to fund. Rather than simply depending on her own future predictions to select companies to fund, she keeps close ties to purchasers. She will not pursue an investment in a start-up project without gauging responses to products from potential users, and she is known for her strong network in the technology industry, most of which she developed through launching Open Systems just as the industry was burgeoning. She got to know other titans of technology like Bill Gates long before most had made their first billion. Each day, she receives 400 e-mails, many from friends in the business.

The ability to network is a hallmark of the highly competitive venture capital industry. The connections an executive has pave the way for deals with entrepreneurs at the earliest phases of their business development and translate directly into successful ventures and IPO windfalls. By staying close to her large network and assessing customer reactions, Winblad can check if a potential product is viable in the marketplace. For instance, she took Jim Dorrian and Bob Earle, the cofounders of Arbor Software Corporation, directly to see executives at Sun Microsystems to offer their pitch. Then Winblad asked the CIO of Sun Microsystems if he would buy their product. Arbor has been a winner ever since—going public, then merging with Hyperion Software. Her network is also crucial in establishing partnerships, such as the Homegrocer.com deal with Amazon.com. "If you want to be part of the future, you want to partner," she says. "So we have high schmoozing capabilities in our industry. Our network is as valuable as the capital we invest."

Winblad is so consumed by her work that she has so far forgone marriage and children. Instead, she's devoted to her two dogs. Although she places future bets on companies that will not come to fruition for years to come, Winblad is comfortable with the risks she takes to make her vision a reality. "We are floating in a sea of data, and it is the people who know how to make choices based on that data that win here," she says. "I turn that data into seeds of success."

3

REINVENTING THE RULES

I learned early on in my career that you could be just as effective, if not more so, by talking to people about what you were trying to accomplish and enlisting them in the decision.

— MEG WHITMAN

If new paradigm leadership is about breaking the rules and reinventing new ones, there have been few better displays of it than Margaret (Meg) Whitman. At forty-two, she is chief executive officer of one of the fastest-growing Internet companies in the industry, yet unlike many of her rivals in the highly competitive field, she has no background in technology. And eBay, Inc., the leading on-line auction company in a market estimated at $250 billion, is profiting with Whitman at the helm—a year after her arrival as president and chief executive officer, eBay offers 3 million items for auction daily, and boasts 10 million registered users. In 1999, the company raked in $2.8 billion in revenues, an increase of 192% over 1998. "People go gonzo over eBay," declared *USA Today*.[1] Unlike competitors and most of the industry, the site has been profitable since its inception, earning $2.4 million in net income in 1998. Seven months after her arrival, she took the company public, raising $735 million. Its stock, though volatile, has surged over 1,000 percent and the company's market capitalization has grown to $22.1 billion in May 1999. eBay is among the top ten businesses on the Internet, although like all Internet companies, its worth can fluctuate daily, depending on the whim and whimsy of Wall Street. In March 2000, Meg Whitman was worth $1 billion after cashing in a portion of her eBay stock, but she still drives an old Buick to work.

The *New York Times* has likened Whitman to Ray Kroc, the founder of McDonald's.[2] While Kroc was a father of fast food who helped usher in a new kind of consumer culture in the early 1960s by making the golden arches an institution across the country, he clearly did not need to understand the chemistry of ground beef to sell a hamburger people craved. Likewise, Whitman does not need to be a computer expert to build a successful Internet company. Instead, and perhaps more importantly, she boasts brand management savvy and the intelligence to learn as she goes, plunging herself into a culture she is cultivating on-line.

Pierre M. Omidyar, founder, chairman, and former chief executive officer of eBay, and Robert Kagle, a partner at venture capital firm Benchmark Capital, handpicked Whitman from among forty high-level executive candidates for the job. Kagle said that she stood out from the crowd because of her long experience in marketing brands. "I was looking for a brand builder to help make eBay a household name," explains Kagle. "Understanding technology was not the central ingredient. You have to have the emotional component of the customer experience in your gut. Unlike the others, she had worked for companies with great long-term brands like Keds, Disney, and Playskool and had a sense of how to promote them. Meg understood that this is a marathon we are running here, and she wants to build eBay for long-term growth."

Whitman is not just thinking outside the box, but building a new box. And she is not alone. All new paradigm leaders share her conviction. Rather than following a standard job description or simply continuing the strategy of their male predecessors, these women are taking risks to reinvent the rules of their businesses. Darla Moore helped redefine Citibank's view that bankrupt companies should be avoided at all costs by turning insolvent firms into reliable customers. Rebecca Mark built her career proving that power projects in the Third World lead to massive profits, especially in politically sticky India. Unlike her husband, Martha Ingram split up the empire of Ingram Industries and even fired one of his trusted lieutenants, former chief executive officer Chip Lacey. Loida Lewis took a separate path from her husband by focusing on improving and expanding the core businesses of TLC Beatrice, and discarding the investment arm Reginald Lewis established to pursue potential takeover targets. Another new paradigm leader, also featured in this chapter because of her ability to break the rules, is Marcy Carsey, cofounder and copresident of Carsey-Werner, the television production studio that launched groundbreaking hits like *The Cosby Show, Roseanne,* and *3rd Rock from the Sun.* Carsey recently joined Oprah Winfrey and Geraldine Laybourne to launch Oxygen Media, a cable channel and Internet site geared for women.

BUILDING A NEW BOX

From an early age, girls are socialized to please people, whether it be parents or teachers, and feel pressured to fulfill the expectations others hold for them. According to a 1991 study commissioned by the American Association of University Women, as girls grow up, their self-esteem plummets. Spirited and aggressive at ages eight and nine, girls begin to lose more confidence than boys do in their abilities at ages thirteen and fourteen. Girls come out of high school with considerably lowered goals and future aspirations. In the poll of 3,000 students, 60 percent of the girls and 67 percent of the boys said they were pleased with themselves in elementary school. In middle school, only 37 percent of girls compared with 56 percent of boys were still pleased with themselves in middle school. Merely 29 percent of high school girls were still happy with themselves, while almost half (46 percent) of high school boys kept a strong level of self-esteem.[3]

Family life has a profound impact on the self-esteem of adolescents. "Parents send contradictory messages that they want their daughters to get good grades in all subjects, but also to exhibit 'appropriate' polite and even demure behavior for a female," explains Dr. Sally Morgan Reis, professor of educational psychology at the University of Connecticut. "The stereotypical behaviors often conflict with the personal attributes a . . . female needs to succeed. Some parents require, or at a minimum expect, their daughters to be polite, well-mannered, and consistently congenial . . . girls are not supposed to be too independent."[4]

But following the rules can be detrimental to a woman's career. Kate White, editor in chief of *Cosmopolitan* magazine, writes that girls learn to be quiet and obedient because they were punished for not doing so, while earning praise from parents, teachers, and almost everyone else when they acted like "good girls." "The real tragedy is that, despite the pats on the shoulder and the compliments, being a good girl actually undermines your career and prevents you from achieving maximum success. . . . The rewards go to women who make their own rules, take big chances, toot their own horns and don't worry if everyone likes them."[5]

New paradigm leaders like Meg Whitman and Marcy Carsey do not feel bridled by the expectations others place on them. Instead, they fulfill their own aspirations, and stand as corporate revolutionaries who topple convention. They excel at formulating a unique vision for their companies, and enlisting employees to support that goal. Although they have thrown off the traditional female focus on pleasing others, they do hold to classic feminine traits that work to their advantage. For example, to motivate employees they draw on such female talents as valuing cooperation and emphasizing relationships. In Sally Helgesen's words, "They are reinventing themselves to accommodate a wider focus, to foster creativity and nurture new ideas."[6]

The ability to build a new box and take in a wider range of ideas arms Whitman, Carsey, and other new paradigm leaders with the tools to break and remake the rules. For such a leader, the goal is not to be a good girl or try to emulate a male model of leadership. Instead, the objective is to bring a new perspective to management. "Before they do anything else, they first break all the rules of conventional wisdom," write Marcus Buckingham and Curt Coffman in *First, Break All the Rules.* "Great managers are revolutionaries."[7]

Reinventing the rules is a crucial aspect of leadership today. When facing common issues plaguing all companies, like reducing expenses, chief executives need to come up with innovative solutions. Without this capability, a company may lose its edge. Ronald Allen wrestled with this issue when he was chairman, president, and chief executive of Delta Air Lines from 1987 to 1997. In 1994, Allen announced that he intended to trim about $2 billion in annual operating expenses, and eliminate 15,000 jobs by 1997 at Delta. His relentless focus on reducing costs by firing employees while trying at the same time to sustain service levels caused morale to plummet and customer service to decline.[8] He was criticized in the press for failing to keep up with the changing times.[9] Delta stock fell after its earnings failed to meet Wall Street estimates, and the board reportedly asked Allen to leave.[10] The stock rose after his departure.

Kay Whitmore, who served as chief executive officer of Kodak from 1990 until 1993, faced similar difficulties. Under his leadership, film profits were weakened by high expenses and losses in various segments of the business.[11] Kodak's standing as the innovation leader of the photography industry suffered as a result. *Forbes* labeled Whitmore as a man who was "cut from the old pattern," and lacked both attention to marketing and a global perspective so necessary for success today.[12]

A NEW TAKE ON WEB MANAGEMENT

Like Darla Moore, Loida Lewis, and all other new paradigm leaders, Meg Whitman rose in a field dominated by men. The high-tech industry still falls significantly behind the rest of corporate America in the numbers of women holding top positions and sitting on corporate boards, according to a 1999 survey by Catalyst, a nonprofit research group in New York dedicated to advancing female leaders in business. The survey noted that women fill only 8 percent of executive suites in computer software Fortune 500 companies, compared with 12 percent overall for Fortune 500 firms. Many women do not rise in computer software simply because they lack the engineering or computer science background of most of the men who lead that industry. While demand for computer scientists has soared during the past few years, only 17 percent of engineering students are women, according to the American Association of University Women.

By taking over the top spot at eBay, Meg Whitman is a surprising billionaire among the technophiles in Silicon Valley. She is a seasoned manager of blue-chip companies, with a strong background in marketing consumer products. Only Carleton (Carly) Fiorina, who became the first woman to head Hewlett-Packard in July 1999, shares the distinction of leading a high-technology company without a background in the field. These two powerful women are taking advantage of a new trend in the industry—the Internet boom has honed the industry's focus on consumers rather than on technology, opening the door to women from nonengineering backgrounds.

"The ability to think strategically is more important today," says Kim Polese, chief executive officer of software company Marimba, Inc. "Women do not have a monopoly on that, but one of the essential ingredients is moving fast and seeing strategy from a completely different point of view. The fact that women are successful at that is opening more doors."

THE EVOLUTION OF A LEADER

The doors to Meg Whitman's office in San Jose, California, are wide open. In fact, her office has no doors. Like the rest of her 200 employees, she is ensconced in a cubicle—they are all the same size. She and Omidyar reorganized the eBay headquarters into cubicles when the company moved to new offices in June 1999. As she sits behind her standard putty desk, with a basic PC on her desktop, her look is classic and traditional. With her blond hair styled in a short bob, she wears a pair of pleated khaki trousers with an orange and white striped Façonnable oxford shirt. Her jewelry is minimal—only a diamond engagement ring with a gold band on her left hand. She has huge green eyes and a broad grin. Whitman appears relaxed, occasionally punctuating her speech with cackling laughter. Her desk and side table are cluttered with the collectible baubles commonly sold on eBay—Pez dispensers and Elvis memorabilia, including a black and white photo of him that reads "All the King's Things." A paperback book called *Meg—A Novel of Deep Terror* hints at her wry sense of humor.

"I haven't been in a cubicle since 1985 because my other jobs have been at more traditional companies, but we wanted to reflect our trading community by having offices that are open and allow for free communication and sharing of ideas," she says of the company's new layout. "If you have an office, you end up closing your doors and spending most of your time in your office. But if you're out in cubes, I think people will feel much more comfortable sticking their heads in and saying, 'Here's what's going on.' Being accessible is really important in our business where information is so valuable."

Whitman took to business early. She grew up in Cold Spring, New York, an affluent hamlet on Long Island's North Shore, as the youngest of three children. Like the families of most other new paradigm leaders, including Darla Moore and Martha Ingram, her family valued education and good grades. Her father worked as a factor, someone who bought receivables from textile retailers. He worked hard and had a strong sense of ethics. "He believed that you treat other people like you would like to be treated yourself," she says. "He thought nothing was so bad as being mean to people."

Whitman's mother had a profound impact in teaching her daughter not to feel bound by convention. A homemaker, she was not afraid to stand out and always supported her children in whatever they pursued. She led by example. When Whitman graduated from high school, her mother, Margaret, traveled to China as part of a delegation of women led by entertainer Shirley MacLaine. Margaret Whitman was one of the early American travelers to the People's Republic in 1973 after Nixon renewed diplomatic ties. At fifty-five, she began a twenty-year career of leading trips to China, while learning a little Mandarin and studying the nation's economy and society. She made over eighty trips to China through 1993. "She was adventurous, outspoken, and a 'can-do' sort of woman," recalls Whitman. "She always encouraged us to do our own thing."

Meg Whitman began breaking the rules at a young age. She excelled both in her studies at the local public school and in sports. From the age of five until the age of seventeen, she was a competitive swimmer, winning a number of statewide championships. She was in the minority on a swim team, she recalls, which was 70 percent boys and only 30 percent girls. She credits swimming with teaching her the values of hard work, discipline, and efficiency. "Swimming is one of those sports where how well you do correlates directly to how hard you work at practice. You can swim 3,000 yards a day hard, or not so hard, and that is how well you will swim in competition. It's all about self-discipline," she explains. "It also taught me how to be efficient and how to manage time. Swimming three hours a day, I did not have a lot of time for homework, so I did it in the car on the way to practice and in any study breaks I had during the day."

Despite little time for homework, Whitman consistently brought home A's. She was compelled to excel, she says, because she always wanted the satisfaction of accomplishing tasks and doing them well. Her parents had no clear career aspirations for their daughter, but they set their sights on the Ivy League. Her father, after all, was a Harvard man, and Meg Whitman did not disappoint. She started at Princeton in 1973, just two years after the prestigious university opened its doors to women. Back then, her freshman class was just 20 percent female. After a summer selling advertising for her college magazine, she ditched pre-med studies for a degree in economics, and graduated in 1977. Two years later, she earned her MBA from Harvard, and married Griffith R. Harsh IV, a brain surgeon, in 1980.

With her thoroughbred education, Whitman was an attractive job candidate who reinvented the rules. She forged a modern path by being versatile and selecting opportunities that may not have made sense to some, as they weren't linear advancements in the same field, but helped her gain the management experience she needed to run a company like eBay. Her ability to be flexible and adapt to new situations quickly, another feature new paradigm leaders share, allowed her to build experience and glean valuable lessons from each of her positions at an array of blue-chip companies. Fresh out of Harvard, she took an entry-level position in Procter & Gamble's marketing department for a first job. "I have always wanted to do as well as I could in whatever job I was in," explains Whitman. "Even when I started as a brand assistant at Procter & Gamble, I wanted to do the best job I possibly could."

At Procter & Gamble, she learned to work within the system, where she was given large assignments, but very little authority, as a junior employee. Her task? Turning Ivory soap into a shampoo. Whitman had to marshal the support of a sales team, a packaging team, an art department, and the scientists and engineers who actually made the product, yet she had direct authority over none of these people. Instead of simply telling them what to do, she presented them with the research she had compiled and sought their input. Her goal was to spur their participation in solving problems and generating solutions. "It was really good training because, in fact, you get things done mostly by influence rather than doing them yourself," she explains. "I learned early on in my career that you could be just as effective, if not more so, by talking to people about what you were trying to accomplish and enlisting them in the decision."

She finds this lesson particularly helpful at eBay, where she relies on technologists both to expand the system's architecture to manage the company's rapid growth, and to solve nagging problems she faces, like the now-notorious service outages. "It's the difference between giving someone an objective, then letting them figure out how to get there, and describing exactly what it is that you think you want done. When you describe what it is you think you want, usually the result is not as good as if the expert thinks about it, draws on his or her expertise, and comes up with something that actually solves the problem. As you get more senior, you cannot personally solve every problem. If you try to, you usually come up with suboptimal answers because you are no longer closest to the data, the customer, or the system."

After learning these valuable skills from P&G, Meg Whitman faced a situation that is common for many women, and again chose to reinvent the rules. Her husband landed a plum position in another state that would mean a move for the family. A strong, Ivy League–educated woman, she never hesitated to relocate to accommodate her husband's career. The couple went to San Francisco in 1981 so her husband could begin a neurosurgery residency at University of California at San Francisco. She, too, grabbed an exciting job as a consultant with a leading firm, Bain & Company. She worked at Bain for the next nine years, during which she had two sons who are now eleven and fourteen.

Her ability to be flexible and efficient helped her juggle the demands of both her clients and her family. When one is a consultant, she explains, clients do not pay you to learn their business, but rather to solve their problems swiftly. This skill also helps her lead eBay. "I got a lot more done than most people by five because I knew I had to be home for the boys. The really interesting thing I learned at Bain was to get to the heart of the matter very quickly, and learn new businesses fast," she says. "That has been really helpful to me at a place like eBay where I'm not really a technology person, but I have to figure out quickly where I can exert influence, and create change and momentum. I also learned how to do great analysis and acquire great analysis from people."

Next, Whitman got a job with the Walt Disney Company. Between 1989 and 1992, she rose to senior vice president of marketing for Disney Consumer Products. At Disney, she learned the value of attracting high-quality people to a company. "In those days, vice presidents would take directors' jobs, directors would take managers' jobs, and managers would take assistant managers' jobs just to work at Disney," she says. "The quality of the people and the quality of the thought, creativity, and imagination went up a notch because every single person that came in was really good."

At eBay, Whitman tries to mirror the excellence of employees she saw at Disney. With a recognizable and profitable technology company, Whitman has little trouble attracting quality people to eBay. She recently hired senior vice president of marketing Brian Swette, who helped develop Pepsi-Cola Company's popular ads, including those featuring Michael Jackson, and others in which two truck drivers delivering Coke and Pepsi meet at a diner, and the driver carting Coke asks for a Pepsi. At eBay, she also tries to emulate the collaboration at the top which Disney chief Michael Eisner shared with president Frank Wells. She works closely with Omidyar, chairman of the on-line auction house. While she offers the big picture, strategy, and analysis for eBay, he focuses on the details necessary to get there.

When the demands of her husband's career as a neurosurgeon caused yet another move, this time to Boston, in 1992, Whitman again reinvented the rules by reinventing herself. She pursued a job as president of Stride Rite Corporation, and won it. She stayed on from 1992 until 1995. This traditional New England manufacturing business was in need of innovation, and Whitman answered that need by reinvigorating its children's line of footwear. She launched the Munchkin baby shoe line and helped reposition the Stride Rite brand as a fashionable, modern line for kids. On the job, she learned a skill that helps her at eBay, too—how to manage creativity. "You are far better off giving creators a box in which to play, so they have some parameters against which they can create," she says. "You end up with much better product. If you are too blue sky, you don't get what you need."

But at Stride Rite, she missed the quality of Disney executives, and felt constricted by a singular vision at the top. She found herself yearning to shake things up. "Arnold Hyatt [former CEO of Stride Rite] had been very successful running a benevolent dictatorship at the company for about ten or fifteen years, but in the last five years, the company had fallen on hard times, and his approach was no longer working," she explains. "No one is smart enough to make all the decisions and make them right over a very long period of time. You have to have a senior team and management structure that can evolve the company with the times and be forward-looking and forward-thinking. What I've really tried to do at eBay is not be the person who sets all the strategic directions and makes all the decisions. I don't think any one person can internalize all the information and trends to make all the choices. It's just too big. Right now Jeff Bezos is making all the decisions at Amazon. But it may not work forever."

In her next job, Whitman saw a limit to her inclination to reinvent the rules—she ran into a roadblock when she tried to take on yet another kind of business. From 1995 through 1996, she was president and chief executive officer of Florists Transworld Delivery (FTD), Inc., a floral products company. Her job was to help ease the transformation of a florist-owned member association to a privately held company. But several important members resisted the idea, rapid decisions were politically unworkable, and competition, especially from online florists, was eroding market share. "I ultimately concluded that if FTD was fixable, it was not fixable by me. I just couldn't strategically see a way out of this thing."

Whitman quit in 1997, but was undaunted by her failure at FTD, and transformed herself again—this time as a toy executive. She moved on to Hasbro as the general manager of the preschool division. Despite her short yearlong tenure there marketing Playskool and Mr.

Potato Head, the job offered her another chance to tackle a turn-around situation. This time, she fared better. After restructuring the division, firing then hiring, she reset the strategy. She gave credit where it was due by pointing to Tinky Winky, Dipsy, Laa-Laa, and Po on her desk. She says signing a key licensee, Teletubbies, showed her that an opportunistic move that's beneficial in the short term can put a company on the right track for long-term growth. "Anytime you sign a licensee, it's risky because you have to sell enough to meet the fee you paid. But I got the deal at such a low fee that it was almost shocking because the deal turned out so well," she says. "What Teletubbies did for the preschool division is that it improved the profitability enough in year one and year two to buy time to execute the long-term strategy of bringing back the Playskool brand."

LEADING AN IPO

Headhunters lured Whitman to eBay in March 1998, after a visit to the person-to-person Web auction company convinced her that the eBay brand wielded power among consumers and offered a new business model for retail. Her mandate: take the company public and manage its fast-paced growth. She led a national road show and attracted investors to eBay by promoting the company's novel and profitable approach to business.

Unlike the vast majority of e-commerce sites, eBay helps individuals transact person-to-person sales of everything from Elvis souvenirs to antiques, rather than selling wares of its own. In that way, the company avoids all the costs involved with inventory, shipping, and handling. With sellers on the site as eBay's source of revenues, the company charges them relatively low listing fees and sales commissions while still making hefty profits.

Six months later, Whitman launched eBay's IPO in the midst of one of the most dismal Wall Street slumps in years. But eBay stock opened at $18 and rose to over $200. In March 2000, the share price was still strong at $163.

Whitman successfully expanded the business far beyond its origins as a ragtag flea market for collectors of Pez dispensers and Beanie Babies created by its founder, Pierre Omidyar. Founded in 1995, eBay was a simple on-line trading post where buyers and sellers could meet.

Whitman brought experience and professional management skills to Omidyar's brainchild, which was originally inspired by his girlfriend's (now wife's) desire to collect Pez dispensers. Often the stuff being sold on the site was rummaged from people's basements. Under Whitman's regime, sellers display descriptions of their wares, prospective buyers e-mail in bids for a set auction period, and when the time runs out, seller and buyer arrange to exchange payment for merchandise. Most users buy and sell collectibles. Some, like doll miniaturist Mary Ellen Gibb, even quit their day jobs to sell full-time on the site. Everything from antique Barbie dolls to Mark McGwire's historic seventieth home run baseball are sold there. In fiscal 1998, Whitman grew eBay to 2.2 million registered users from 341,000, increased net revenues 724 percent to $47.4 million from $5.7 million, and nearly tripled net income to $2.4 million from $874,000.

FORGING A LINK TO CUSTOMERS

Whitman also further developed the unconventional and innovative model for e-commerce offered by eBay that makes it profitable, unlike many competitors and struggling start-ups in the field. eBay takes 6 percent off the top with few costs to bear because it serves as a broker for buyers and sellers, incurring none of the distribution expenses that come with handling merchandise. As a result, its gross profit margins are in the ethereal realm of Microsoft's at 85 percent. The company was expected to quadruple gross merchandise sales in

1999. Fifteen percent of all consumer e-commerce spending in 1998—$1.42 billion—occurred at auctions, according to Gomez Advisors in Concord, Massachusetts. That total is more than the on-line sales of books and music "eBay is a lot like Disney in terms of its magical appeal to consumers and the emotional connection to eBay that users have, but we are pioneering something that is entirely new. What's fascinating is the impact we have had on the community," says Whitman. "Not only did eBay enable individuals to do business with one another, but there is an emotional connection to eBay that is very rare in good companies. It's the thrill of the hunt, and finding people who like the same stuff you do."

Whitman's hands-on approach to understanding her customers sets her apart from other managers by providing yet another example of her ability to think out of the box. Unlike traditional retailers who spend costly sums to mail surveys to customers with the hope of a response, Whitman has forged a direct link to the eBay consumer via e-mail. She set up a consumer insight and analysis group to open communication lines. Twice a month eBay posts customer surveys on the site and receives about 4,000 responses to each one. Each day, the company answers 6,000 e-mail queries, and Whitman receives a daily report breaking down the questions into categories so she can tell where customer concerns lie and address those issues. She also con-ducts quarterly focus groups to listen to users talk, and speaks on the phone to ten to fifteen customers a week. "We get calls from people who are really angry. I'm interested in talking to those people—because if you understand what you've done to anger customers, you can fix problems," she says. "It's one thing to read the data, and another to hear it—it's pretty visceral. I'm a people person who likes listening to consumers."

Like Martha Ingram and other new paradigm leaders, Whitman is a leader who wants to hear the bad news. For instance, 1.8 million new users registered at the site in just the first quarter of 1999. eBay's policy to answer all e-mail questions within twenty-four hours suffered as customer support services failed to respond quickly enough and the queue of queries grew to seventy-two hours. Rather than criticize Brian Swette, the senior vice president for marketing who oversaw the customer support area, Whitman added reinforcements by asking a colleague to help. "It was no reflection on Brian or any of us. It was just a problem we needed to fix. Stuff happens, particularly in this environment," says Whitman. "The problem you have as a chief executive officer is that everyone only wants to tell you the good news. They never want to tell you the bad news. You have to show people that it's okay to talk about bad news because you are not going to jump down their throats or fire them if they do. You need to know to help them solve it."

MANAGING GROWTH

Managing the company's rapid growth is a pressing need for Whitman, who has to execute new strategies and tactics for the company all the time. She says her strong analytical skills and ability to cut to the chase help her achieve this goal. When she arrived, there were only nine engineers at eBay who made all the decisions, while also writing the code and maintaining the system. That structure worked well when the company was small, but would not suffice as the business grew. One of her first decisions was to put together a professional management team of five senior managers who report directly to her. She meets with them three times a week. "When I came, everyone did everything and it was a disaster. Now, we meet as a group to vote on decisions and I am the tie breaker. The worst thing for a company like eBay is to avoid making decisions because you can't agree. Someone has to make the ultimate call here, and I am more than happy to do that."

Whitman also calls the group together every three months to reassess company strategy and priorities. In these meetings, she encourages her colleagues to be honest and lay both their problems and their ideas out on the table. "At Hasbro or Disney we used to do this once a year, but we are growing at 40 percent to 50 percent per quarter, so every three months we are a different company. And every three months our top management meets to take stock of the strategy and ask, 'Hey, are we doing the right thing?'" she says. "Making these decisions together is important because without that involvement you never really get anybody to totally buy in. I'm not a screamer. I'm very much a listener. If I'm in a meeting with my senior team and I have a point of view on something, but someone says something that sounds better, I'll say, 'Good point. I was wrong.' That sets a tone for the organization that people don't paint themselves into corners, and can speak their minds."

Unlike old paradigm leaders such as Linda Wachner, Whitman sees herself at an advantage over male executives. She says that being a mother gives her a leg up in forging trusting relationships quickly with her colleagues. When she arrived at the company, she saw a rift between the engineers, who serve in effect as gatekeepers for the site, and the rest of the organization. Rather than simply leaving the matter alone, she tried to bridge the gap. Like Martha Ingram, Meg Whitman exhibited an ability to lead people to discuss problems with one another, helping to smooth things over: "I have been able to engender a sense of trust far faster than a man would have because of my experience as a mother. That sort of 'getting the kids to play nicely together' is similar to getting people to talk about concerns that divide them, like turf issues. It's a female trait. I sort of force people to talk about issues that they might not be willing to talk about. And it's been extraordinarily helpful in building this management team quickly. You know men, they stay at a superficial level longer than women do."

Like Shelly Lazarus, Meg Whitman doesn't just listen to her associates, she gives them responsibility. She gleans good results from her over 200 employees by offering competitive salaries, bonuses, and stock options, but the money alone is not enough. Rather than placing them on a prescribed career path, she tries to match skills of staff members to the right position within the company. She sees her primary task as CEO just as authors Marcus Buckingham and Curt Coffman describe: "Help each person find roles that ask him to do more and more of what he is naturally wired to do. Help each person find roles where her unique combination of strengths—her skills, knowledge and talents—match the distinct demands of the role."[13]

Her ability to place people successfully, coupled with eBay's soaring stock price and the heaps of money associates have tied up in options, allow her to retain staff. Only three employees have left the company over the past three and a half years. "I would say that half of our employees are volunteers because they are already millionaires," she says. "But that doesn't stop them from coming to work."

Whitman also places a premium on communicating with staffers—not just senior-level management—about her goals and strategy for the company. Every two months she holds a company-wide meeting to discuss recent changes. She has found that clarifying objectives and making employees accountable for reaching them, while allowing the workers themselves to determine exactly how, is an important source of motivation. Staffers say her ability to stay focused and positive amid a roller-coaster ride on Wall Street sets her apart. "She is relentlessly optimistic," says Steve Westly, eBay vice president of marketing and business development. "She stands out with a combination of drive and executive maturity."

Like Loida Lewis and Martha Ingram, Meg Whitman has shown courage under fire. Her most difficult challenge so far came in June 1999 when eBay's systems crashed and the site was out of service for twenty-two hours. In addition to millions of angry, disappointed customers, the shutdown cost the company up to $5 million in revenues. On Wall Street, however, that loss ballooned to 1,000 times that figure as eBay's market value plummeted $5 billion. Afterward, Whitman blamed herself for not developing eBay's infrastructure and technology talent quickly enough to meet customer demand. She intensified her focus and worked 100 hours a week for the next three months on solving the problem, handing off nontechnical duties to a marketing executive to free up her time. Soon the stock price rose again.

"She showed terrific leadership and composure under a lot of pressure," recalls investor Bob Kagle, general partner of Benchmark Capital. "She picked up very quickly on complex technology issues and made clear decisions in a trial by fire, and eBay came out stronger for it."

Whitman's accomplishments have made her the one to beat in the on-line auction business. Fending off rivals is a tough job for every CEO, but eBay is particularly vulnerable because it is so successful and the Internet has no barriers to entry. Whitman has to stay on her toes to take on the likes of Jeff Bezos's Amazon.com—the largest on-line department store with over 17 million customers and $1.6 billion in sales in 1999. Amazon.com offers auctions on its own site, as well as a joint site with traditional auction house Sotheby's. Amazon is user-friendly, offering customer conveniences like credit card acceptance and one-click ordering, while buying on eBay is still cumbersome. Nearly 90 percent of customers have to send a check or money order, wait for it to clear, and receive the merchandise up to two weeks later. Other major rivals have come on the scene. In September 1999, a team of Internet sites, including Lycos, Inc., and Microsoft's MSN, agreed to share on-line auction listings, allowing customers at one site to bid on items on another.

Technical problems have also persisted at eBay. Fraud has been a problem as well, with New York's Consumer Affairs Department investigating the site. A thirteen-year-old New Jersey boy bought $925,012 worth of merchandise on eBay before his parents found out. Whitman has since instituted an insurance program and offered escrow accounts for items over $200.

Despite intensifying competition and technical issues, sales have continued to mount at the company, and Whitman is reinventing the rules once more. Although she has a booming business, Whitman wants to reach into higher-end markets where competition is even more intense—expensive collectibles from $500 to $10,000. In April 1999, she acquired a regional auction house based in San Francisco, Butterfield & Butterfield, for $260 million in stock. Whitman plans to expand into untapped regional as well as foreign markets. She is also encouraging retailers, including Lands' End, to open storefronts on eBay, and has added the capability to handle credit cards on the site.

Being out in the forefront of change is a comfortable position for Whitman, who stays focused amid the turmoil of her industry as she reinvents the rules and forges a path across the new frontier of the Internet. Although she was brought into eBay because of her conventional management experience, she does not run the business like an old-line firm. Decisions need to be made more quickly—in a matter of days or hours. Being on the run makes mistakes unavoidable. Many question the future of eBay as it faces increasing competition. They wonder whether Whitman, with her lack of technology skills, can continue to succeed with her brand-conscious approach. To be sure, even if the company's fortunes sink, she will still emerge with a solid record for her courage to reinvent the rules of the game. She tries not to focus on the constant hum of competitors starting up their engines. "This is a revolution," she says. "It's on the scale of the Industrial Revolution."

A DRIVE FOR INDEPENDENCE

Like Whitman, independent television producer Marcy Carsey is known for reinventing the rules. When Carsey was trying to sell *Roseanne* to NBC in 1988, the network was not interested. "Why would anybody want to watch this really obnoxious woman who is grating and not very attractive?" Carsey remembers an executive from the network asking her. NBC's reaction was a little surprising considering Carsey's production house, the Carsey-Werner Company, previously sold that network *The Cosby Show*, one of the most successful shows ever run.

Undaunted, Carsey sold the series to ABC instead. *Roseanne* depicted one of the boldest women television has ever seen, and became one of the top-rated shows during the 1988–89 season. In 1997, the series ended its run after nine successful years. Why was it such a hit? "There was nothing on TV about the absurdity of being a working mother," Carsey recalls. "There were wives on TV. But the shows were not about them. They were about the husbands."

By acting on their instincts, Marcy Carsey and her creative partner Tom Werner have built one of the most successful independent television production companies in the industry's history. For these producers of *3rd Rock from the Sun, That '70s Show, Cybill,* and *Cosby,* iconoclasm has paid off handsomely. Their company is worth a reported $1.2 billion today. Carsey is among the fifty wealthiest residents of Los Angeles according to the *Los Angeles Business Journal,* and one of the wealthiest individuals in the country, with a personal fortune of $600 million.[14]

"Marcy defined breaking the rules for all of us," says Geraldine Laybourne, the former chief of Disney/ABC Cable Networks who made the Nickelodeon channel a success and became a mighty force in cable. "She worked her way up to the top of ABC, but said I need my own organization. Her first show out of the box was *The Cosby Show* even though she was told minorities and comedies didn't work. She proved that they do. She was completely guided by her own independent voice and her own sense of the audience. With *Roseanne,* she showed that television could be relevant, helpful, and treat the audience with respect."

A BREATH OF FRESH AIR

Now Carsey is breaking the rules yet again. She recently joined with popular icon and reigning queen of daytime television, Oprah Winfrey, and Laybourne to create the Oxygen cable network. Apart from creating original shows, Carsey and her partners Tom Werner and Caryn Mandabach will be supplying reruns of their hit shows for the network. With plans to invest $400 million in programming to get the company off the ground over the next five years, the powerful triumvirate is shaping Oxygen to appeal to women. Currently only one cable network is already doing that job, Lifetime Television. That channel already extends to 72 million homes, virtually every household that receives cable television across the country. Last year, Lifetime's prime-time ratings rose to 13 percent—making it number one in delivering the critical category of women to advertisers.

It's a market that's difficult to enter. To make Oxygen viable, Carsey and her colleagues are indeed up against the prevailing wisdom. Time Warner dropped plans for a women's cable channel in August 1999, reportedly due to high programming costs. Analysts say that starting a new cable channel is nearly impossible because securing distribution is difficult in today's crowded cable landscape.

Unlike Lifetime, the goal at Oxygen is convergence—the simultaneous broadcasting of programs on cable TV and the Internet, with one medium supplying the other—similar to the scheme of MSNBC, the TV and Web joint venture between Microsoft and NBC.

Big boys of technology and media like Time Warner and Bell Atlantic have tried convergence schemes and failed before.[15] Bell Atlantic head Raymond W. Smith launched Stargazer in 1993 to hook up 8 million homes in six states by 2000 for interactivity. After spending a reported $200 million on the project, Stargazer languished, and Smith retired in 1998. In May 1993, Gerald Levin led Time Warner to partner with US West to offer multimedia to cable customers. In 1995, they constructed a network in Orlando as the basis of a national project. Two years later, only 4,000 households received the service, and Time Warner closed the Orlando experiment in late 1997. Even Microsoft took a stab at the market with its Tiger, a "media server" type of product costing upward of $100 million.

Carsey and her partners are undeterred by the failures of those who have gone before her. In February 2000, the Oxygen cable network debuted with an initial presence in close to 10 million homes. By 2001, the company hopes to reach 20 million homes and 30 million by the following year. Laybourne, who formerly oversaw Lifetime while working at Disney, says women need more cable choices and that Oxygen will appeal to a "more active" (meaning younger) audience than Lifetime, where the average viewer is 43.5 years old. "Cable programming for women today consists of heartfelt movies and formulaic shows," says Laybourne. "It's low-hanging fruit geared for the lowest common denominator. We think women deserve more, and we are trying to break the mold."

Powerful investors including Disney, America Online, TCI, and Microsoft cofounder Paul Allen believe that the driven founders of the ambitious project will make the company a success. Allen has already invested up to $100 million and will supply close to 6 million cable subscribers from his growing cable empire for the launch of Oxygen's TV channel. Tom Werner, who is a minority as a man among the female-dominated leadership of Oxygen, is also excited about putting innovative shows on the new network.

"Oprah is going to do a thirteen-part series for Oxygen on how to work your way around the Internet that will help women learn how to do it," Werner says. "Hopefully our programming will be rowdy, ballsy, funny, and intelligent so that women will want to watch. We don't want to be preachy or grim like some other networks. I never feel out of place among smart women. Some men feel intimidated by that, but I'm happy they allow me to hang with them."

BEING PART OF THE AUDIENCE

Like Patricia Russo of Lucent Technologies, Meg Whitman, and other new paradigm leaders, Carsey has beaten the odds before by reinventing the rules. Everything from her appearance to her company offices are anathema to the glamour and glitz of Hollywood. She and her partner share an office on the second floor of a small bungalow on the former MTM lot in Studio City. Eschewing the power lunch, Carsey picks up a plate in the commissary line downstairs. Her conference room, filled with knotty pine furniture covered with green and white striped cushions, looks more New England than L.A. The wallpaper is green, white, and maroon plaid, and small prints of sailboats gliding across the sea hang on the walls. Carsey drives a modest Mustang convertible to work, and lacks that surgically altered look so common in her industry. At fifty-four, she wears her dark blond hair in a no-nonsense bob with bangs. She dresses in a relaxed manner with loose-fitting black pants and a casual long black sweater striped in brown and sprinkled with white dots, tied at the waist with a black sash. Her look is alpaca, not designer. The temperature is seventy-five degrees and sunny, but she has a cold. Sneezing, she reaches for a tissue as she sits down cross-legged in one of the pine chairs.

"Success hasn't been about working my way through the system or having the most projects in development. And it hasn't been about trying to give a network what it wants or what it says it wants," she says. "It's about being part of the audience, and not separating yourself from that. Then you develop shows from the point of view of the audience rather than the network or whatever trends are in the air."

That formula has been a good one for Carsey, and her company has had a hit show nearly every season since 1984. Years ago there were a lot of independents—production companies that are not aligned with networks or studios—including MTM, which made *The Mary Tyler Moore Show* and *Hill Street Blues*, and Garry Marshall, which put out *Happy Days* and *Laverne and Shirley*. By the late 1980s, the increasing costs of producing television shows made support from big studios highly desirable, if not necessary. Media mergers proliferated, leading most small producers to huddle under the umbrella of a studio. Competition from cable and dwindling earnings for traditional networks only exacerbated the problem, making the move in-house alluring and often inevitable for both parties.

THE LAST INDEPENDENT

But Carsey and her partner have reinvented the rules by opting to retain their independence. Over the years, Disney chief Michael Eisner has tried to lure Carsey-Werner to run the entertainment division at ABC, but the pair refused. Joining a network would have meant giving up their company and abandoning new shows in the midst of development. NBC also made an offer to attract the team to run its programming, but the two rejected that offer as well.

"Being the last independent left feels right to us because the problem with being partners with a studio is that you then give over a piece of your creative control and then everything starts to get a little mushy," says Carsey. "I have confidence in what I am good at and I am good at crafting shows. I would rather live and die by my own decisions, not those of a network."

Carsey and Werner prefer the freedom to produce the shows they select and have the option of selling their programs to all of the networks. If they had arranged an exclusive deal with ABC, *The Cosby Show* never would have made it to television because ABC rejected it. The show wound up on NBC instead. Later, NBC passed on *Roseanne*. The producers then sold the idea to ABC. The same happened to *Cybill:* ABC refused it, but the show ended up airing on CBS. And ABC execs nixed *3rd Rock*, so the series became a hit on NBC.

Oxygen is the first partnership with a network that Carsey and Werner have pursued, but the new convergence scheme is a bold and risky venture in itself. It presents an opportunity for Carsey to help write the rules—because the channel is new, Carsey can help mold the business. Although they will be spending much of their time handling the programming aspect of Oxygen, Carsey says the company will still be selling programs to the networks. After all, they currently have four series running on three networks. Carsey and Werner have demonstrated that a couple of smart programmers with good instincts and enough confidence to fight for their convictions can still be a success in prime time.

With Oxygen, Carsey is focusing on a largely untapped market she understands: women. Women are an alluring market for advertisers—American females control 85 percent of all personal and household spending decisions, make 75 percent of their family's financial choices, and contribute $3.5 trillion to the U.S. economy, according to the Washington, D.C.–based Women's Consumer Network. And Carsey has long cultivated the female audience with shows like *Roseanne, Grace Under Fire,* and *Cybill.* In fact, she has created programs with some of the strongest women to ever appear on television. "There's a lot of us in all of this," she says. "We try to do what's not on the air."

CARVING HER OWN PATH

Like Meg Whitman, Marcy Carsey grew up on the East Coast, and always hit the books. She went to a local public school, and was placed in an accelerated group. Raised in Weymouth, Massachusetts, Carsey came from humble beginnings. Her father worked at the Fore River shipyard in Quincy, Massachusetts, and always brought home a small paycheck, under $250 a week. Her mother worked in a bank until she began to have children in her early thirties, then stayed home to raise them. Although money was tight, Carsey never felt that she lacked anything growing up because her mother always maintained a sunny attitude. "Without ever saying anything in particular, she gave my brother and me a sense that the world was a place where you could just grab hold of whatever you wanted and do with it what you will," she recalls. "I remember admiring a red velvet dress for my ninth-grade prom that was $50—in the fifties, that was not chopped liver. And my parents bought it for me somehow. I never heard them talk about money or worry about it. As a result, I guess I've never had an attachment to money, so I was never afraid of losing it."

Carsey's parents also reinvented the rules in their own way. Despite their modest income, her family was the first on her block to buy a television. She used to sit on a stool watching *Father Knows Best* and *I Remember Mama*. As a girl, Carsey developed an instant attachment to television. She was drawn to the tube originally because she was a self-proclaimed nerd; never a prom queen, a cheerleader, or one of the "cool" kids, she took refuge in television. "I loved the storytelling. I fell in love with the guys, and admired the women," she remembers. "On those long winter days in Massachusetts there wasn't a lot to do—especially when you weren't the cutest girl in class—you would say, 'Thank God, *Maverick* is on or else I'd just have darkness, slush, and homework to look forward to.'"

Unlike Whitman, who worked in an array of different kinds of businesses, from a young age Carsey focused on a single industry— television. After graduating from high school in 1962, she went on to earn a bachelor's degree in English literature from the University of New Hampshire. The first job she landed out of college was as a tour guide for NBC in New York. She quickly progressed to production assistant for the then New York–based *Tonight* show. In 1974, she relocated to Los Angeles with her husband, John Carsey, a writer for *Laugh-In*, and Michael Eisner hired her as a general program executive at ABC. She was three months pregnant with the first of her two children during the interview. Eisner was understanding. "My wife is going to have a baby, too, and I plan to come back. Don't you?" he said. Needless to say, she took the job.

In just five years, she was named senior vice president handling prime-time programming for ABC. One of the few women to rise in network television during the late 1970s, Carsey recalls that women were absent from top management, but common in the typing pool and the sales department. Even then, Carsey was willing to be controversial. *Barney Miller* was one of the first shows she put on the air, and another program she made, *Three's Company,* was one of the riskiest at the time. "I was motivated by testing the boundaries of what was possible," she says. "That has always been the fun part."

Carsey's fearless nature inspired her to take risks in business. Like Darla Moore, she had a laser focus to achieve. In 1980, she decided to quit her top programming job at the network just when ABC was one of the top networks and she was at the height of her powers there. "Guys were more patient with the corporate process than I was," she says. "I was impatient. I never particularly identified myself or my ego with the corporation. The bosses like Michael Eisner who had inspired me were gone. And my ideas about how to do my job were different from the ideas of the new guys in charge. Women have always been more comfortable with finding their own way within the workforce." So she started her own production company, and never doubted she would be successful.

In severing her ties with ABC, she bucked convention. Even then it was common for former network executives to link themselves to a studio or network, simply because it was the best way to ensure survival for a new company against the imposing start-up economics of television production. All television series are produced at a deficit because the networks do not pay enough in license fees to cover the expenses of creating a show. A typical episode of a half-hour comedy runs up a tab of between $500,000 and $600,000 to make and incurs a deficit of $100,000 to $200,000. Without hefty sums of money in the bank, it is almost impossible to assume those deficits while waiting for the payoff a big hit brings. To get the company off the ground, Carsey took out a second mortgage on her house. A year later, her former colleague at ABC, Tom Werner, joined her.

Why? He was attracted to her iconoclasm. "After she left, it didn't take me long to realize I had made a mistake," he says. "She was my boss at ABC and I wanted to move into her old job, but it wasn't smart because I was missing the genius who had made it exciting and stimulating. She is so clear-thinking that her point of view is like a piercing arrow. At ABC, even though the president of the company would say he liked a pilot, she would get up in front of forty people and say, 'Are you out of your mind?'"

Carsey joined Werner because their skills mesh well together. She is often considered the more discerning judge of material, particularly skilled at molding a series during its formation, while he is known for spending more time on post-production and managing the networks.[16] But the pair stays unusually close to their projects. They both have a keen eye for casting, which helps because they cast and read each script, offering suggestions even on set construction. Although they are executive producers who could remain distant from their projects, they choose to work like "line producers," meaning that they are on stage when episodes of their shows are taped or filmed. "He is more thoughtful, and I rely more on instinct," explains Carsey. "It's a good combination because without him I can be too impulsive, and without me he can be a little too logical."

BUCKING CONVENTION

Strong and independent like many of the company's TV protagonists, and at the same time family-oriented, Carsey helps set the tone. She lets her instinct for the audience and what will entertain it guide her. To keep those sensibilities fresh, it is important that she remain a part of it. Unlike other television studios, Carsey-Werner avoids rushing lots of shows into development to see what works, but focuses instead on creating a few winning programs. They persevere. Carsey and Warner waited six months for John Goodman to be ready before they forged ahead with *Roseanne*, even though ABC was demanding the series. And they kept staffing costs down by staying small—even today the company has only 120 employees.

Although they have produced a few bombs, such as *Oh Madeline* and *Townies*, the hits have far outweighed the misses. The company's first big success, *The Cosby Show*, went against prevailing tastes. Back then, shows featuring a kid's point of view, like *Family*, *Diff'rent Strokes*, and *Family Ties* dominated the airwaves. And images of African Americans on television included streetwise characters like George Jefferson and J. J. "Dyno-mite" Walker. The series was the first to depict an affluent middle-class African-American family, and became a huge hit. The series is among the most profitable shows in television syndication history, earning over $1 billion. "There was no comedy in the top ten," Carsey recalls. "Of course, that made us want to do comedy. And we were interested in doing domestic comedies because we were living it. My partner and I were raising kids. We knew there had to be billions of others going through the same thing."

She is always looking for fresh ideas to fuel the company's success. No comedies about aliens were currently on television when Carsey launched *3rd Rock from the Sun* in 1996. The sitcom, about creatures from outer space who observe the oddities and silliness of human behavior, was a surprise hit. Recently she wanted to launch a lighter, "less earnest" series and came up with *That '70s Show*—another success. That popular nostalgic comedy will soon be syndicated as well.

Perhaps more than any other company in Hollywood, Carsey-Werner is an equal-opportunity employer, according to *Variety*. While groups of white men knock out many sitcoms, Carsey's company mentors talented young women and minorities, many of whom remain with the company for years in executive roles. Women are also likely to be well paid at the company. Bonnie Turner, who helped create *3rd Rock from the Sun* with her husband, Terry, has an ownership stake in the show.

"It's a company that is totally open to women," says Joanne Curley Kerner, a producer on *Cosby* who has been producing for Carsey-

Werner for eleven years on three different shows. "You couldn't be in that company and be a sexist."

Carsey credits her success to being stubborn enough to stick to her vision of a show—thus reinventing the rules. Cash from winners like *The Cosby Show* has allowed Carsey-Werner the cushion they need to stay independent and go their own way. She has also avoided the conspicuous consumption prevalent in Hollywood and managed company profits closely. Although Carsey-Werner reserves the right to create shows independently for the networks and continues working on existing programs, she has pursued the partnership with Oxygen because the business climate has changed. Facing a declining audience, increasing competition from new channels, consolidation in the industry, and spiraling costs from the price of shows to expenses for keeping talent, the networks are under intense cost pressures. Cable channels have been snatching market share from them—capturing 38 percent of the national audience during the 1998–99 season, while the four big networks (ABC, CBS, NBC, and Fox) and the two smaller ones (WB and UPN) together drew 62 percent.[17] She complains that the networks now own all the programs they air so that independence has become increasingly difficult for her company to maintain. "Without direct access to distribution, we are at the mercy of the networks," says Carsey. "The networks are really our production competitors and they are the gatekeepers, too, so having our own distribution system is important. A cable channel is such a thing."

With Oxygen, Carsey feels she is partnering with two women who agree with her approach to programming—offering the audience something they cannot find on their television screens. And she is not entering an established network with a defined image, but a new venture she can help shape. You can bet that Carsey will continue on her contrarian path, just by means of a different conduit. "You have to have balls. Courage is really important," she says. "You have to have the confidence to do it in the best way regardless of how that's going to sit with management or the outside world."

4

A LASER FOCUS TO ACHIEVE

If the LBOs were the rising sun of finance in the early eighties, bankruptcy was the dark side of the moon ... the graveyard, the knee-breaking, bill-collecting backwater of the financial forum. In other words, an undiscovered opportunity.

— Darla Moore

When she was a budding thirty-year-old trainee at Chemical Bank in 1984, Darla Moore's superiors assigned her to what was considered Siberia in the financial world. While all the hotshots in the field were angling to get into the booming leveraged buyout (LBO) business, she was asked to handle loans for Chapter 11 bankrupt companies. Traditionally, banks are loath to finance these corporate losers. But Moore's drive to achieve helped her rake in big returns and forge a path to success out of what many considered a dead end.

In 1990, Moore, who would grace the cover of *Fortune* magazine as "the toughest babe in business,"[1] reeled in $1.3 billion in so-called debtor-in-possession (DIP) loans, estimated to be more than all other bankruptcy lenders combined.[2] In that dismal year for bank profits, Moore's unit earned a reported net income of $25 million to $35 million, vindicating her will to win in an unsung sector of the industry. With her independent vision, she pioneered this highly specialized area of lending, handling more than $4 billion in financing throughout her thirteen-year career at Chemical, now Chase. She was hailed as the secret weapon that propelled her bank far out in front of competitors in a surprisingly profitable business. By the time she left in 1994, she was earning more than $1 million a year as a managing director at the bank.

"I so wanted to be in the LBO business, but I couldn't break into that," remarks Moore in her deep Southern drawl. "Ultimately there were no women there because the men never let any of them in. If the LBOs were the rising sun of finance in the early eighties, bankruptcy was the dark side of the moon . . . the graveyard, the knee-breaking, bill-collecting backwater of the financial forum. In other words, an undiscovered opportunity."

Moore was not content to be in the hinterland of finance, but she recognized immediately that she had the will to turn a path to anonymity into a route to success. Her ability to envision possibilities when others only see the words "game over" is an invaluable quality she shares with the other women featured in this book. Fueled by her success at Chemical, her next job only enhanced her reputation as a shrewd deal maker who could reap rewards by going against the grain. She became president of Rainwater, Inc., the investment company owned by her new husband, renowned financier Richard Rainwater. When she took over, her husband had $700 million in assets. After three and a half years, she nearly tripled his net worth to $1.5 billion. Although his portfolio fell to $1.2 billion in 1999 after suffering stock market losses, he still retained a hefty chunk of change. Now forty-five, Moore has become one of only a few women across the country to have a business school at a major university named after her. She is also working currently to alter the finances of South Carolina, the state where she was born. Not surprisingly, she was ranked among the fifty most powerful women in American business by *Fortune* magazine in both 1998 and 1999.[3]

Like all new paradigm leaders, Darla Moore is able to recognize chances where others see a conventional dead end, then tap into her drive to succeed to turn the situation to her advantage. That laser focus coupled with an ability to spot opportunities others fail to see is another powerful quality that defines the women in this book. Meg Whitman helped build eBay into one of the leading Internet businesses in the country by concentrating on her strengths—her marketing savvy and financial skills—rather than her technological shortcomings to generate revenues and profits as well as a successful IPO. Shelly Lazarus reeled in some of the biggest clients Ogilvy & Mather Worldwide ever serviced by keeping her eye on the firm's talent rather than concentrating on its high client turnover. Patricia Russo refocused a $3.5 billion AT&T business unit, and has since become one of the most powerful executives in the telecommunications business as a high-ranking executive at Lucent Technologies. Another new paradigm leader, also featured in this chapter because of her impressive ability to develop a $20 billion global energy business for energy giant Enron Corporation, is Rebecca Mark. And rather than resting on her laurels, she is taking on a daunting and not so glamorous new project as chairman and chief executive officer of Azurix Corporaton, Enron's new subsidiary. At her new company she is tackling the world's $300 billion drinking water and sewage treatment market.

DISTINCT FROM THE CROWD

Moore is never too distant from her Southern roots. She is a lot like a modern-day Scarlett O'Hara. A floor-to-ceiling oil painting of her dressed in a voluminous white blouse and a flowing burgundy taffeta skirt is prominently displayed in the foyer of her condominium on the Upper East Side of Manhattan. Although she can look the part of the quintessential Southern belle, Moore speaks her mind in a direct tone that demands attention. At Rainwater's satellite office on Madison Avenue, she is fond of asking employees, "So how much money did you lose for me today?" Slender and elegant, she is liable to look for inspiration behind the wheel of a backhoe at her family farm in South Carolina when pressures of business mount. An avid collector, she stocks her apartment with rare books about the philosophical underpinnings of capitalism by authors like Henri Rousseau, Adam Smith, and Alexis de Tocqueville. But she has a soft spot for ornate and a bit overdone eighteenth-century French furniture that embodies the antithesis of American capitalism. She wears a gray flannel pleated skirt and burgundy cashmere twin set, but the skirt is short—above the knee. Moore sits calmly in an armchair while her frisky keeshond puppy, Doodle, shreds her business documents at her feet.

The contradictions inherent in Moore manifest themselves in her style of leadership, and she offers a fascinating portrayal of what can only be described as a hybrid of the old paradigm and the new. While her laser focus on accomplishment places her in the new paradigm, her style of managing people positions her in the old. She handles employees in a traditional style—she issues orders and demands compliance. Although she is a blend, Moore acknowledges the opposites in her corporate character, and makes them work for her, as her rapid rise illustrates. She appears in this book because the skills that drove her route to success are intrinsic to new paradigm leadership.

Moore concedes that a white-shoe financial firm like Chemical Bank, with its roster of Fortune 500 clients, seemed a surprising place to find a woman who excelled and broke new ground by asserting her own style of management. Like Meg Whitman, Moore is something of an unexpected leader in her field. But new paradigm leadership appears in a wide array of industries, and often finds champions in unlikely places. All new paradigm leaders, including consultant Orit Gadiesh and venture capitalist Ann Winblad, share Moore's counterintuitive wisdom.

Moore's accomplishments contrast starkly with the dismal status of women in banking. While females comprise close to 70 percent of the workforce at banks, according to 1996 Equal Employment

Opportunity Commission (EEOC) statistics, they're still a minority in high-level positions. These figures show that women exceed men in all bank-related job categories measured except for one: officials and managers. What's more, the agency's data demonstrate that the industry's lower-paying office and clerical positions are held by women at nearly a five-to-one ratio.

"Banking has a lot of women in the pipeline in terms of the percentage of women in its workforce," says Mary Mattis, senior research fellow at Catalyst. "But it doesn't have a significant level of women in the very highest levels of leadership." On Wall Street in 1996, just 8 percent of managing directors of major investment banking and brokerage houses were women.[4]

FROM BANKRUPTCY TO PROFITS

Like other new paradigm leaders, Moore refused to look at her low-profile assignment as a dead end. In 1984, while she toiled in bankruptcy, the dollar amount of completed LBOs rose fourfold to reach $18.6 billion.[5] But the LBO era wreaked havoc on many leading companies. Some of America's best-known businesses, like Texaco, Macy's, Federated Department Stores, and Eastern Airlines, fell into the abyss of bankruptcy, as the LBO business began to dry up. These insolvent companies needed funds, called debtor-in-possession (DIP) loans, to meet daily operating costs and bankruptcy fees while they restructured their existing debt. A careful reading of the law by Moore's boss, Robert Conway, revealed that such distressed companies repay DIP lenders before other creditors, so he assigned Moore not just the task of attracting clients, but the job of convincing the bank to fund the troubled companies it had long avoided. At Chemical, such loans ranged from $20 million (Cook United, Inc.) to upward of $800 million (Carter Hawley Hale Stores). Indeed, it was a small nugget that Conway gave her, but Darla Moore turned it into a gold mine. And what began as a sideshow for the bank in the go-go eighties became, in fact, a critical and profitable star act that Chemical Bank featured in the early nineties under her leadership.

The reason? Moore had a keen understanding of the needs of her customers. Her ability to provide big loans quickly was also a vital asset in loaning money to bankrupt companies. Her biggest asset in winning business was the self-confidence she transmitted to corporate honchos who were struggling through the most difficult period of their professional and personal lives. Meeting with executives whose companies were in disarray was challenging, but Moore put these men at ease in a manner that went beyond traditional banking services.

"Let's face it, going into bankruptcy is scary business—especially to a businessman who doesn't know what failure means, who sees himself as a pillar in the business world and the community. Suddenly, his world is collapsing," drawls Moore. "These were some of the whitest shoe, WASPiest places you ever saw, and I would listen to all this self-importance for a while. Then I just leaned over like a doctor and said, 'I know this is the worst thing you have ever experienced in both your personal and professional life. I understand that, but this is not the end of the world. Nobody has died. Let me tell you what is going to happen. And let me tell you what you are going to feel. And let me tell you how people are going to react to you.' Then I went through every constituent from his employees to his family to members of the golf club. And I would tell him how to handle each one. He had tremendous confidence that I would take care of him. A guy could never go in and talk to him like that."

As more and more giant corporations slid into bankruptcy, most requested Darla Moore's services at Chemical Bank—so much so that she became known as the "queen of DIP." Her mastery of the business coincided with the end of the high-flying LBO era, and she adapted to economic change with ease. "In banking, being female gave me a competitive edge," she explains with a wry grin. "Clients would rather have lunch with me than with the men."

Also because of her shrewd insight, Moore avoided the pitfalls that many Wall Street deal makers fell into after Black Monday, October 19, 1987. In the aftermath of the crash, debt and leverage were branded as tools of excess. Heavy hitters like Salomon Brothers and Drexel Burnham got bruised by scandal and decline, while former investment titans including Michael Milken and John Gutfreund paid a handsome price for their hubris and reckless management. The number of business failures reportedly jumped 20 percent in 1990 to 60,122 from 50,388 in the prior year. And the scope of the financial distress grew, too—assets in bankruptcy, a paltry $1.6 billion in 1980, reached $43 billion in 1989 and jumped to $84 billion in 1990. In what *American Banker* labeled "a generally horrible era for bank profits," Moore's prosperity was remarkable.

"In banking, major decisions are still made by fifty-six-year-old white men with wives in Greenwich, who can't understand why a woman wouldn't rather be playing tennis," explained a former colleague of Moore's from Chemical who spoke under condition of anonymity. "But Darla surprised people because she was so confident, and that confidence was addictive to those around her. She would walk into a room full of gray-haired men, and she's there with her blond hair and perky personality saying, 'Gentlemen, I'm here to save you.' The reaction is 'Whew! We've been saved.'"

A SORE SPOT—MANAGING PEOPLE

Although Moore's laser focus to achieve was an asset for her as she rose at Chemical Bank, the old paradigm features of her leadership style made it difficult for her to manage others. Extracting the best results from employees is a constant challenge for all managers, but executives who cling to old paradigm techniques of managing people find it a particular chore. As she advanced in her career, however, she saw the error of her ways. Even now, she is working to improve this aspect of her style.

Her past inability to manage people is legendary—when Moore was thirty-three, most of her employees at Chemical Bank quit. Her domineering style sent subordinates running out the door. "Darla is so demanding of herself that she is too hard on those around her," says Charlotte Beers, chairman of advertising company J. Walter Thompson.

The meritocracy approach, a holdover from her upbringing, failed Moore in managing others. Her philosophy was basic: "Capitalism is man's deepest desire to better himself," she explains. But her belief that if you were a good person you worked hard left her with little patience for employees who could not make the grade. Like Linda Wachner, she issued orders to underlings and was intolerant of those who could not respond: "It's not that I was a screamer or that I overtly beat people up," explains Moore. "I just sapped the individuality out of my employees and made people feel stressed by my expectations because I not only wanted to control the form, but also the substance of their work. I was just too rigid."

Her boss tagged her a "management problem." After her employees kept packing, she saw a need to make a change. As she racked up more successes at work, she lured workers who performed better. As a result, she gave them more leeway. In the technical area of bankruptcy, she grew to rely heavily on the expertise of her staff. "It was a natural progression," she says. "The more successful I got, the more confident I got, the better the people I hired. And the more I backed off those people, the more they could do."

She learned a joke here, a little levity there, could also win points. One of her favorites, drawing on her Southern roots, was to threaten to wrap employees in a Confederate flag and hoist them up a flagpole in midtown Manhattan if they failed to sign a particular client. In the end, she says, she recognized that a real leader can walk away from a company and not be missed. "The legacy you leave are the people you hire and leave behind."

OVERCOMING OBSTACLES

Like Orit Gadiesh and all the new paradigm leaders in this book, Moore exhibits an intense drive to succeed that helped her face up to conflict and stare down obstacles that got in her way. Contrary to the stereotype that women managers are strictly focused on building consensus, the women featured here don't mind stirring up a bit of trouble. In fact, Darla Moore is renowned for her ability to handle and even precipitate conflict. She feels comfortable when embroiled in battle, speaks in military terms, and believes that a woman cannot be successful without engaging in conflict. "Men can often avoid conflict on their path to senior levels, but women can't do that or they will be pushed aside," explains Moore. "Women cannot be afraid to fight because they've got to engage in conflict and confrontation from time to time. Some women I've noticed just go in and they're ready to fight on anything and everything—big mistake. You have to have the intuition into what fights to pick and what confrontations to take on."

Moore has handled disputes throughout her career, and has tussled with a few corporate titans since she took over management of her husband's assets. Legendary investor Rainwater lays out the strategy, while Moore inks the deals. Despite a recent investment slide in his real estate, energy, and health-care assets, she has proven tough enough for the job. She played a pivotal role in pushing out two formidable players who led companies in which Rainwater had sizable investments, even when her husband opposed her. "My greatest strength is seeing clearly through chaos," she says.

In 1996, Moore deposed infamous corporate raider T. Boone Pickens as chief executive officer of Mesa, the oil and gas company he founded. Pickens was legendary for his ability to terrify chief executive officers of companies like Unocal and Gulf Oil Corporation in the eighties when he came calling with a hostile takeover bid. In the past, Michael Milken had funded his corporate raids, but now he was in trouble. Moore was undaunted. The stock of Mesa had plummeted from $48 to less than

$3, and Pickens was in danger of proxy fights and hostile takeover. Moore and Rainwater proposed buying some stock, selling new equity, and refinancing Mesa's spiraling debt. It appeared to be an amicable alliance. But Moore was convinced Pickens's infamy was damaging Mesa and told him to resign. "It's nothing personal," she says. "I'm just not afraid of knock-down-drag-out fights."

And in 1997, it was she who led the board in dismissing Columbia/HCA CEO Richard Scott over her husband's objections. Rainwater had founded the health-care giant with Scott in 1987, four years before he married Darla Moore. Moore replaced Rainwater on Columbia's board of directors in 1994 when the company was thriving. With $20 billion in revenues in 1996, Columbia was one of America's leading health-care companies. Despite the strong results, she was concerned about Scott's leadership style. She was particularly disturbed about press reports that the company's cost reduction jeopardized the level of medical care Columbia offered, and industry gossip that interactions with management were notoriously difficult. She voiced her concerns to her husband toward the end of the year. The federal government had concerns of its own. In March 1997, federal agents descended upon company offices in El Paso under suspicion that Columbia was overcharging Medicaid and Medicare. Scott insisted all was well. But Moore led the board to oust Scott after the government investigation expanded to cover the company's operations in seven states.

Moore is tough so her husband doesn't have to be. Rainwater vows that she is a more effective presedent of the company than he would be: "By the time I'm ready to act," Rainwater told *Fortune*, "Darla will already have the job done."[6]

RUGGED ROOTS TO AMBITION

Moore discovered her drive to achieve while growing up on a farm. She took pleasure in hard work, and unearthed her will to succeed.

She was raised in the poor tobacco town of Lake City, South Carolina (population 8,398). But she passed summers at her grandparents' 125-acre farm, where five black families worked as tenant farmers. The word "traditional" hardly defines this rural, agrarian hamlet in the Deep South, which was among the last American towns to be integrated. "I think you're born with a clock or a mechanism of drive, and your environment either fosters it or kills it," says Moore. "And my environment was one whereby the cornerstone was hard work. I farmed. If you're a good person, a person of character, a person of quality, you worked hard. And it wasn't complaining work. It was a positive thing."

An appreciation for hard work wasn't the only quality Moore picked up during her upbringing that helped her succeed. She learned that an education was essential. Despite their decision to farm, both of her grandparents were valedictorians of their high schools and college-educated. Her parents were college graduates as well. Her grandfather, a Civil War aficionado, created his own brand of leadership—at the end of each year, he sat down with each tenant farmer, most of whom had not been educated, and explained what the farm had earned that year, and what percentage belonged to him and his family. "They were one of, if not the only, farm family of that level of education. And yet they chose the farm life," Moore recalls. "Because they were educated, they had a different kind of attitude. Fairness was a major character trait that I watched and was taught."

At school and in church, Moore also learned what was to be a girl's most important goal: to have and raise children. Further, if girls dared pursue careers, they should become teachers or nurses so their work would enable them to follow their husbands. Her younger sister, Lisa, followed the more conventional wisdom and became a nurse, and now lives with her husband and two sons in Boston. But it was not from the clergy or her sister that Moore learned the lesson that became the most important to her; it was from the mother of a child-hood friend. She told thirteen-year-old Darla Moore something she never forgot—that her biggest mistake was to marry, because she had three children and was "stuck" with an alcoholic husband. "I would look around and see women in my hometown and the lives of quiet desperation they led, even though they had followed all the rules," says Moore, who went on to reinvent the rules in a number of ways. "Right then I realized that doing what was expected of you is a dead end, and that I was not going to do what I was told because I didn't want that kind of life."

It was at the dinner table that Moore discovered another skill that fueled her desire to achieve—communication. She recalls that her mother often kept information from her that she thought would upset her daughter. For example, even as a young girl, Moore opposed racism, so her mother once chose not to tell her about an incident when a librarian would not allow a boy who was black to borrow books. "I was never told what was real, so I got good at recognizing when a spin is being put on something, and I have become painfully direct in my communications," she says. "I like to say to my employees, 'So, what are you wasting your time on today?'"

In many ways, Moore's parents played a profound role in helping her build the self-confidence to become a focused, successful leader. Her father, Eugene Moore, was a schoolteacher and coach, and his wife, Lorraine, worked as an office administrator at the local Methodist church. Eugene Moore had been an all-star athlete in college at Clemson, and wanted his elder daughter to excel at every sport. He made a track on the lawn of the Moore house and timed her fifty- and hundred-yard sprints. He also measured how fast she swam laps in the pool, and gave her pointers on the basketball court. He even took her fishing and hunting. She killed rabbits and birds. "He treated me like a boy," says Moore, who grew to believe she could do anything. "When I was three years old we sat down with a blackboard with X's and O's all over it. He taught me the football formations, and I am still knowledgeable about that. No one ever said you're really pretty or you're really ugly or anything like that."

Her mother pushed her as well, but in other disciplines such as music (piano) and academics. She was a stern disciplinarian, with rules on everything from the length of Darla's skirt (knee-length) to her grades. At times, Lorraine Moore literally put her daughter in a corner, not simply because Darla did not get an A but because she *could have* gotten one but didn't. "I was never very competitive in a traditional sense—against [classmates] or [colleagues]. The competition was always in me," explains Moore. "My parents set an internal standard so I was never competitive against others, but with myself."

Moore never desired to be part of a group, but felt destined to achieve greater things on her own. In her all-white high school, she didn't have many friends. She rejected established routes to popularity like becoming a cheerleader or a beauty queen. She went on to earn a bachelor's degree in political science from the University of South Carolina in 1975, and then worked as an intern for Republican South Carolina senator Strom Thurmond on Capitol Hill. After graduation, the senator helped her land a job as a researcher for the Republican National Committee. But politics held little allure for Moore because power in that arena was always fleeting. It was money and a career that she craved. So she chose to go to business school at George Washington University, and received an MBA in 1981. Then she entered finance.

A WILL TO ACCOMPLISH

Moore's will to accomplish helped her define an unconventional path in her field. Unlike many women who had come before her in banking, Moore steered clear of staffing posts. Instead, she sought to advance her career in a revenue-generating job. She blended the old paradigm tendency to command employees with the new paradigm characteristics of a clear-cut vision to achieve and direct communication with staff and with clients. She also forged close relationships with her customers and adapted flexibly to change in the financial arena, creating a winning formula for success. "It's the package," she explains. "Although the feminine qualities are powerful, you don't lead with them and you don't wear them on your shoulder. I've learned to wear both silk and steel with equal aplomb over the years . . . because leadership is far more powerful than either gender alone."

The skills Moore used as she rose in banking provide lessons in leadership for all executives, be they male or female. Her ambition and competence in the lending field garnered attention. But Moore realized early on that competence alone did not assure growth for her business. Instead, she combined these attributes with the traditional feminine quality of empathy toward clients, and rose to the top of her field while adjusting skillfully to a transforming marketplace. This mix put her in a unique position to satisfy customer needs and to assure her own progress. "Darla does not know the language of business that men know—she is blunt and direct while men are more polite," explains Charlotte Beers of Moore's appeal. "She marries boldness to substance. She is bold not to shock but to say the unsayable. That makes people curious. But she combines it with major substance because she has mastered her subject, and that makes her a factor."

And Moore's leadership role is only expanding as she enters a realm typically reserved for aging male captains of industry. In March 1998, the University of South Carolina business school was rechristened the Darla Moore School of Business, making her one of very few women to have her name attached to a business school at a major university. With an enrollment of 3,000 and a $10 million endowment, the business school at her alma mater ranked second in international business in 1998, according to *U.S. News & World Report*. Although she wrote the school a $25 million check for the honor, it is part of her renewed focus on her home state. She recently spoke before the state legislature urging finance reform for South Carolina as well. That the university sought her out in the hopes of raising its visibility signals the wide reach of this unique "Wall Street wizard." "Every psyche has both feminine and masculine characteristics to it," Moore says. "Some women go in and they're warm and loving and compassionate. The difference I had with other women is that I lead with the masculine characteristics."

THE EMPRESS OF ENERGY

Rebecca Mark, known as the "doyenne of deal making" and "the empress of energy" in the power industry, is another new paradigm leader with a strong will to succeed. Her spacious office on the fiftieth floor of Enron Corporation's Houston skyscraper shows that she's arrived. The rich mahogany furniture, lush Oriental rug, supple beige leather chairs, bold city views, and wide expanse of the room all say one thing: This woman's one powerful player. But her huge brown eyes, broad smile, and blond hair distinguish Mark from most of the graying white men who lead her industry.

No corporate Brooks Brothers suit or casual uniform of jeans or khakis and a blouse for this chairman and CEO of Azurix Corporation, Enron's water subsidiary. She strolls across her office wearing an Escada mustard blazer over black pants and three-inch pumps to give a firm handshake. Her jewelry is shiny and big— David Yurman earrings and rings with hefty citrine stones, and a gold Ebel watch with diamonds. On trips to India, China, and Brazil where she has launched power projects, she is known to change outfits two or three times a day. "If you don't distinguish yourself from the crowd, you'll just be the crowd," says Mark. "I'm not going to spend as much time as I do in business and forget that I'm a woman."

As for Darla Moore, an iron will to achieve and a laser focus on how to do it propelled Rebecca Mark, one of the few women who is a top candidate to run a leading energy company, from the farm to the top echelons of business. A keen sense of feeling out of place in her hometown of Kirksville, Missouri, coupled with a hunger to excel and a desire for adventure, led Mark to rise in her field. There is talk she may be tapped to guide Enron after current chief executive officer Kenneth Lay's contract runs out in 2001. She has also appeared prominently on *Fortune* magazine's list of the most powerful women in American business in 1998 and in 1999.[7] Like all new paradigm leaders, she combines traditional male qualities, such as ambition and aggressiveness, with more feminine qualities, including collaborating and forming collegial relationships with clients and colleagues. A self-made millionaire, she has never let social convention about a woman's role in society put a lid on her dreams. "I never had money so the desire to have money and attain financial security were a big part of my drive," Mark explains. "And the desire to be somebody different—to figure out where it was that I did fit in."

As in banking, men have traditionally dominated the operations side of the energy industry. Some argue that a lack of female candidates assures that women will always play a supporting role in the field. Twenty years ago, few women studied engineering, much less worked in typical entry-level operations jobs. In addition, the industry historically has observed a code of keeping women from oil fields and other rough environments, further reducing the number of women reaching its senior levels.

Don't tell that to Mark. At just forty-five, she has jetted the globe to build a career selling pipelines and power plants to developing countries for a largely U.S.-based company. Because of her ability to find opportunities others may have missed and her will to succeed, she built Enron International from nothing to $20 billion worth of projects around the world. Now that unit has 11,000 employees in about thirty different countries. She has become an icon at Enron by forging new paths in far-flung countries and by demonstrating a striking resolve to preserve these assets from destruction. In India, she has mollified militant groups, withstood bombings, placated politicians, and gracefully overcome government turmoil to keep projects intact.

"Rebecca is so effective because she has a good strategic mind to create value where it doesn't exist, and she is persistent enough to make it happen," says Joe Sutton, former president and chief operating officer of Enron International, who was her second in command in the Dabhol project in India. "We worked there for four years straight, twenty hours a day, seven days a week. We were sick the whole time with bronchial problems from the poor air quality and diarrhea from the food. We made it through the Bombay bombing in 1993. The Sheraton hotel we stayed in was bombed, and our whole team was shook up and crying. Rebecca calmed everyone down. Then we worked in the building by candlelight when all the elevators were blown out and everyone else had evacuated. I was a ranger in the army and I would say ranger training is one of the most difficult things you can do, but India was more difficult yet. Rebecca never backed down."

Her will to achieve earned her a promotion in 1999 to become vice chairman of parent Enron Corporation, the $31 billion (1998 sales) energy company. And she is a leading candidate to become chief executive officer of Enron, the company that the *New York Times* recently dubbed "a model for the new millennium because entrepreneurship and innovation are prized."[8] According to the corporation and Bloomberg Financial Markets, Enron stock has outpaced the Standard & Poor's 500 through the nineties, while many of its rivals in the gas business have fallen behind the market. From the end of 1988 through June 24, 1999, the return on Enron shares, including reinvested dividends, reached 972 percent.[9] The total return on the Standard & Poor's 500 stock index over the same period totaled 518 percent; and the S&P index of natural gas stocks has returned just 209 percent. And Mark's influence on the stock price hasn't gone unnoticed.

As a result, she recently took on a new assignment: helping her company get a piece of the estimated $300 billion global water market as chairman and chief executive officer of Azurix, the water utility arm Enron formed in January 1998. Although her new job promises to be challenging, competitors are shaking in their boots at the prospect of Mark stirring up the water business. "She thinks big and is a real global player," says Chris Mellor, group managing director of Anglian Water. "Her roots are in the American utility sector, but she has thought and acted globally from the beginning, pursuing asset development and privatization opportunities around the world as she developed new business for Enron. Rebecca is definitely one to watch, a formidable competitor."[10]

She took her new company public in June 1999 in an IPO worth nearly $700 million, and reached a $2 billion market cap in October 1999. Her 2 million shares were worth $14 million in March 2000. She has signed contracts to provide water services to more than 8 million people and raked in revenues of $618 million by October 1999. Enron chief executive officer Ken Lay reportedly expects that water will become as important to the company as its core natural gas and electricity businesses.

"Good people and successful people work very hard for their success," says Mark. "It's typically not because you're smarter. It's because you work harder than the guy next to you."

RISKS AND REWARDS

Even at the dawn of her career, Mark dared to take risks some might deem counterintuitive, another hallmark of new paradigm leadership. Like Orit Gadiesh, she has a reputation for being intrepid, but her approach is to face her fears and overcome them. She landed her first job out of college at First City National Bank of Houston, a bank that is no longer in business. She joined the commercial bank training program, and rose quickly from trainee to loan officer, financing energy projects. "I had offers for more money from several large energy companies to do marketing work, but wanted to go into banking because I didn't understand finance and was petrified of it," said Mark. "I thought, 'That's what I don't know so that's what I'm going to do.' I knew I would see a broad range of things at the bank and be successful there. I always want to take the choice I perceive to be the brightest opportunity."

Early on, Mark found that while skill and effort could get her far, charm would get her farther still. Loan officers who schmoozed with clients had an edge when it came to winning business. Putting customers at ease and impressing employers became a focus for her. Although she hates the word "mentor" because of the subordinate relationship the term implies, she remembers her boss at the bank's loan department filling that role for her. Among other things, he taught her how to motivate people. Always well-dressed and sociable, he would look her in the eye, smile, and say, "Well, Rebecca, what have you done that's brilliant today?"

His attention and praise had a profound effect on Mark. "When things are low and you don't perform to the standard that you want, you have that out in front of you, and it's motivating," she says. "It's a kind of encouragement and cheerleading that everyone needs—somebody to say, 'I know you have it in you.'"

Like Moore, Mark avoided support positions at the bank and mapped out her own path to success. She focused on getting into commercial lending. Although Mark was one of a handful of women to hold a professional job in banking in the late 1970s in Houston, she didn't realize that fact until later. "I didn't even recognize that there were fewer women than men, I just thought women weren't interested," said Mark. "I thought it was terribly exciting—this world of big money and big business with all these men doing things. I was used to it from growing up in an agricultural community where men got to run everything."

Working at the bank, Mark felt a sense of belonging she had

sought all her life and an outlet for her ambition. "I was there, all of a sudden, at a real job, making real money, and having real responsibility. For the first time, I knew how I fit in," said Mark. "I could understand my performance relative to other people doing the same kinds of things I was doing. I just never knew how to be second best."

By 1982, however, Mark felt her bank was taking on what she considered too many risks. Instead of compromising her principles and goals, she looked among her clients, who were mostly power companies, for a finance position. That year, she took a staff job in the treasury department at Continental Resources Company, a natural gas pipeline business, which proved to be fortuitous. Continental was bought in 1985 by Lay's Houston Natural Gas, the predecessor to Enron. Lay, one of the few executives who foresaw the possibilities that deregulation presented, aggressively worked to exploit that potential.[11] It meant that his company could take on a more important role than just making and transporting gas for others to transform into usable energy. New laws now permitted outsiders to construct independent power plants and market their products to utilities, so Lay created a business in 1986 to build some of those plants, and to reap the rewards of transforming gas into electricity.

Mark saw her opportunity, and used her talents as a new paradigm leader to turn potential into profits. At Enron, her skills as a leader flourished. "Women who are really good in this organization tend to think a bit more like the men do than perhaps a traditional woman's role, and men who are good here tend to be more interactive and more open and communicative and instinctual than most of the men you find in corporate America. We're kind of converging in the middle somewhere."

Mark learned to hone her laser focus on accomplishment from many of her colleagues at Enron who previously served in the military. At first, banks were queasy about funding Enron and utilities refused to purchase power from the firm. So Lay hired two men who were used to handling difficult situations—John Wing and Robert Kelly, both West Point graduates and Vietnam veterans. Mark worked for the two as the unit's finance chief.

The trio built the company by nailing down contracts with utilities, fuel suppliers, partners, and contractors, and winning over wary lenders. Fourteen-hour days were the norm. "They were my first introduction to real high-performance high achievers who wanted to get things done and understood a lot more than I did about how the world worked," she says. "From Bob, I learned how to delve into the details of things and grasp the analytics, and from John, I learned how to form a vision to lead people and motivate them."

In the midst of a budding career, Mark made a choice that could have halted her climb up the corporate ladder. In 1986, she gave birth to twins, and decided that she did not want to work full-time for the first year of the babies' lives. Instead, she worked half days ironing out the financing on deals on a project basis. Determined to stay on the fast track, she relocated to Wellesley, Massachusetts, ultimately earning an MBA with distinction from Harvard University. After the twins' first birthday, she was back working full-time on an Enron project in Milford, Massachusetts, while still going to school part-time to get that Ivy League degree. Her marriage strained, she filed for divorce, knowing she would have to work even harder to support her young family while paying for school.

Like many women who rise to the top, Mark has faced rumors that she had a romantic relationship with a colleague. Word spread that Mark and Wing had had an affair, but Mark denies it. And yet, despite the gossip, she gained a reputation in the industry for her diligence, acumen, and strong results. She and her partners inked five major deals in as many years, including a 50 percent stake in a $1.2 billion, 1,875-megawatt plant in Teeside, England, that was up and running by 1993. Enron has already earned over $200 million in profits and gains from the project, a watershed for Mark as well as the power industry. Teeside also carried the distinction of being the first power plant built abroad by a nonutility company, and opened Mark's eyes to the opportunities waiting in less established foreign markets.

Spurred by her will to achieve, Mark built a lucrative business by striking deals where others feared to tread. In 1991, at age thirty-six, with her passport filled with visa stamps as she traveled to Latin America, Asia, and the former Soviet Union, she faced two challenges: figuring out which emerging markets might open, and determining how to get Enron involved. Unlike many engineers who excel in energy firms like hers, Mark was a talented MBA who was driven to develop a profitable business because of her inner drive to excel. The biggest coup of her career so far turned out to be the establishment of a plant in India— a tantalizing market of 950 million people. She began by knocking on doors of political officials in the world's second most populous country, and eventually signed a $2 billion deal to build a power plant at Dabhol, 100 miles south of Bombay in the wealthiest state in the nation, Maharashtra. But internal politics soon thwarted her plan. Voters elected a Hindu nationalist government that canceled the plant four months into construction, after alleging that Enron had bribed officials to secure the deal. Mark, in return, filed for international arbitration and sued the foreign government for $300 million in compensation.

OPEN LINES TO SUCCESS

While others might have given up, Mark's determination to excel only fueled her further to come up with a solution. She got creative. Unlike Moore, who relies primarily on her masculine traits in business, Mark skillfully blended classic female and male characteristics, typical of new paradigm leaders, to win the Dabhol deal. After some saber rattling on both sides, Mark spent the next fourteen months trying to get the deal back on track through a campaign of shuttle diplomacy. She made concessions on the price of Dabhol's power and developed a rapport with the new political leader, Balasaheb Thackeray. She heard that Thackeray, a former cartoonist, was a Walt Disney fan, and gave him a present she knew he would appreciate—a videotape of Disney's *Sleeping Beauty*. She also offered Maharashtra state the opportunity to buy 30 percent of the Dabhol project. With so much at stake, Mark made a symbolic concession: She hung her short Western skirts in the closet and began wearing Indian jewelry and native clothing, such as flowing salwar khameezes.

She zealously pursued a compromise in which the nationalist government won its concessions, and she landed a lucrative deal. Mark took a risk and reopened dialogue, but grew quiet and listened to nationalist concerns. She satisfied their goals—the new government had demanded cheaper electricity rates and a percentage of the deal—while getting what she needed. Constant and open communication was vital to reaching a positive outcome.

Listening is a consummate female trait and a component of effective communication that all new paradigm leaders like Mark exhibit. "Even when they find their voices, and start to speak assertively as leaders, women nevertheless retain a strong value and talent for listening," writes Sally Helgesen. "It is a skill intrinsic to their values for responsibility, interconnection, and inclusion, not simply a result of their position as 'the second sex.'"[12]

Mark also had to wage a battle of public opinion. Many Indians view foreign companies with suspicion because of the nation's history: India virtually closed itself off from the world since independence was achieved in 1947 because of a devotion to a socialist model of self-reliance. In 1991, however, the government changed course and began to invite foreign investment to lure capital and spur growth like its Asian neighbors. But many of the foreign companies who entered the country since 1991 have met with disappointing results. Mercedes-Benz, for instance, opened a plant in 1995 to produce E-class sedans for India's burgeoning business class, but is running at less than 20 percent capacity because sales of the vehicles have been sluggish.[13]

Mark was fixed on making the Dabhol project nothing short of a huge success for Enron. Her best weapon was not muscle but patience. She talked with as many people as she could, including members of the local press, business leaders, organizations, politicians, and bureaucrats. Resolved to make the plant a "good neighbor," she also launched a newsletter that the company sent to 2,000 policymakers and editors. With slogans like "power to the people," she redirected the dialogue to focus on the ultimate customer, the Indian people. Enron granted CARE, the U.S. aid organization, $500,000 for development programs close to Dabhol. The funds reach fifty-six villages. In addition, Enron planted more than 100,000 trees on the project site to help prevent erosion. Despite not having a local partner on the deal, Mark promoted Sanjay Bhatnagar, a Harvard-educated native of India, to run Dabhol.

From a virtual catastrophe, helped in no small part by her strong will to succeed, Mark emerged with a major triumph. She not only saved the plant, she expanded the project by 9 percent to 2,450 megawatts and $2.5 billion. Her success in India cemented her status as a leader in the power industry.

Mark put in the travel time to meet with India's power brokers about the deal. "I can count every airplane mile on my body somewhere," she said. "I even took the boys with me." Mark travels with her sons throughout the world. She has a live-in nanny, whose daughter, Yolanda, also lives with the family in their 8,000-square-foot Houston home. Mark helped pay for Yolanda's private school education, and is now assisting in sending her to college.

A DRIVE TO GET OFF THE FARM

Even from an early age, Mark would always achieve whatever goal she had in mind. She had a knack for keeping up with the boys since she was an eight-year-old girl playing cowboy and Indian games with her older brother on the family farm in Kirksville, Missouri, a small town about 150 miles east of Kansas City. The two children would build forts, then use machetes to hack escape paths through the fields.

What they didn't notice was that they eventually cut their paths through twenty acres of corn, destroying part of their family's livelihood. When their father discovered the damage, he was furious. He figured out how much their antics had cost, and made the pair work six hours a day for the next month to pay for the lost corn. "It was about $400 for each of us, which was an outrageous amount of money at that time," explained Mark. "We had to work it off."

Like Darla Moore and other new paradigm leaders, Mark didn't follow convention. She grew up in a home of Southern Baptists focused on farming, church, and family. Most of her family remains in her hometown today. Education was also highly valued in Mark's household. "It was assumed from an early age that we'd go to college and be successful at something, but I come from a place where people stay—they're rooted," she explains. "Everyone in my environment was self-employed. Everybody was independent and wouldn't think of working for a salary. It was all about taking care of yourself and figuring out your own life."

Mark also embraced hard work as a path to her own success. Close to five months out of the year were cold and often snow-covered at the family farm. Before and after school, she had a plenty of chores to do. She mucked out stalls, fed the hogs, and used a hatchet to chop the ice off the tops of water tanks so that the cattle could have water to drink. When she was a child, there were many tough years when a drought, a dive in crop prices, and livestock disease brought her family to the brink. Everyone worked and didn't mind getting their hands dirty, including Mark. "You learn that discipline really matters, and that you just work until the work's done," she recalls. "You learn about responsibility at a very early age and you learn about business in a unique kind of way—you know the value of money. You understand the relationship of what it costs to plant a crop and what happens when it gets damaged."

With her own independent vision, Mark also identified with male role models rather than female ones. Cooking and sewing, tasks her father and grandfather encouraged her to learn to be a good housewife, held no interest. She preferred her chores instead. She also liked to talk about the family business with her father. She was always playing with boys, and even learned Morse code. As a child, she pretended to hunt, but as a teenager she developed a taste for the real thing. "Playing with real guns was much more fun for me," she says. "I think I may have had a few dolls, but I don't know that I spent a lot of time with them."

Mark was always eager to escape to a wider world where she felt she could flourish. Reading broadened her horizons beyond her Missouri farm. She began reading at age four and grew to love a variety of books, including novels, biographies, and historical works. She devoured whatever she could get her hands on, and developed a passion for Ayn Rand. "I tried to figure out why I didn't fit in [my] environment. I could not understand why the world was divided into two parts, boy parts and girl parts," she says. "I loved anything that took me to another world—out into other peoples' lives and other arenas."

A seventh-grade Spanish class and a ninth-grade French class taught her to look abroad to fulfill her aspirations—an unconventional path compared with most of her peers. "It was like living someone else's life—by studying languages you learn the culture and the nature of how people interact with each other," she explains. "It was like traveling without boarding a plane. I'd never seen a big city other than St. Louis or Kansas City."

Her hunger to travel was no doubt rooted in the alienation she felt from her own environment. She had few friends. Unlike her peers, she never saw herself marrying one of the other farm kids, settling down, and having children in Kirksville. She also did not feel "unduly attached" to her family, nor did she need the support or security of being near her parents or siblings. "I was really a loner in a lot of respects. I didn't fit into the church that my parents attended," she explains. "I was always a little bit different, always questioning whether the place we were was where we needed to be or whether we needed to be thinking about the world a little bit differently. I remember questioning the world and my surroundings and assumptions about the world since I was three years old."

College was Mark's escape hatch. Her parents couldn't foot the bill, but with the help of a scholarship, she went to Baylor University in Texas. While attending school, she worked up to forty hours a week to earn her living expenses. She also held down summer jobs. "I drove a school bus for a while and waited a lot of tables," she says. "Work was something I knew how to do, and I knew how to make money to take care of myself."

After earning a B.A. in psychology in 1976, Mark concluded the degree was a mistake. Ironically, the field depressed her. Business, she reasoned, suited her personality better. "I just could not commit to psychology and put that kind of energy into other people's lives. It wasn't a lack of interest or sincerity, but I was much more of an organizer. I'm all for helping people as long as I can tell them what to do to shape up and do it right. I like to say, 'Let's lay out a plan, and now you follow it,'" explains Mark, who took away an M.A. in international management from Baylor in 1978. "It sounded to me like business."

MANAGING PEOPLE BY GETTING OUT IN FRONT

Not surprisingly, Rebecca Mark has been more successful than Darla Moore in managing employees—because, like other new paradigm leaders, she collaborates with them. Mark looks for unconventional ways to get the job done in her efforts to find opportunities that others simply do not see. At Enron, her goal is to foster the innovative and entrepreneurial spirit exhibited by Silicon Valley start-ups, just as the company does. She allows for a lot of autonomy in her search to uncover new ideas.

A culture that rewards ideas helps Mark motivate employees, as does her ability to listen closely when staffers present their proposals.

"A skill I learned from men is the value of leadership. Leadership really means just getting out there in front and doing it, and doing it is the way to show other people how to do it," explains Mark, who points to her plant in India as a primary example. The uncertainties of doing large deals in India, where government stability is shaky, nuclear tensions with Pakistan are escalating, and cultural norms differ dramatically from those in the United States, scare off some of the most experienced American executives. When the new government rescinded Enron's contract, the project appeared to be dead. But Mark's boss, Lay, continued to support her, and she refused to let the project die.

She found that she had to work harder to keep not just her own laser focus on accomplishing her goals but that of her employees as well. She recalls how morale on her India team hit a low point when the deal fell into question. "I believe that people will grow to the demands placed on them," says Mark, who said she concentrated on keeping her team members focused and positive. "It really is a matter of heart."

She views being a woman as an advantage when dealing with employees. "I think women are instinctual and listen carefully to emotions and feelings, and they are probably better caretakers of their people. We don't end our business lives when we leave the office. You'll see us bringing our kids into the office or leaving for a doctor's appointment, or maybe being more aware of the things that affect the lives of our associates—the spouse who has cancer or the aging parents."

AMBITION, VERSION 2.0

Keeping a laser focus on achieving their goals helped power the careers of Moore, Mark, and the other women featured in this book. While aggressiveness is worthy of praise in a man, society often writes off the aggressive female as "pushy." Both feminists and scholars have noted the trend for decades. Intelligent girls with potential for success are often criticized for being ambitious. Those with aptitudes in science, math, engineering, or even literature are often disparaged by their peers in school. Dr. Sally Morgan Reis, University of Connecticut professor of educational psychology and the principal investigator for the National Research Center on the Gifted and Talented, notes that girls start to be "perceived negatively" if they are too smart. By grade six or seven, they begin to look at themselves in terms of other girls who are more popular. "They start to perceive, correctly, that many teachers are uncomfortable with girls who are too ambitious, too smart or too outspoken. . . . And their achievement starts to be [lower] than what would be expected given their level of ability."[14]

The laser focus on accomplishment that Moore and Mark exhibited as young women can overcome these destructive elements. While the ambition that enables new paradigm leaders to execute is similar to that which many successful men embody, it differs from that which old paradigm leaders exhibited. Many in the first wave of female leaders did not share power with those around them. Old paradigm leaders, like Linda Wachner, were autocratic and distanced themselves from colleagues and employees. Others, like Jill Barad, had problems relating to powerful managers and an unwillingness to listen to bad news.

But ambition takes many forms, and new paradigm leaders draw on different sources of motivation from those of their old paradigm predecessors to fuel their drive. Some want to assure financial independence for themselves, and others are driven to assure livelihoods for their families. Still more seek to strengthen themselves while also building leadership qualities in their colleagues. New paradigm leaders understand that to achieve their lofty goals, they must share that determination with those around them. Not only will they reach their objectives more quickly, but they will build leaders to follow in their footsteps.

5

MAXIMIZING HIGH TOUCH IN AN ERA OF HIGH TECH

I start from a point of view that says to lead people, they must be engaged. One way to engage them is to issue orders, make demands, and frighten people. To me, that does not get you the best result.

— SHELLY LAZARUS

In May 1994, International Business Machines Corporation (IBM) dropped a bomb on the advertising world, and Shelly Lazarus was one of the few industry executives not blown away by the news. That's because, as part of a new marketing strategy, the world's largest computer maker consolidated its $400 million advertising account, divvied out among forty different shops, into just one. That new account went to Ogilvy & Mather Worldwide, where Lazarus was a senior executive. It was the largest account switch that had ever been made.

Why? The IBM executives who made the call, chief executive officer Louis Gerstner and vice president of corporate marketing Abby Kohnstamm, could have picked another agency, but they selected Ogilvy & Mather primarily because of Lazarus. These executives believed that not only did her agency have the global reach, but she had the right stuff to help their company, a lumbering giant that brought the world the mainframe computer, revamp its image at a critical time. As they saw it, she had something of a counterintuitive approach that made her comfortable rebuilding the rules to achieve good results for clients. "I had been their partner years ago when they were both at American Express, and I ran that account for Ogilvy," says Lazarus. "We worked together closely and successfully with outstanding result. And now [Gerstner and Kohnstamm] were taking this huge risk because the company was in great trouble. They were under fire and the world was watching. The nod was in our favor because they chose to go with an organization with whom they had a positive experience. And they trusted me to deliver."

IBM's switch was not only a coup for Lazarus, but also emblematic of how she gets her job done. Building trust with clients and colleagues has been a hallmark of Lazarus's career. With IBM, her potent combination of business ingenuity mixed with the warmth to forge enduring professional relationships helped her score the largest account in the fifty-one-year history of her advertising agency. Today, that remarkable consolidation is worth over $750 million in billings to her firm each year—nearly double the account's size when it first arrived.

AN ADVERTISING GIANT

Capturing IBM's business helped catapult Lazarus to the chairman and chief executive officer post of advertising giant Ogilvy just two years later in 1996. In an industry that peddles primarily to female consumers, she is only the second woman ever to run a top international advertising agency. At fifty-two, she directs the world's eighth-largest advertising company with $10 billion in 1998 billings, and takes home over $1 million a year. Her global empire currently spans 359 offices with over 10,000 employees in 100 countries. She has boosted billings 10 percent each year since rising to the top spot at the company. One of the few female chiefs of a major communications company, she has earned accolades from the *New York Times*, *Vanity Fair*, the *New Yorker*, and *People* magazine. *Fortune* magazine named her the fourth most powerful woman in American business in 1998 and 1999.[1] She has thrived in a pressure-filled business by building trust with clients, empowering employees, and striking a chord with consumers. Some colleagues describe her management style as "nurturing" and "distinctly female." Her agency won more than $700 million in new business in 1998, adding Miller Lite and Kraft's Post cereals unit to the company client list. Apart from IBM and American Express, she services other blue-chip clients including Ford, Mattel, Unilever, and Maxwell House, part of Kraft's coffee and cereal unit.

"[My successor] had to be Shelly," says Charlotte Beers, the former chief executive officer who passed Lazarus the baton in 1996, when the firm took in $7.6 billion in annual billings. "I would not be as good as her at taking the momentum we had and turning it into capability. Besides being a twenty-six-year Ogilvy employee, Shelly has a powerful strategic capability and operations sense. But she can walk into a room and disarm everyone in it by opening with a nice story that everyone can relate to. It's a subtle way for her to take ownership."

USING OLD-FASHIONED SKILLS

Key to Lazarus's success has been her reliance on a signature new paradigm trait: the ability to roll up her sleeves and get involved with her clients and her employees in a meaningful way. She inspires employees by giving them projects to handle, and she lures clients by taking the time to understand their businesses, push for new concepts to build their brand image, and build relationships with them as people. "Sometimes advertising executives want so much to please the client that there's pandering, but there's none of that with Shelly," says Ann Fudge, executive vice president of Kraft Foods overseeing its coffee and cereals division, who has been Lazarus's client since 1991. "She listens and she's honest. Like Jack Welch [chairman of General Electric] or Larry Bossidy [chairman of Allied Signal], she creates cultural values about winning and delivering the best work, challenging clients to think more broadly, and pressing for new ideas. And she learns about my customers. But it's the little things she does, like calling me and sending me little notes. She makes me feel important as a client by staying linked to my business."

Business is not just business for Lazarus, and the bonds she forms can get personal. "When my mother died this summer, she was incredible," adds Fudge through tears. "She was there for me."

New paradigm leaders like Lazarus capitalize on the use of seemingly old-fashioned skills, like nurturing, displaying warmth, engendering loyalty and respect, and having a "bedside manner," at a time in business when most executives are fixated on managing bits and bytes. Of course, new paradigm leaders are not just touchy-feely types who make others feel good but let the serious aspects of their work slide. They are extremely competent in their jobs. And their skill in collaborating with staffers and connecting with customers on a very human level ensures that they will excel in this highly competitive digital age in which partnering is a vital competitive advantage. What defines the women featured in this book is that they reach into their hearts and treat people like people, which sets them apart.

Top venture capitalist Ann Winblad plays the role of "coach" to help budding entrepreneurs of the software start-ups she funds shape their ideas into successful companies. Ellen Gordon's move to group employees of Tootsie Roll Industries in teams has enabled her to improve the candy maker's results for each of the last twenty-one consecutive years. Orit Gadiesh changed the entire structure of Bain & Company to a partnership to revitalize the consulting company by giving its employees a greater stake in its progress.

Another new paradigm leader featured in this chapter because of her ability to strike bonds with employees and clients to help them achieve success is Marilyn Carlson Nelson, chairman and chief executive officer of the privately held $22 billion (1998 revenues) travel behemoth Carlson Companies. Nelson heads one of America's largest private companies, and appeared on *Fortune's* list of the most powerful women in American business in both 1998 and 1999.[2] She, too, is famous for building a loyal employee base of over 180,000 people in more than 144 countries through profit sharing and liberalizing benefits at her sixty-one-year-old company.

New paradigm leaders all share the philosophy of Geraldine Laybourne, chief of Oxygen Media, that leading executives need to look for opportunities to really connect with employees, rather than operating at a distance from them: "The glass ceiling is not nearly as dangerous as the glass floor that most executives stand on," she says. "It's a guard they all use as a shield that divides them from their employees, so that employees only tell them good news. When I hear bad news, I am grateful because I know we are going to learn something that will help us avoid mistakes."

USING NATURAL FEMALE TALENTS

Women are widely known for their ability to collaborate with others and nurture those around them. According to anthropologist Helen Fisher, girls are more nurturing with each other when they play than boys are. This distinction between the sexes continues into adulthood. "Females have a natural tendency to form lateral connections to others, and spend a lot of time working these ties because women regard these connections as power, while men regard power as rank," says Fisher. "These natural gender differences occur probably as a result of testosterone. Young men have seven to ten times more testosterone than women do, and they form hierarchies, whereas women don't. Because they are nurturing, women are naturally great at attracting clients."

But qualities like "nurturing" have new meaning in today's workplace as managers face the twin difficulties of luring talented employees in a labor market with unemployment at record lows and wooing increasingly demanding clients. Developing talent through allowing personnel the opportunity to take on more autonomy and a greater level of responsibility seems to be helping the leaders reach their objectives. Building leadership from within is a vital skill in any thriving business, and new paradigm leaders view this as an integral part of their role.

"When faced with the challenge of turning talent into performance, why do so many managers choose, instead, to dictate how work should be done?" write business analysts Marcus Buckingham and Curt Coffman of the Gallup Organization. "In the end it is probably that the allure of control is just too tempting. On the surface [the] temptation seems justifiable, but play [it] out and [it] soon saps the life out of the organization and shrivels its value."[3]

The ability to form collegial relationships with employees and customers is not only vital to motivating employees and drawing customers, it's essential to a company's growth. When this feature is absent, a chief executive's job is at risk. Eckhard Pfeiffer held the chief executive officer position at Compaq Computer Corporation from 1991 to 1999, but was removed by the board of directors after he imposed a rigid hierarchy and fostered a contentious atmosphere. Faced with a highly competitive and diminishing PC market, Compaq's earnings declined in the first quarter of 1999, and the company lost almost half its market capitalization by May of that year.[4] Renowned for his imperious nature, Pfeiffer installed executive perks at a company that had fostered an egalitarian culture in the past.[5] He was criticized for becoming distant from customers, employees, and shareholders.

Wolfgang Schmitt became chief executive officer of Rubbermaid, Inc., in 1993, but lost his job in 1998 after being blamed for the company's decline.[6] Company earnings per share fell 58 percent during his tenure as Rubbermaid failed to counter a price slide due to retail industry consolidation and a rise in production costs from increasing raw material prices. But Schmitt was widely blamed for the company's woes because of his "tyrannical" management style, which drove away key employees and sealed his fate at the company.

DEFYING STEREOTYPES

From the start of her career, Lazarus was often the only woman in meetings. Even in 1999, only 5 percent of the highest corporate officers among Fortune 500 advertising firms were women, according to Catalyst. While advertising agencies gear their pitches primarily toward women, who control 85 percent of all personal and household spending,[7] few females fill executive suites. But Lazarus quickly learned to turn this apparent drawback into an advantage. While her male colleagues looked to her to reflect customer opinions, she also defied stereotypes about women. "We'd be talking about what women would buy, and then suddenly everyone would look at me—it was amazing, there I was, suddenly representing all women, everywhere," she recalls. "Early on in my career, there was a presumption that women weren't as strong, weren't as capable as men. So if you were capable it magnified the performance relative to the expectation. I had enormous power in that way."

When she took over the chief executive position, Lazarus made a small but significant decision that subtly built goodwill among her employees in classic new paradigm style. She opted against moving into the spacious CEO suite and remained in her old, single-room office on the tenth floor of Ogilvy's Eighth Avenue building. Her decision was partly a practical one. After all, she had already personalized the place. Walking into her office is like jumping onto a lily pad. Frogs are everywhere. Ceramic frogs and wooden frogs lounge atop her desk. Plush Beanie Baby frogs from local drugstores and crystal frogs from Baccarat adorn her coffee table. She points with pride to one frog that plays the song "London Bridge Is Falling Down." "I gave my husband a toy frog on the first anniversary of our engagement, and soon we began trading them," she says. "Now I get two to three frogs a week from employees, clients, and friends from all over the world."

But her decision on office real estate also speaks volumes about her management style: "Men like to feel powerful, but I get no thrill out of that," she says. "I start from a point of view that says to lead people, they must be engaged. One way to engage them is to issue orders, make demands, and frighten people. To me, that does not get you the best result. I think it's all about surrounding yourself with people in whom you have total trust and whose minds and abilities you respect, and then inviting them in and allowing them to participate with you in decision making. First of all, you come to better decisions because you're including people whose brains you respect. But also you've already prejudiced the outcome in your favor because they are now invested in the decision and the outcome. If you just issue orders, the person receiving the orders spends most of his or her emotional energy proving the order was wrong in the first place. So to me, that's just a complete waste of time."

Lazarus's office is loaded with family photographs of her husband, highly respected and sought after Manhattan pediatrician George Lazarus, and their three children, Ted, Samantha, and Ben, ranging in age from twelve to twenty-five. The dominant color in the room is salmon pink. She settles into a classic wooden chair with a salmon and blue striped upholstered seat. Practical and modest, she has combed her natural ash blond short hair back behind her ears. She wears an elegant black dress with a deep red blazer accented by a classic single strand of pearls and large pearl earrings encircled with gold.

MANAGING WITH HUMILITY

Lazarus has spent the past twenty-six years working at Ogilvy, and her journey to the top was a steady climb. Her skill with people and her ability to execute helped her thrive at the topflight agency, where she feels just as comfortable managing freewheeling creative colleagues as meeting the needs of bottom line–oriented corporate clients.

Like Rebecca Mark and Darla Moore, Lazarus turned an area many considered a dead end into a launching pad to rise higher in the company through her laser focus on achieving success. In 1989, she was asked to lead the agency's American direct marketing unit, O&M Direct U.S., where, in her words, she was in charge of producing "junk mail." But few of her mailings actually ended up in the trash. In just one year, 1990, she led the unit to billings of $354 million, a 15 percent gain over the prior year. She made Ogilvy a leader in the industry by changing its focus. "When I came to O&M Direct, there was much less emphasis on overall strategic marketing," she says. "I emphasized getting involved in the guts of our direct clients' businesses."

Her results got noticed. By 1991, she was promoted again, to president of Ogilvy's prestigious New York office. Like Pat Russo and Ellen Gordon, she was given a classic new paradigm leader fitness test: Could she turn around the business? Once a "class act" of the industry where red carpeting lined the hallways to welcome clients, the agency's flagship New York office had descended into turmoil during the early 1990s.

Back then, the office garnered about $700 million in billings from high-profile clients including American Express, General Mills, and Lever Brothers, but its parent company, the WPP Group PLC, was choking from debt. Since buying Ogilvy for $860 million in 1989, chief executive officer of WPP Martin Sorrell had imposed strict financial discipline and trimmed staff by close to 10 percent. An advertising recession combined with Sorrell's pressure to cut costs damaged morale further and endangered big accounts. During the first half of 1991, client budget cuts from companies such as Duracell and Joseph E. Seagram & Sons drove agency revenues down a reported 5 to 10 percent, according to *BusinessWeek*. Making matters worse, longtime client American Express, whose $60 million account was a backbone of the business, fired Ogilvy that year. Other clients soon abandoned the firm as well. What's more, several key executives walked out, including Gordon S. Bowen, the top creative executive on the American Express account, and Bill Gray, the senior account executive for the credit card company. "We had lost our way," recalls Gray. "Once WPP took over, we suffered an identity crisis, and there was a fair amount of turnover at the top."

FOCUSING ON PEOPLE

Rather than follow these senior members of the company out the door, Lazarus dug in her heels. "I used to have these nightmares that I would go into the office and no one would be there. I would be all alone," she recalls. "We were losing business left and right, and we were losing people. Everyone was despondent, but that word did not even do it justice. It was like clinical depression. People looked physically contorted. We made like no money—maybe a few million dollars. Lots of accounts were at risk. I was told that every person in the New York office had their résumé out on the street."

When faced with customer flight and an in-house brain drain, Lazarus, like all other new paradigm leaders, showed courage under fire. Instead of hiring new staff, her first move was to sit down and talk individually with the thirty employees who were leading account executives at the firm.

"I had to hear what was on their minds, what their issues were, and why they felt so overwhelmed by the problems," she said. "It struck me that the biggest challenge I had was this group of people who had no hope. I asked, 'How could I restore it?' First, I had to make the problem seem scaleable. So I didn't ask, 'How can we turn around the New York office?' Instead I asked, 'Do you think you could improve the work on Maxwell House in the next six months?' Second, I put control in their hands. This was an extremely hierarchical organization. The president of the agency made every decision. That was obvious to me because in the first five days I was in the job I was getting papers on my desk asking for authorization for everything—for having a Christmas lunch or for hiring an entry-level assistant account executive. So I just sent all these papers back to the account executives, and asked them to make all the decisions. They didn't even know what their costs or profits were. Because they had no responsibility for it, this information was irrelevant. I returned all the salary budgets and expense budgets to them and said, 'Listen, I don't care if you have three people and pay each one of them a million dollars, or if you have a hundred people whom you hire freelance. Just spend what you need to improve the work on Maxwell House.' And third, I offered bonuses for those who could win back business. They hadn't had a bonus in over two years at that office. But it wasn't about the money. That was not their focus at all, but it made the game more fun because there was actual reward. It was another source of pride in the work."

Like Martha Ingram, Loida Lewis, and other new paradigm leaders, Lazarus took some hefty risks while displaying her courage under fire. To offer bonuses meant haggling with her tightfisted boss, Martin Sorrell, for money. But using a bonus as an incentive would also send a message to employees that the company believed they could, in fact, fix the problems on their own. Lazarus put together a one-hour presentation explaining the situation and how she intended to use the funds as part of an incentive plan. She knew nothing about structuring such plans but took the plunge anyway.

"It was tough at the time because the office was losing money and he had his own debts to pay, but I had to ask for money," she said. "Aside from saying no, I knew he was going to say, 'What do you know about building an incentive plan?' But after the whole talk was over, he asked, 'Is that enough?' The result was newly inspired people because what you're saying by offering a bonus is that the power is in your hands, and I believe in you. Here's a stretch goal, but I know you can do it once I've given you ownership of the project. Within nine months we turned around the business. And I didn't have to bring in one new person. The same exact people who had their résumés out on the street got the job done."

WINNING BACK CLIENTS

Lazarus was charged not only with rejuvenating the languishing office, but winning back leading clients like American Express, an account she had worked on for ten years. Rival agency Chiat/Day had lured the financial services giant away from Ogilvy in 1991. Rather than giving up, Lazarus only worked harder to regain the business. As a first move, she wooed back Bill Gray and put him to work on the American Express account.

"We still retained one small part of the [Amex] business, the unsexy part, the service establishment stuff. This means the cooperative advertising the company does with restaurants and stores that accept the card. It's work people aren't very much interested in because it's mostly smaller budget ads for restaurants. I deliberately left a group of very high-powered people there to work on it. The obvious response might have been to take all of the senior people off because this portion of the account did not require such top people, but I didn't," she recalls. "Instead, I told everyone what we needed to do was to give the client great work and prove that we were of value. We didn't moan or whine or say how unhappy we were. We just worked away on our small assignment, and said we were going to earn our way back to the table through great work. And the relationship has never been as good because it's like when you go through a bad patch and you make it up. The relationship just gets stronger."

Thanks to her high-touch sensibilities, Lazarus was able to calm her employees as well as the client to smooth this rough period. Rival Chiat/Day trotted out hip and trendy ads that were irreverent and cynical, but American Express executives disliked these because they conflicted with its timeworn brand. Lazarus, instead, tried to remain true to the card's traditional image, but update it. Taking the cue from her, Gray made a counterintuitive proposal to American Express: "At the time, a lot of establishments were publicly denouncing the card because they were paying a premium they thought was unjust to accept it, but we went in and said your greatest threat is your greatest strength," he recalls. "Our ads pictured the founders of Home Depot, Cypriani Restaurant, and other famous merchants testifying that they used an Amex card personally just like their customers."

Lazarus also encouraged her team to lay out a counterintuitive approach for the client. "Shelly is always very relaxed in the face of extremes, and she kept everybody calm and confident in themselves," recalls Gray. "Her presence alone is enough to kick-start things. She made it clear to me and to Amex that she wasn't going to look at this period as anything but a momentary pause."

After eleven months, Lazarus succeeded in regaining the entire American Express account. Memorable celebrity spots with comedian Jerry Seinfeld followed. With a similar focus on clients and on relationships, she also wooed back other important clients who had ditched her firm, including Ponds, NutraSweet, and Shell Oil. Her efforts helped reverse client and staff losses and paved the way for IBM's arrival.

The strides she made at the agency's flagship office led to further promotions for Lazarus. In 1994, she became president of Ogilvy's North America unit, marking her tenure there by obtaining the gigantic IBM account. A huge boost for Ogilvy, IBM became one of its three largest clients, and lifted the firm's total worldwide billings to $6.3 billion from $5.8 billion that year.

ENGAGING COLLEAGUES IN DECISION MAKING

Lazarus used her collegial management style to help her run the North America region more effectively. When she began in her new position, she found that the area was split into six separate units, located in major cities across the United States and Canada, with each acting independently. She saw immediately that the existing structure was flawed and inefficient. She believed the company could better serve clients and staff by working as a single unit, where one could tap creative resources from the appropriate location and gain access to research from various offices. What she wanted was cooperation between the individual offices within the region, but how could she get it? She called on her new paradigm trait of high-touch management to get the desired result.

Lazarus brought all the office heads together to ask them if they thought that current conditions were unwieldy, and if forming a single unit could remedy the problem. When all these executives backed her plan, she went a step further. She questioned them about ways to implement this new approach. After four hours of open discussion, the group together came up with a plan to measure the region financially as a single office, through one profit-and-loss statement.

"I could have just issued a set of orders that said from this moment on, this is the way we will work. But by bringing these people together, I was startled by how much faster we made progress. I saved two years by engaging everyone in that first conversation because there were real turf issues I thought would take at least that amount of time to resolve," Lazarus explains. "There are people who disagree strongly with me. They say you must just tell people what to do and then they'll do it, but that hasn't been my experience. Not when you're managing people who are smart, talented, creative, and question everything. So I've learned to manage in a very collegial way. In my business, if I order you, humiliate you, and make you fearful but I get the result, I actually haven't won in the long run because I know you will be leaving soon."

By 1996, Lazarus's string of successes at Ogilvy led to her naming as chief executive officer of the advertising agency. True to her management style when she led the New York office, she put her collaborative approach into effect by handing decisions down to employees throughout the firm. In doing so, she broke down hierarchies, and handed the power to run client accounts directly to her senior managers. To keep the company growing, she draws on their expertise to service demanding global clients while offering dramatic creative work that is typically the forte of smaller shops. She has tried to strengthen Ogilvy's focus on global branding and nurturing growth for Kraft, Finnish telecommunications firm Nokia, and Kodak. She has also worked to broaden the agency's cachet with Internet clients by reeling in companies like MotherNature.com, Tickets.com, and WebMD.com.

Yet another outcrop of her new paradigm focus on high touch is her strategy of "360-Degree Branding." This phrase is her term for her approach to advertising—which means making all contact with customers—whether through a Web site, brochure, or television commercial—communicate what the brand is and what it means. As an example, she points to the "e-business" campaign for IBM, in which a whole range of media is used to communicate the idea that the company is "friendly," "accessible," and plays a major role in the wired world. By featuring humorous scenarios of people from countries like the United States, Japan, and Germany grappling with technology, the campaign strives to give the computer behemoth a warm image with worldwide appeal. This message appears on billboards, in newspapers, on television, direct response, and the Internet. "The company went from the dying IBM in 1994 to this highly successful leader in the business," she explains. "We have taken the communication role in that and evolved it."

Showing respect is a key part of Lazarus's high-touch approach. Lending trust is another basic component of her management style. Combining these two elements allows Lazarus to both strengthen herself and boost the prospects for those around her. "I'm a great delegator. I don't think you can do everything yourself," she says. "I think you have to find people you trust, then just hand off whole objectives to them and let them get on with it. Then you never second-guess them, you just support them. And if they don't deliver, then you get someone else who can. If you get the right people, it's very liberating. Usually, at the beginning, they check back with you all the time. I always say, 'I've given you the whole project, and I support you in your decisions. You don't have to check with me.'"

Instead of a pyramid hierarchy beneath her, Lazarus structures power at Ogilvy by placing herself at the center of a web with spokes connecting her to circles of management teams that surround her. She installed creative executives as copresidents along with account executives (noncreative management) on every team serving clients so that both artistry and finance are afforded equal strength. "I like to invest power in small groups of very strong people," she says. "I don't have a lot of staff people around. But in the circles, there is a decision maker everywhere. That decision maker usually acts to break ties, but it rarely comes to that. The power of the one more powerful is not felt all that often."

If Lazarus has a goal to meet, she does not bark out orders to her management staff. Instead, she involves employees in solving the problem. For instance, when Martin Sorrell, CEO of parent company WPP, urged a hiring freeze in 1998 to cut costs, Lazarus had a better idea. Rather than tell her regional heads to stop hiring, she sent out a memo calling for their ideas on how to cut costs. She got a slew of responses back that she put in place, and saved the company over $1.5 million. Her approach saved the company $500,000 more than Sorrell had planned with his initial headcount freeze. In short, as a new paradigm leader, she treats her staff the way she likes to be treated. "Give me a directive, and let me loose," she says. "But don't just give me an order."

RELEASING PEOPLE TO BE CREATIVE

Like Orit Gadiesh espousing "True North," Lazarus promotes her vision for Ogilvy's corporate culture because she believes it creates an environment that allows employees to do their best work. She defines the environment as one that places a premium on respect for the individual, accountability for the quality of one's work, and the ability to experiment to achieve the best ideas. Although Lazarus does not collect retention rates, she says the average tenure for senior executives is eleven years. She adds that lengthy tenure is important to clients who get to know and rely on staffers as well. "It's all about releasing people to be creative and motivating them to take risks, and getting rid of traditional structures, roles, and office politics," she says. "There are times when this is an arbitrary business, but my role is to pick everyone up and not let them take it personally. After all, you are only as good as the people you employ, and so many of our people have been here for fifteen, twenty, and twenty-five years. This is a place people want to be."

With an appreciation of her colleagues in mind, Lazarus gives her employees a stake in the company so she can keep good talent in the notoriously cutthroat advertising industry. She worked with her parent company to set up new programs so that each Ogilvy employee could receive equity and stock options in WPP for the first time. "We were acquired hostilely so we hadn't yet established new equity accumulation programs for our employees when I took over," she says. "So I worked on developing programs so that all Ogilvy employees could have stock options in WPP. I want to give them an equity stake so they can have a secure financial future."

Apart from ownership in the company, Lazarus offers challenges to her employees and accommodates their lives outside work. "If you want to attract and keep talent, you have to create opportunities that match that person's desires and ambitions," she explains. "You cannot dictate how a person's career will evolve. If you want that person's talent, you're probably going to have to get it on their terms rather than your company's. You keep them because you give them added responsibility, added impact. And you compensate them fairly."

BORN WITH A BUSINESS SENSE

Like Meg Whitman, Shelly Lazarus developed her own talent for business early. She grew up in suburban Oceanside, New York, as the eldest of three children. She had two younger brothers, who are both attorneys today. Her father, Lewis, was a CPA, and her mother, Sylvia, a homemaker. In Brooklyn, where her family moved in 1960, Shelly always brought home straight A's from Midwood High, but not just to please her parents. She says they were not the types to live by the achievements of their children. "My parents didn't need me to do well in school because it made them feel good. So I was pretty free to set my own values in a way. School came easily to me because I liked to learn," she says. "I was always passionately interested in whatever I was doing at the moment. I never did anything halfway. Whatever it was, it would just consume me. I loved working on the school newspaper, and the next thing I knew, I was chosen to be editor in chief."

Charlotte Beers has her own description of the ease Lazarus possesses. "She is one of the most whole people I know," Beers explains. "She was blessed with a very balanced and nurturing upbringing."

Always fascinated by her father's work, Lazarus got an introduction to the stock market when she was ten years old. Her dad bought her stock in ITT, and she would dutifully check its share price every day. "Even though I had brothers, he never ever told me not to do something because I was a girl," she says of her father. "I didn't even have that conscious thought. I just enjoyed the moment and whatever interested me. I never planned to be a CEO because it was just so easy for me to stay focused on what I was doing, and then good things would happen as a result."

Her love for advertising developed in her senior year at Smith College, during the fall of 1967. A psychology major, she joined a friend for a road trip to Manhattan to attend a career conference sponsored by the Advertising Women of New York. "I had never been interested in advertising before," she says. "But I was just fascinated that you could communicate something in an advertisement that could actually influence people's beliefs and behavior. The desire to get a job in advertising is what sent me to business school."

ACHIEVING A BALANCE

After completing Smith, Lazarus earned an MBA from Columbia University Graduate School of Business in 1970. After earning a business degree, she took a job in Manhattan as an assistant product manager at Clairol, the beauty product concern. She was looking to put bread on the table for herself and for her husband, George Lazarus, a medical student she had met at a Yale mixer while in college. But in 1971, she got an offer from Ogilvy to work as a junior account executive, and she jumped ship. Soon after joining the agency, her superiors noticed her management potential. In 1973, she became the first female account executive at the company when she was six months pregnant with her first child. "I always felt I was being promoted before my time," she says.

Today, at Ogilvy & Mather, Lazarus is also tolerant of work/life balance issues, but she does not offer special treatment for women at her business. She does not provide specific family-friendly policies at Ogilvy, nor does she believe affirmative action programs assist women. She told the *New York Times* in 1997 that there is an "inverse relationship" between the number of special programs a company offers and how open it is toward people who are "different."[8]

Lazarus, instead, leads by example. She makes time for her family, and speaks openly about being a wife and mother as well as being a topflight executive. She never misses birthday parties for her three children. She often kicks back and watches the famously irreverent show *South Park* with Ben, her youngest son. Despite working long days, often until 10 P.M. when she attends evening client meetings, she has always taken time out to spend with her children—to attend a school play, shuttle the children to a doctor's appointment, buy them shoes, or take them to camp.

"Balance is important to me because my family has always come first. How I spend my time and how I communicate my values and my own priorities extends to my employees, who don't have to account for every minute of their time," she says. "We agree on objectives and I trust them to execute. No one has to come ask me whether they can go to the school play. I don't care. Just get the work done. How you go about doing it is your business. At our company we have such a concern for individuals. You tell us what you need of the organization to do your work superbly well, and we'll work around you. It's more of a philosophy than a set of rules."

SUCCESSION STORY

Chairman and chief executive officer of the Carlson Companies, one of the world's largest private businesses, Marilyn Carlson Nelson shares Lazarus's skill in forming relationships as a means of helping her to broaden her business. In a dramatic break with her firm's tradition, Nelson sealed a partnership in 1998 with one of the oldest and best-known names in travel, the British firm Thomas Cook. The merger combining the two private firms was valued at more than $1 billion. Before the two parties signed on the dotted line, Nelson hosted her new colleagues for dinner at her French country-style home on the shores of Lake Minnetonka. Then, after the deal was signed, she flew to the U.K. to meet personally with hundreds of executives both from Thomas Cook and Carlson's offices to assure them their jobs were secure.

Nelson's domineering father, who preceded her at the helm of the firm, would never have pursued such a combination with Thomas Cook. Fabled for his difficulty with sharing power, he only sought acquisitions and wholly owned projects. His style may have been right for the time period in which he rose. But the partnership Nelson forged would make her already giant travel company a major force in leisure travel, with annual revenues over $42 billion. The deal marked nothing short of a new era at the firm.

Despite inheriting the top post at Carlson, Nelson, sixty, is working to put her own stamp on the company, and alter its culture to suit her personal style of leadership. Her father, Curtis L. Carlson, ruled the company with a firm grip for six decades, and, to his credit, built a powerhouse. Founding the business in 1938 to sell trading stamps, he turned it into one of America's largest private conglomerates, which includes travel agencies, marketing services, hotels, and restaurants. Systemwide revenues in 1997 from branded operations both owned and franchised reached $20 billion. Carlson's operating revenues from companies it owns were $6.6 billion during that year.

BUILDING PARTNERSHIPS

But Nelson, who took over in 1998, is focusing with new paradigm flair on forming alliances and partnerships to help speed growth at her Minneapolis-based company, whose businesses include Radisson Hotels, TGI Friday's, Radisson Seven Seas Cruises, and Carlson Wagonlit Travel agencies. Her strategy appears to be working. She has already increased the company's worldwide travel agency business by 200 percent.

A French speaker, Nelson has skillfully broadened operations in Europe. And she's building luxury cruise liners and expanding the company's hotel franchises, including its Radisson chain. Apart from travel, she is also extending her $1 billion business that counsels companies like General Electric and Merrill Lynch on employee incentives. She plans to double Carlson's operating revenues to $14 billion in the next five years and achieve 20 percent annual growth. One of *Business Week*'s Top 25 Executives of 1998, she is on target to reach her goal. In 1998, the company grew to $7.8 billion in operating revenues, an increase of 20 percent. A year later, *Forbes* ranked the company ninety-first on its list of the world's top 500 private companies, and estimated her personal fortune at $1 billion.

Like Pat Russo and Orit Gadiesh, Nelson is partnering not just with other companies but with colleagues. Since she rose to direct corporate expansion in 1996, she has built a remarkably devoted employee base through her progressive policies. A charismatic and powerful speaker, she added an on-site day care facility, profit sharing, and expanded benefits—often over her father's protests. At the same time, she lured important managers to join the company from outside the business. Confident and motivated, she downplays her own ego while surrounding herself with strong executives on her management team. Under her tenure, the number of women in Carlson's executive ranks rose from 8 to 23 percent, and the number of female vice presidents increased from fifteen to forty-two. By 2001, she plans to invest more than $1 billion in technology as part of a strategy to provide greater efficiencies for the conglomerate, integrate the company's separate operating groups, and offer improved training opportunities for employees. She has even hosted Christmas parties for employees of the technology department of the company at her home. These programs are all part of the soft touch she employs to glean better results from employees by engaging and motivating them in ways that their salaries alone cannot.

FOCUSED ON CUSTOMER SERVICE

Like Darla Moore and Rebecca Mark, Nelson also collaborates with corporate clients and individual customers to provide better service. One longtime client, Merrill Lynch, began by using Carlson to plan incentive travel awards for leading clients and top-performing staff members. After the initial contract, Nelson's firm provided the hotels and cruise ships through which those awards would be redeemed. Recently, Carlson began consulting with Merrill Lynch on ways to lay out a new cruise ship her company is building to suit the Wall Street firm's needs and specifications. She is even tweaking Carlson's technology, so that client preferences, even their allergies to down pillows, can be registered throughout the system.

"We want high touch and high tech," says Nelson. "In a service company, you have to have both. The key to the twenty-first century for me is the need to work together and optimize opportunities together. The challenges are so great that mutual respect is the key. In my experience, women have this peripheral vision, and a systemic approach. Clearly relationships are an early part of a woman's being. We've been socialized to be the keepers of the flame. Our heightened sense of responsibility for relationships extends to whatever business we are in. It makes women very valuable when you're looking to build relationships with customers, build relationships internally, and build teams. The more wired the world becomes, the more relationships matter and the more being a woman becomes an advantage. Women recognize that by sharing recognition, you increase your power and your effectiveness."

EARNING THE TITLE

There was a time when being female was a distinct liability for Nelson. Her father was dissatisfied that he lacked a male heir to take over his company upon his retirement, and he made no efforts to hide it. In fact, he was legendary for berating his daughter publicly, once reportedly calling her a "goddamn fool" in the presence of senior managers at the business.[9] She was not his first choice as a successor. Instead, he opted for his son-in-law, Edwin (Skip) Gage, who is married to Nelson's younger sister, Barbara. Gage was named chief executive of Carlson Companies in late 1989 when Curt Carlson was considering retirement, but Gage left the company by the end of 1991 to start his own business. He took a $600 million piece of Carlson Marketing Group's business with him, and launched the Gage Marketing Group. As a Carlson spokesman put it, "To the credit of both of them, they realized there could only be one CEO—and it needed to be Curt."

In search of a successor once again, Curt Carlson hired Jack Murrin, a former partner with management consultants McKinsey & Company, to be his second in command in 1992. Murrin departed a year later, reportedly because of Carlson's meddling in his affairs.[10] Then Curt Carlson set his sights on Juergen Bartels, who was leading Carlson's hospitality group, including the Radisson hotel chain and TGI Friday's restaurants. But in 1994, Bartels quit to run Westin Hotels amid another flurry of press reports about the patriarch's proclivity for micromanaging.[11]

After Bartels moved on, Marilyn Carlson Nelson proved to be better suited to working with her father, overcame skepticism, and emerged as the heir apparent. She showed courage under fire by ending instability at the company and surrounding herself with a strong management team. In 1997, Curt put her in charge of the daily workings of the company as chief operating officer. One year later, she became chief executive officer.

As she rose to the top, she continued to lead in a collegial way despite opposition to her high-touch approach. Her father fought with her against adding perks for employees, such as a bonus plan and a $2.5 million day care center, and bringing in board members from outside the family. But Nelson stood her ground. "Curt was always competitive with his own executive team just as you read about in certain animal cultures where the leader is competitive with those around him to maintain his leadership," she says. "I take a different view. I'm far more outgoing and intimate with people. I focus on jumping into other people's shoes, and identifying who they are and what they care about. Once I understand that, I can engage them in a job. Rather than just paying them for their time, I really engage their heart and soul in something that we could do together, but could not accomplish alone."

PUSHING BACK BOUNDARIES

After withstanding nearly ten years of tumult at the company, Marilyn Carlson Nelson is taking risks to lead her business into the future. Her deep brown eyes gleam at the prospect, and her energy for the cause seems limitless. She starts her average day at 6 A.M. and often does not quit until 10 at night. With her chin-length chestnut brown hair and broad smile, her grandmotherly looks belie her hunger for risk. A trim figure with a broad smile, she is known for breezing into annual employee meetings on in-line skates. She skis the expert black-diamond slopes. And to celebrate taking over as chief executive officer in 1998, she flew nine Gs, the limit of human stamina at nine times the force of gravity, in an F16 jet with the Air Force Thunderbirds. "I've just begun," she says enthusiastically. "I like to push back boundaries."

Her office, awash in pink with blond wood furniture on the fifteenth floor of the gleaming glass twin tower company headquarters in Minnetonka, Minnesota, contrasts starkly with the serious gray leather and dark mahogany woods filling her father's former office across the hall. He died at age eighty-four in 1999. Rather than move into his imposing chairman's suite, she opted, like Martha Ingram, Loida Lewis, and Shelly Lazarus, to remain in her cheerful corner room, where a pair of canaries named Cordon and Bleu perch in a cage by the window. Looking out, she takes in a view of carefully manicured lawns surrounding the company's corporate office park located on the outskirts of Minneapolis.

Her primary goal is to keep family members allied behind her—a tough challenge for any leader of a family business who is not the founder of the firm. When Curt Carlson died, he left each of his surviving family members an equal stake in the company. Her strategy for keeping the family united: surpassing her father's 15 percent annual growth rate and doubling operating revenues over the next five years. To reach these goals, she intends to increase travel-service operations in Europe and Latin America and sell Carlson's services to businesses around the globe.

She is busy priming her son, Curtis, to succeed her, while also assuring nonfamily executives that there is room for them to rise in the company. Her collaborative approach with colleagues is key in helping her achieve these objectives. Not only does she involve associates in decision making, but she has already expanded benefits and profit-sharing schemes, including creating "phantom stock," a system of bonuses for employees linked to revenue growth. Her flex-time program is another perk designed to please personnel. "I want to lead with love, not fear," she told *BusinessWeek* in 1998.

A WILL TO WIN

Although heading the family business was not Nelson's initial goal in life, that became her main aspiration as she matured. To date, she has spent the last thirty years at the company. Like other new paradigm leaders, her success in her field is striking—only 11 percent of top corporate officers in the travel industry are women, according to Catalyst.

Like Martha Ingram, Marilyn Nelson got her start in business by working in the nonprofit sector. In 1980, the governor of Minnesota gave her a daunting challenge—to bring the Super Bowl to her hometown of Minneapolis despite its frosty January weather and subzero temperatures. She handled the task in her typical fashion—she worked to build the right relationships with the twenty-eight National Football League owners. All told, it took her nine years to get the job done. The night before the final selection in 1989, she delivered little yellow duck bathtub toys to the rooms of each of these owners. She attached a personal note to each duck that said, "For a great game and wild life, play indoors in Minnesota." The owners finally caved in to her persistence and persuasion. Her laser focus on achieving never waned. "I just don't like to lose things once I start them," she says. "I stick at them a long time. It was nine years before we convinced them to bring the Super Bowl here. 'No,' for me, is just a deferred 'yes.'"

When she was fresh from her own Super Bowl victory, her father urged her to expand her role at the family business beyond her position as director of community relations. Nelson entered the fold as a senior vice president, and asked to chair the vital audit committee. Her father gave her the position. "If I was going to be in the company, I needed a role where I was allowed to make an impact," she said.

Like Ellen Gordon, Nelson soon concluded that Carlson needed a system of financial controls. Her high-touch sensibilities were an asset in helping her lure top talent from Sara Lee, Walt Disney, and Starwood Lodging to help her grow the business. In 1993, she hired Martyn Redgrave from PepsiCo, Inc., to become chief financial officer of Carlson. She asked him to develop a more advanced company-wide accounting system like those public corporations use.

"PepsiCo is one of the greatest marketers in the world, but I would put her up against any of the best at PepsiCo, and she would beat them all hands down," explains Redgrave about why he switched to work for Nelson after fourteen years at the soft drink and restaurant giant. "She has a unique combination of a sharp intellect, a global view, and a natural enthusiasm and warmth that she delivers to every forum. She is genuinely concerned about people in comparison to her father's legendary interpersonal style. Her style was certainly a factor in bringing me here. Her unique characteristic of conveying a caring for people is important to enabling people to do their best work. That's attractive to any senior team member or employee."

ADOPTING NEW STRATEGIES

Nelson vowed to give the company a more global and collaborative focus. In the past, as Curt Carlson developed the company into a vast empire, there was little pressure on its various divisions to communicate with one another. A sign of the disarray, the company until recently had twenty-four different e-mail systems, and executives at the firm's diverse units did not even know which customers they shared.

Nelson moved to adopt a new policy of integrating the notoriously divided company she runs in the hope of better servicing clients. She believes that as clients consolidate their businesses and become more global, the opportunities for cross selling—the practice of peddling a variety of company services to a single client—will expand dramatically. She hired an executive to oversee collaboration among the various segments of the business. The plan was to set up councils bringing together personnel from different departments, such as marketing and hospitality, to discuss client needs and develop new proposals to win more business for Carlson. Like Lazarus, she believes decisions made jointly by groups save time because employees are more invested in implementing these choices than in those foisted on them.

Nelson's strategy seems to be working. General Electric and Merrill Lynch already purchase global travel arrangements and marketing/hotel services from her company. Even the government of Aruba uses a variety of Carlson's products. For its 500th birthday as a nation in 1999, the Caribbean island hired Carlson to plan a celebration through its marketing arm, make arrangements for visitors through its travel agents, provide transportation via its five-star luxury cruise ships, and host guests at its Radisson hotel.

"My father's style was command and control. All the information came to him," recalls Nelson. "He processed it, then pretty much unilaterally made decisions. He wanted sole control of all our investments. He ran it like a holding company with each unit reporting to him separately."

"I run things differently and have changed the culture at Carlson. You can't move fast if everything funnels into one individual. At the top, we are a team. I am collaborative and have good partnering skills. That fits with an increasingly powerful trend for our global multinational clients to narrow the number of suppliers they use and to integrate their travel services. They want to access our expertise as if it was an arm of their own business."

"When [my father] ran the company, he worshiped financial capital. But now that we are in a knowledge economy, I worship human capital. My combination of learning to partner with and motivate people, my international exposure, and my sense of the value of human resources are all things at this particular moment that are helping me make good decisions on behalf of the company, in large part because we are spending a lot of money to attract and maintain people."

FUELING GROWTH

Nelson's high-touch way is helping to power the Carlson Companies' growth. She is partnering both within the company and outside it to expand and reduce risk. In 1997, she persuaded France's Accor to merge its Wagonlit corporate travel business with her own. Through the joint venture, she created Carlson Wagonlit Travel, a $9.5 billion global corporate travel management company with 3,000 locations in 141 countries. The move allowed Nelson to quickly pick up major clients with high levels of international travel. Partnering enables Carlson to achieve international scope faster, add expertise that it might have taken years to achieve, and obtain the financial support to be aggressive in markets that are rapidly consolidating. "My dad opposed it, but I convinced him of the strategic value of the deal," she says. "We've enjoyed twenty-three percent sales growth since then and added premier customers."

In 1998, Nelson's leisure group unit acquired Travel Agents International, a transaction that made Carlson the largest franchiser of leisure travel agencies in the country, with 1,300 locations. She also launched a strong Internet presence with a consumer Web site called enQuest, which features on-line bookings routed through Carlson agencies. Investing in technology to spur Internet bookings cuts costs for Carlson—hotel reservations made electronically are four times cheaper than those handled by a phone agent, according to travel industry trade magazines.

HIGH TECH AND HIGH TOUCH

Many argue that the private nature of the company hampers Nelson's ability to attract talent to the firm during an economy close to full employment, and that she may need to spin off assets of the business in the near future. While not ruling out an IPO for parts of the company, she counters that she has achieved high retention figures through her high-touch sensibilities—maintaining competitive bonus programs and salaries, and adding perks. She spends $400,000 a year to operate the on-site day care center she built at Carlson. She invested $1 million in a four-week training program for Carlson executives, and has sent more than 1,000 employees to seminars on Stephen Covey's "Seven Habits of Highly Effective People."

In the past, top executives could earn up to 50 percent of their annual compensation through an incentive plan. Nelson has raised that figure to 100 percent. Among some of her other goodwill programs, she has increased the number of people in executive posts to twenty-five from four. She has also expanded the bonus plan she devised beyond the top levels of the organization to include all of Carlson's 400 technology workers. A gym, coffeehouse, relaxed dress code, and flexible hours all came into being during her tenure. She invented a program she calls Club Carlson to give employees discounts on all products the firm offers around the globe, from a European cruise to their own telephone service.

As Nelson sees it, high touch can go a long way in a high-tech world. "Instead of expecting our employees to fit some mold, they tell us what they need to be productive and it's paying off," she says. "In the past, the chief of technology reported two or three levels down at the company, but now he reports directly to me. I made that change because technology is key to our future. I did the same for heads of the human resources and communications department. In technology, we have a turnover rate of 12 percent, which is extremely low right now. And we have a turnover rate at TGI Friday's of something around 77 percent, which is low for the retail industry as well. Our phantom stock is linked to company progress rather than the stock market so our options never go underwater as they do in a public company. I take our employees seriously as experts, and help them to hone their expertise and build equity. I always ask everyone what we can do to provide a more stimulating and rewarding environment."

Communicating openly and constantly is a hallmark of Nelson's leadership style, and that of other new paradigm executives. One of her first steps as chief executive officer was to set up an international satellite feed so that she could address staff members all over the globe. Historically, the company released news, such as information about an acquisition, to the public before announcing it internally. She reversed that process and simplified e-mail at the company while adding a video conferencing studio to help her speak with her international partners and employees. "I use communication tools my father never dreamed of using," she says. "He didn't even like to use voice mail."

A DRIVE TO COMPETE

Having grown up in a traditional home in South Minneapolis, Nelson was not always a technophile. Her father was a Swedish immigrant, and her mother's family came from Germany and England. Outgoing and bright, Nelson was the elder of two daughters. Both parents encouraged their daughters to work hard, and expected the girls to bring home top grades. Nelson studied hard. In a sign that she enjoyed academics, she and her best friend in fourth grade would often sit in her bedroom closet reading Shakespeare to each other by candlelight. One of her first memories of her father was his teaching her iambic pentameter.

Because her father started the family business a year before she was born, growing up with Carlson Companies was like having another virtual sibling. Many family conversations around the table inevitably centered on the business. "When we would go out to dinner, my father would always say if we didn't order dessert, we could reinvest that money into the company and over time it would compound and become more valuable," Nelson recalls. "So we gave up dessert."

While her father taught her about economics, he also encouraged her to develop a taste for competition. Because she did not have the option to take athletics in school as a girl, he set up a competitive environment at home. He would race his daughter at shoveling snow off the driveway. There was a Carlson family Olympics with competitions ranging from the three-legged race to poetry writing. "He would never let me win when he and I raced, but expected me and my sister to perform better than the other kids in our family at the Olympics."

Nelson's mother, Arleen, encouraged her daughter to be sensitive to issues of inequality and to help those in need. Nelson volunteered at a local nursing home, and performed plays there. "I always went out of my way to talk to and bring home the person in my class who seemed left out, less capable, or that others somehow were being hard on," she says. "My mother taught me to try to build bridges between people."

Both parents wanted their daughter to stand out in a crowd. She became the editor of the newspaper at Edina High School, and held a seat on the student council. She was also captain of the cheerleading squad. "They would always encourage me to lead, whether it was a Girl Scout project or a theater production at school," she says. "They supported that by taking me seriously as a leader."

Thanks to her strong record, Nelson got into Smith College in 1957. Upon her father's urging, she pursued a degree in economics. During her junior year, she studied in Paris at the Sorbonne and in Geneva at the Institute des Hautes Études Économiques Politiques. In 1961, she graduated with honors from Smith with a degree in international economics and a minor in theater. She landed her first job out of college as a securities analyst at PaineWebber, Inc., in

Minneapolis. At work, she was told to use her initials to hide the fact that she was a woman.

Like Martha Ingram, Nelson let her family life take her off the career track for a while. After marrying Glen D. Nelson, a surgeon and currently the vice chairman of medical products company Medtronic, Inc., she had four children. While they were young, she took up fund-raising for the Minneapolis Symphony and the local public television station. She served as president of the United Way as well. And, like Ingram, who also worked in the nonprofit sector, Nelson picked up skills that would help her motivate employees in the private sector at Carlson Companies.

"Because I could not hire or fire or even pay people, my power came from personal resources and the ability to engage, involve, and motivate large groups of people through communicating a vision and collaborating," she says. "I understand that engaging them in a job is more important than paying them for an hour of their time. It's really engaging their heart and soul through establishing a big stretch goal, then relaying my confidence that they can do it. It's an unwavering sense of support that leads me to invest in their training, and of respect that people really do rise to the occasion when they set their hearts and minds to it."

That spirit has buoyed Nelson in her work at Carlson Companies. She is concentrating on fostering the company's evolution from a first-generation entrepreneurial organization into a corporation that will continue to grow in the next millennium. She expects to lead Carlson for the next ten years before retiring and handing over the reins to her son, Curtis, who currently runs Carlson Hospitality Worldwide. She expects a smooth transition: "We struggled to get along early on, but have really come to an understanding," explains Curtis Nelson about working for his mother.

The new paradigm features that have solidified Nelson's success are clearly being recognized as a foundation for keeping the company humming well into the future. Her collaborative leadership style, which honors input from clients and employees alike, gives executives an advantage because they are able to keep pace with ever-changing demands. "She has taught me how to sell ideas to an organization so that people are willing to stand behind them," says Curtis Nelson. "A single style is no longer appropriate, you have to have a style that is agile and adjusts to the times."

6

TURNING CHALLENGE
INTO OPPORTUNITY

I was asked to step into the president's job . . . I knew the buck would stop with me, and that this business was in deep trouble. But I was committed to a turnaround.

— PATRICIA RUSSO

While Patricia Russo, forty-six, gladly joined AT&T's Global Business Communications System (Global) unit in 1990, most executives would have run the other way. This $3.5 billion business, which supplies communications systems, including phone, voice mail, and voice messaging technology to companies like American Express, General Motors, and the *New York Times*, was hemorrhaging nearly $200 million a year. The unit employed a staff of 26,000 people in 450 locations around the world. At the time, Russo was entrenched in the sales department at the profitable network services division of AT&T, but when the chance to join the struggling Global business unit came her way, she jumped at the opportunity. She wanted the new job, vice president of sales and service, because it was a promotion, and she wanted a crack at improving a troubled business. She quickly climbed its sales ranks and won the top job in 1993.

As president of the unit, Russo faced some daunting tasks. Apart from stemming huge losses, she had to bolster customer service, shore up the morale of a demoralized staff that had suffered through numerous chiefs and rounds of layoffs, and overcome a bleak financial picture for an industry poised for more downsizing.

As the first woman to run an AT&T business unit, she tackled these problems valiantly and turned an area that the company was considering divesting into a thriving business. Russo jettisoned unrelated divisions such as financial trading support, concentrated the group's efforts on communications systems, and moved to bolster sales abroad. And she achieved a dramatic cultural change at her unit by placing a priority on staff and their empowerment as well as on pleasing customers. For instance, she began conducting employee evaluations of managers in the unit, and based executive compensation in part on results from such surveys. She focused on transforming the mentality at Global from a heavily bureaucratized unit into a nimble technology business of knowledge workers and "shareowners." She followed her instinct: If employees were satisfied, customers would be, too. And she was right. By 1995, with over $4.3 billion in revenues and $300 million in earnings, she made Global the most profitable division in Lucent Technologies, AT&T's soon-to-be-spun-off $20 billion (1995 sales) systems and technology group. Before being promoted in 1997, she built the Global unit into the telecommunications giant's second-largest business with more than $5 billion in revenues (1996 sales) and 20 percent sales growth a year.

"I was asked to step into the president's job," says Russo. "It was a huge step. I knew the buck would stop with me, and that this business was in deep trouble. But I was committed to a turnaround. People believed that I knew what had to be done, and asked me to take on the challenge."

TURNAROUND QUEENS

Russo further enhanced her reputation while serving as executive vice president of strategy, business development, and corporate operations for Lucent from 1997 through late 1999. *Fortune* magazine labeled her one of the most powerful women in American business in 1998 and in 1999, and awarded her the title of "proven turnaround champ."[1] In what some would consider a counterintuitive move, she bolstered Lucent's top position in communications networking by leading the company on a buying spree. She has overseen twenty-seven of Lucent's thirty-one acquisitions, worth close to $41 billion.

As a result, her success has driven her farther up the company's corporate ladder. In October 1999, she became chief executive officer of the highly lucrative core business of the largest telecom equipment company in the world with 1999 revenues of $24 billion—65 percent of Lucent's annual revenue. She will run the company's service provider networks unit—the job formerly held by Carleton Fiorina, now chief of Hewlett-Packard. But Russo's current job has a much wider scope than Fiorina's did—encompassing the corporation's major technology groups, including wireless systems, optical networking, switching, and access systems.

All new paradigm leaders share Russo's abilities to lead and succeed throughout periods of profound and rapid change. Rather than seeking modest challenges and attainable goals, these women shoot for the top, becoming "transforming" leaders who are, in essence, turnaround queens. They not only embrace change, but foster it in their roles. Orit Gadiesh saved Bain & Company from bankruptcy by reinventing the business and by adopting new core values for the company that inspired her employees to excel. Ann Winblad foresaw the growth of software start-ups when the area was still overlooked by many in the industry. With her vision, she helped make software a robust driver of the economy. Loida Lewis revamped TLC Beatrice from a sputtering far-flung empire to a healthy business. Rebecca Mark helped drive growth at Enron by developing its international arm and turning it from a business fraught with risk to one awash in rewards. Another new paradigm leader, also featured in this chapter because of her ability to turn around a business by initiating radical change, is Ellen Gordon, who leads Tootsie Roll Industries. Her financial skills helped transform a company badly in need of modernization into a highly profitable business that has been a winner on Wall Street ever since she became the company's president nearly twenty years ago.

CHANGE MAKERS

New paradigm leaders, like Russo, Gordon, and Carsey, are not hampered by the need to enforce age-old hierarchies because of their more collaborative approach to doing business. And they tend to strike a closer relationship with employees because of their willingness to communicate openly with staff and draw information from them. They embody what Pulitzer Prize–winning historian James MacGregor Burns calls "transformational leadership." In his studies of political leadership, he described two types of leaders. The first are "transactional" leaders, who generally adopt modest goals and manage the challenges they are given. Such leaders obtain cooperation through deals—jobs for votes, bonuses for meeting sales targets—and maintain the status quo at their companies. The second are "transforming" leaders, who have far-reaching plans that fundamentally change the organizations they run. A transforming leader "looks for potential motives in followers, seeks to satisfy higher needs, and engages the full person of the follower."

What does that mean? In his powerful book, *The Leadership Engine*, Noel Tichy explains that a transformational leader's job in business is to "energize" others: "[L]eaders are energized not just by the goals of the team or the organization, but by transforming and coaching individuals to be leaders themselves."[2] Tichy identifies Jack Welch of industrial conglomerate General Electric Company as a transformational leader. Shelly Lazarus of Ogilvy & Mather Worldwide with her collaborative approach, and Meg Whitman, for

her pioneering role in the development of a new kind of business—
the on-line actioneer, could also be included. The particular objectives executives set vary based on company needs, but to dramatically
improve results at a business, new paradigm leaders cannot focus on
incremental change. They remake corporate cultures and seek innovation to unlock employee potential. In that way, such leaders can
radically alter and revitalize companies.

These skills are needed in businesses across the country. In all
industries, companies have determined that the competitive nature of
the new economy—the necessity for speed and global growth, the
struggle to respond to the increasing demands of customers, and the
need to capitalize on information technology—are too important and
too pressing to be addressed by anything less than change on a grand
scale. New paradigm leaders provide an example of just that. Many
reengineer or alter power structures in their organizations from traditional hierarchies to teams. To bring about such profound and rapid
changes, these leaders realize they need to enlist cooperation from
associates.

The ability to transform organizations and turn them around by
inspiring employees is not only essential to leadership but vital to a
company's health. When these qualities are lacking, a chief executive's
job is in jeopardy. Joseph Antonini learned these lessons the hard way
when he was chief executive officer and president of Kmart
Corporation from 1987 until 1995. Antonini was known for his
inability to tolerate bad news and his failure to recognize merchandising, customer service, and cost control problems.[3] Under his leadership, Kmart suffered a dramatic loss of market share, declining profits
for more than two years, rounds of layoffs, and more than seventy-
two store closings.[4] These setbacks cost Antonini his job.

Arnold Langbo served as chief executive of Kellogg Company from
1992 to 1999, but quit after failing to turn around the world's largest
cereal maker.[5] Langbo was nicknamed the "cereal killer" because
Kellogg's market share in North America fell to 32 percent in 1998

from 38 percent in 1991. He was criticized for focusing on trimming expenses rather than growing the business through advertising, developing new products, and promotions. The company suffered layoffs and falling earnings as a result.

RISING TO THE TOP

Russo has been energizing employees since she began her rise in telecommunications, a field where few women have reached top levels. Among Fortune 500 electronics firms, a category that includes Lucent Technologies, women represented just 6 percent of top corporate officers in 1999, a figure that has barely budged since 1996, according to Catalyst, a nonprofit research organization. That figure is less than half the average for Fortune 500 companies, where women comprise 12 percent of leading corporate officers. At Lucent Technologies, Russo is one of two women among nineteen senior corporate officers, an above average, but hardly stellar, statistic. Few women rise to the top because they lack the credentials: an MBA or a degree in engineering. Instead, many were steered toward stereotypical female positions, including human resources and staff positions.

Russo caught on to this pattern, and actively sought jobs where she would have profit-and-loss responsibilities to boost her chances of rising. "I wanted jobs where results were measurable, where I could demonstrate that I could produce just like anybody else, female or male. So, I've spent 90 percent of my career in line-operating jobs. As a woman, I felt disadvantaged for quite some time early in my career that I had to prove I could do it," she says. "There was always this sense that you're in a typically male role and you're going to have to prove that you can do the job effectively."

Despite her corporate deep red tailored blazer and black slacks, Russo has the look of an athlete with a trim build and long limbs. Five-foot-nine and an avid golfer, she obviously likes to win, and usually breaks ninety on the links. Quick with the sports metaphors, she likens confidence in athletics with confidence in business. Both, she says with a knowing smile, come from "demonstrating ability." Her brown hair falls just above her shoulders, curling under at the ends, and her bangs sweep across her forehead. When she speaks, Russo occasionally pounds her hand on the desk to punctuate a point she is making. She wears a large diamond engagement ring, and a gold necklace and earrings sprinkled with diamonds. Her office is spacious but nondescript, with beige furniture and a spare maple desk. She has placed few personal touches in the room except for a photograph of her husband, Frank, who is a director at AT&T, on top of her desk. Married for sixteen years with two stepsons, she has remained focused on her career.

Although they are plain, her digs stand out from those of most of her neighbors at Lucent's Murray Hill, New Jersey, headquarters. The rest of the sprawling complex is full of tiny offices that resemble minia-ture high school chemistry classrooms from the 1950s, with their pale blue tile walls outlined in white, small scale, and government-issue quality furniture. One feels the need for a bathroom pass, or expects to open one of the doors and see Jerry Lewis concocting a formula to turn from Dr. Jekyll to Mr. Hyde as he did in *The Nutty Professor*. But Russo is not about to whip out a Bunsen burner. Like Meg Whitman, she has risen to the top of a cutting-edge scientific company without an engi-neering background. Instead, she offers lessons learned from an advanced management program at Harvard, professional pedigree, and considerable business acumen.

Russo joined AT&T in 1981 after being recruited. The stint at Harvard came in 1989, when she decided to beef up her academic credentials to improve her chances of advancing in the company. "I remember attending the program, and out of 160 people from the United States, I was the only woman," she said. "I have always believed that the way to deal with being a woman in business is to perform and not talk about it. I've never made a stink about women's issues. It does not mean I have not addressed them. My approach is subtle. My focus is to do the best job I can."

With her top-notch education and unshakable will, Russo rose at the telecommunications behemoth through her courage under fire. She shifted to the Global unit in 1990, and made a big splash in 1993 when she was promoted to run it. "I had a lot of people asking me about my sanity when I took it over," she said. "But sometimes your greatest opportunities are the challenges nobody else wants."

GIVE THE PEOPLE WHAT THEY WANT

Assuming control of the Global unit at AT&T presented stiff challenges for Russo. Engineering a financial turnaround at the business meant nothing less than changing the rigid company culture. For decades, this business that is now part of Lucent Technologies had been the stodgy producer of phone equipment for AT&T's customers. A history of providing the country's phone monopoly made Global a lumbering giant vulnerable to competitors like Northern Telecom Ltd. and Siemens Rolm. AT&T's engineers were known for championing surefire reliability rather than rapid innovation. Even current employees admit that Bell Labs, the research and development arm of AT&T and now part of Lucent, earned a reputation as an ivory tower of scientists who often took years to develop products and were apt to work on what they—and not their customers—wanted.

"What we were trying to do was to move from a culture that was driven by internal requirements, hierarchical in its thinking and bureaucratic in its approach, simply because the company had been a monopoly that, by definition, had no competition," explains Russo. "It wasn't that any organization has people who intend to be that way, but they are a product of the way they need to work, and the drivers of how they work. We needed to create a culture that could win in a deregulated, increasingly competitive industry. So we wanted to get people externally focused on competitors and on customers. We needed to put a premium on speed, and leveraging the talents of every single person in the business. This organization was full of people who felt pretty beaten down, and they needed a big dose of self-esteem."

And AT&T's Global unit was in turmoil. Trade publications forecast the demise of the business and predicted that many, including AT&T, would abandon the enterprise that was hitting the company with centimillion-dollar losses.[6] A trend of steep discounting gripped the industry since the mid-1980s and led to a price war among producers that made eking out a profit virtually impossible. Shipments of the voice mail systems declined an estimated 7 percent in 1991. Repeated employee cutbacks plagued AT&T and other major suppliers in their efforts to reduce operating losses estimated at over $250 million in 1991. In 1992, sales were flat and industry operating losses totaled an estimated $125 million.[7]

When Patricia Russo took over the operation for AT&T in 1993, she was determined to make big changes at Global—an intimidating task for someone promoted from within the organization. Her predecessor, Jerre Stead, had come from outside AT&T with much fanfare as a turn-around specialist, but he failed to make the unit profitable, and the business was losing market share to Northern Telecom during his tenure.[8]

Instead of poring over papers on her desk, Russo spent her first few months out "among the people." She met with over 5,000 associates. She wanted to focus on employees because she knew the business was deeply flawed and in need of dramatic changes to return to profitability. She would have to elicit the cooperation of all personnel to bring about that radical transformation. "Turning around a $5 billion business with 27,000 people is more than a one-person job," she says. "I was the leader of a team of people I had to motivate for us to succeed."

Rather than simply telling workers what she wanted them to do, she listened to their concerns. She recognized right away that employees were deflated by repeated layoffs at the company, and feared pink slips were around the corner because the business was still unprofitable.

"Back then, people didn't feel free to say what they thought because we came from a history of hierarchy, level consciousness, and communications that were not really open," said Russo. "People were treated differently based upon their level in the business hierarchy. And I wanted to get rid of all that. I wanted an environment where people are engaged, where people feel empowered, where we push decision making as close to the customer as possible, where we have open communication. That way, if you disagree with something that's going on you feel like you can say, 'I think that's wrong' without any fear of retribution. I wanted an atmosphere that's externally focused, not internally focused. One that focuses on customers and competitors, where people don't spend their time talking at the watercooler about what happened to them that day, but rather, 'Gosh, did you hear that Cisco did this?'"

Employees quickly noted Russo's refreshing emphasis on *people*. She brought in a new management team to help her execute these changes. With the exception of some downsizing in late 1993, company tallies of employee satisfaction more than doubled from 30 percent to over 70 percent after she became president of the unit. "Before she came along, there were two classes of people—management and nonmanagement at a company that was very elitist with huge offices and limousines for officers," said Fred Lane, then vice president of human resources at the Global unit. "So the common folk–type leader was almost unheard of. But she opened compensation plans and bonus plans that had only been available to the top five percent of management and tied them to performance so that everyone from the stockroom to the president was treated the same. She felt it was critical to send a strong signal that showed we believed in our people, and that we believed in this business."

PAINTING A PICTURE

Russo described her role at the time as "painting a picture" for both managers and employees. She clarified objectives and clearly linked them to key results of customer or shareholder satisfaction and prof-itable growth. For the first time, she gave people even at the lowest levels access to financial results, and held open meetings so that each month a couple hundred people would have contact with her and be able to ask questions. At staff meetings, she placed a graph on the board that showed where the company was, and where she wanted to take it: "One goal was to achieve a financial turnaround which had to include happy customers. There's no long-term sustainability if your customers aren't buying and you aren't improving share. And I wanted to create an environment that had people enthused and was a very different place than it had been. My message was this is what I'm passionate about and committed to. And by the way, if you're not, that's okay, but you won't be successful here. So I created an idea of what the environment needed to be like in order to help people real-ize their full potential."

Changing behavior at an institution is a tall order. Russo set out to be a good example. She spent three days a week on the road talk-ing to customers and staff. She returned phone calls from people at all levels of the company within twenty-four hours. She also speci-fied objectives and evaluation procedures so that individuals would be held accountable. "I laid out goals, but tried not to be prescriptive about how to achieve them, because we were trying to create an environment where the people who really knew how to get things done were closer to the problem than I was," she says. "In that way you engage people to use their expertise, their skill, and their knowl-edge. I didn't want to say, 'Leave your brain at the door because I am a higher-level executive than you are.' When you create a sense of commitment—that you're in it with them and we're all working together toward a common goal—the loyalty that you can engender in people is incredible."

Russo met with her direct reports once each month to discuss results and problem areas, and she incorporated critical goals into how she measured and paid employees. For instance, she developed specific methods to track customer satisfaction and rewarded employees based on those data. After putting these systems in place, she communicated results to the ranks through quarterly broadcasts. She also met with 7,000 employees each year in groups ranging from twenty to 500 at a time. And she set up ways for employees to rate their managers and give them feedback. Any manager supervising three or more people has to undergo an evaluation every year by his or her employees, and must share the results with colleagues both up and down the pecking order.

"If you say cultural change is important, you have to model those changes," she said. "I didn't just call people back who were above a certain level at the company. Otherwise it's a joke. And you have to repeat the message. You have to constantly communicate results to people so they will know you are serious, and feel good about their progress. And unlike my predecessors, I shifted the focus from me to us. They all knew I was the one in charge, but my focus was on us."

Russo also spent much of her time with customers. The Global unit had 1.5 million customers that were primarily businesses. She hit the road, visiting many of these companies, including Home Depot, Citibank, Merrill Lynch, and Prudential Insurance. She traveled abroad to meet with customers and employees from China to Britain. Russo formed a users group of 2,000 members and led quarterly meetings with them, too. And she would call managers of the 450 offices around the globe and ask their thoughts on customers and competitors. "I had tentacles everywhere to stay in touch, and keep a pulse on what was really going on in the business," she said. "It gave people an opening to share issues and tell me about problems that I would otherwise not know about. The result is that employees and customers know you are really committed. In large organizations, people are willing to follow a compelling vision and support what you are trying to do if they believe you are in it with them. You have to work at the human level."

Within two years, Russo had reinvigorated the business. In 1995, it was earning hefty profits of $300 million. After years of losses, she managed to turn the Global unit around, shoring up its leadership position in market share by achieving 20 percent sales growth without steep layoffs. By 1996, she built the business to over $5 billion in revenues. At the same time, she increased prices over 8 percent, and helped reverse the industry trend of steep discounting. Her efforts ended the price war straining the business since the mid-1980s, and gave Global a stronger outlook for the future. "I was gratified when I ran [Global] because I felt the team I assembled, the choices we made, and the culture we tried to create made a difference, not just for the performance of the business but for the possibilities for the people in the business," she says. "Supporting and helping people so they can thrive while we achieve our goals is what drives me. To be an effective leader, you must answer these questions: Do you have a vision and can you articulate it in a way that has people in your organization, no matter what level, saying, 'Sign me up'?"

STRIKING A DELICATE BALANCE

With Russo's success at Global, she shot up the ranks at Lucent Technologies, the newly public communications equipment vendor with rapidly growing sales. In 1997, she was promoted to executive vice president of corporate strategy and operations. The skills she gained at Global helped her grow the business internationally and identify acquisition targets, such as cutting-edge technology firm Ascend Communications, Inc., and computer consulting player International Network Services, Inc., that are likely to boost sales.

Mirroring Meg Whitman's tenure at Procter & Gamble, Russo used the power of influence to excel at Lucent. "In my job I have to be collaborative because I have to get a lot done through influence rather than through direct mandate. You have to be able to persuade to get things done," said Russo. "Rather than try to tell people what to do, it's much more effective if you can get the key leaders of the organization to buy in because they are the ones who have to execute. So you have to be engaging and get input. You also have to be willing to change your mind and learn."

Russo worked to strike a balance between collaboration and decision making. She oversaw departments, such as corporate strategy, business development, human resources, public relations, and global procurement for the company. When making choices, she elicited not just facts, but opinions from those she supervised. All the while she was aware of the time factor—she gathered information, but was careful to make her choices quickly. "What's important is knowing my timing, so that I can invest enough time to get adequate input and have people feel like they've had a chance to weigh in, while still making a decision when I need to make it. My expectation is that when everybody has had a chance to weigh in, they are all signed up even if a decision doesn't go their way," she said. "People understand that the process is fair. I don't just sit up here with blinders on, but get different inputs so I can make an informed decision. Rather than relying on position power, I think about my opportunities to influence others in the organization."

One of her goals was to attract and keep good employees amid a war for talent. To that end, she broke with the past and helped develop a plan to offer equity and stock options to all Lucent employees. When Lucent was first spun off from AT&T, each employee was given an option on 100 shares of stock. Those options vested in October 1999, and were worth over $20,000 to each staffer. She has tied Lucent's 401(k) plan to match company performance so a dollar in the retirement program will earn more if the company achieves better results. She also invests in training sessions to teach staff members new technical and managerial skills for at least two weeks a year, depending on the employee's position. "We've increased our granting of stock options both in terms of number and in terms of people. We are creating a culture of ownership deeper into the organization," she says. "People want to feel valued and valuable. Being competitive is more than just paying people well, it's offering them the chance to feel like they are making a contribution."

A TEAM PLAYER

Russo knows something about being a team player. She grew up in a family of nine—large enough to fill a baseball field. Like Marcy Carsey and Ann Winblad, she knew that finances were tight, but never felt deprived of anything. Her father was a doctor, and her mother was a homemaker. The second of seven children born within six years of one another, she learned to be independent at an early age. She also learned to help others. She had twin brothers who were handicapped, one with cerebral palsy and the other with hearing problems and brain damage. "My twin brothers required a tremendous amount of attention, compassion, and support, not only from my parents but from all of us. So I grew up with an appreciation of the importance of keeping real inconveniences and tragedies in perspective," she said. "It helped me in looking at problems later."

Jockeying for position in a large family also kept Russo on her toes. With so many children at home, her parents put her in school a year early so she was always the youngest in her class. When she was eleven, she wanted to go to a school dance, but her father nixed the idea, saying she was too young. She argued with him, eventually convincing her father she should attend because she deserved the same opportunities as her peers. "In a large family, you have to be able to sell your ideas," she said. "I learned early about the power of negotiation and persuasion. I had to be aggressive to thrive in an environment of many children close in age, and to carve out a little attention from my parents, but not in a negative way. We couldn't be in constant conflict because we all had to collaborate as well. After all, we had to live together."

As a girl growing up in suburban West Trenton, New Jersey, Russo put her aggressive nature to good use in sports. Her parents valued education but encouraged their children to be well rounded, and "not nerdy," adds Russo. Soccer, tennis, golf, and skiing—she loved them all. "My parents never tried to compartmentalize us, so my mother never said, 'You really should be playing with dolls instead of kicking a soccer ball with the boys in the neighborhood,'" she recalls. "It was important for me because sports was one of the things that helped me gain confidence, and it was a metaphor for business. Athletic confidence comes from doing something well, and so does confidence in business. I always felt I could play, whether it was raking leaves in the yard or kicking a soccer ball. I knew I could compete in anything that was classified as what little boys did, instead of what little girls did. And my parents encouraged me to take my licks, get up, and go do it again."

Russo worked hard in school and excelled. In 1973, when she was just twenty years old, she earned her undergraduate degree in political science from Georgetown University. Her first job out of college was selling mainframe computers for IBM. Striking out in the computer business wasn't easy for a woman in those days, and several clients gave her the boot. "There were quite a few instances where men said, 'We don't want a woman on the account,'" Russo said. "They didn't even know me so it was not a matter of me personally. I can remember saying to myself: Why do these customers feel this way? I can do this job. So I moved on to other customers."

Although she had no role models working in business in her family, Russo believes her mother's optimistic attitude was a fundamental influence that helped her become successful. Neither of her parents steered her toward any particular career. They encouraged her to pursue her own interests rather than become a homemaker, nurse, or teacher—typical jobs for women of her generation. "Even though my mother underwent a lot of misfortune with my brothers, she always felt she was the luckiest woman in the world," Russo recalls. "That ability to be positive was really important at [Global] because the business was in such trouble. If I lost my confidence, then I would not perform as well, and that becomes a self-fulfilling prophecy. So a positive attitude is very important in preventing the negative spiral from occurring. You have to appear confident to pass that on to the people you are guiding."

PUTTING THE CUSTOMER FIRST

Aside from providing a positive work environment for employees, Russo has a good handle on perhaps the most important thing in today's economy—customer service. Instead of viewing herself near the top of a standard organizational hierarchy at Lucent, she places the customer atop her chart. In heading up her company's aggressive acquisition strategy against rivals like Cisco Systems, Inc., and Canada's Northern Telecom, her main objective is to improve service to customers. She draws on her experience of catering to a global network of customers when considering opportunities. "Power is with consumers. Customers make choices every day about who to partner with and how to spend their money," she says. "The companies that get that, that understand they need to be customer-centered, solutions-oriented, and knowledgeable about what their very formidable competitors are doing are the companies that are going to win."

In her new job as chief executive officer of the company's core business, she will work to retain the unit's preeminent position and rapid expansion. Lucent grew rapidly after it was spun off from AT&T in 1996. The company achieved revenues of $38 billion in 1999, and nearly quadrupled shareholders' money, compared with a 20 percent return for the S&P 500, according to Lucent. Since the company went public, its shares soared from 13 ½ to a high of 120 in January 1999. A two-for-one stock split followed in February. The stock became more volatile toward the end of 1999, and reached $68 in March 2000.

Russo is part of the team working to transform the business from a musty 123-year-old maker of phone equipment into a fast-track behemoth providing vital communications tools for the Internet age. Lucent scientists have won eleven Nobel prizes. "Our customers want solutions, not just products," she says. "So we focus on understanding what customers want, understanding where the market opportunity is, and massing our capabilities against that set of opportunities," she says. "At the same time, we've worked on creating a high-performance operating environment, a culture where people can take risks and make decisions, where they're empowered to do what's right for the customer and they're connected to the success of the business through our reward and compensation structures. We've done a lot of things to create a very different culture across Lucent than we previously had at AT&T."

Russo is one of the few senior executives to remain with the telecommunications giant after rising through its ranks, but her future remains to be seen. *BusinessWeek* labeled her a possible successor to Lucent's chairman and chief executive officer, Richard McGinn. At Lucent, she is still part of the extended AT&T family. AT&T, the biggest U.S. communications company, is famous for grooming many topflight executives but infamous for retaining few of them.[9] Many industry titans began at the company, then moved elsewhere, such as Carly Fiorina, chief executive officer of Hewlett-Packard Company; George Fisher, chairman of Eastman Kodak Company; and John Malone, former Tele-Communications, Inc. chairman. With the rapid growth of the communications industry, AT&T talent has embarked on the digital frontier to guide start-ups and established players alike. Perhaps Russo's new promotion will keep her happy. "Change creates opportunity and ought to be embraced," says Russo. "You just have to adapt and be willing to take risks, and change course when you've made a mistake. If things aren't changing, then you probably ought to ask 'What's wrong here?'"

ROLL MODEL

Like Russo, candy manufacturer Ellen Gordon is a skilled turnaround artist. While Abigail Johnson, daughter of Edward (Ned) Johnson III, may be inheriting a mint in Fidelity Investments, Gordon was heir to Tootsie Roll Industries, a mature company badly in need of modernization and fiscal discipline. When she became one of the first female presidents of a major public company in 1978, Gordon pulled down gender barriers, built a family fortune, and has been overseeing production of candy by the ton ever since. Her career illustrates the importance of financial savvy in executing a turnaround for a business.

Before she took a leading role in the corporation, the Chicago-based confectioner that makes Tootsie Rolls, lollipops, and other candies needed a boost—sales were flagging, and production systems were outmoded. "Tootsie Roll had lost its way before she came on board as president," says analyst David Leibowitz, managing director of Burnham Securities in New York. "Under her watch, the company has been on quite a tear, and the numbers have improved tremendously. Tootsie Roll has had a twenty-two-year string of record sales gains. The stock has been a magnificent performer. She has increased earnings and dividends every year since 1980."

Gordon has revitalized the classic mom-and-pop organization she runs with her husband, Melvin, who is chief executive officer, and made it more than just a piece of Americana—it's also a champion on Wall Street. *Forbes* labeled the highly profitable operation a "hot growth company" in 1998 and likened it to a Silicon Valley player.[10] Shares of this 103-year-old business increased nearly 70 percent in 1997 alone. Revenues hit a record $389 million and earnings reached $68 million in 1998. The near 50 percent stake the Gordons own in Tootsie Roll was reportedly worth $675 million.

The couple works as a team. Their offices at the Chicago plant face each other, and a conversation in one can be heard in the other. Each must convince the other of the benefits of a new acquisition before they undertake it. Though each inherited enough family money to live a life of ease, neither considered it. "We both came from families who had a very strong work ethic," says Ellen Gordon. "I was brought up very frugally."

Like Marcy Carsey, Gordon has adopted a strategy of staying small and independent that many would consider counterintuitive. This strategy is unique in the candy industry, where she faces immense rivals with billions in sales such as Hershey Foods Corporation and Mars, Inc. She had the foresight to increase her family's holdings of stock to nearly half the firm's shares in the 1970s. She also secured close to 75 percent of the company's voting stock for the Gordons. She anticipated that other candy manufacturers would be swallowed up by larger industry players like Nestle and Hershey, and protected her business from takeover. "Ellen was primarily interested in making sure nobody wrested control of Tootsie Roll from the family. This was years ago, way before takeovers became common," recalls her husband. "It was back when people with twenty, twenty-five percent of a company felt very secure. Ellen didn't."

A FOCUS ON INNOVATION

Gordon focused on bringing innovation and technology to the capital- and labor-intensive corporation. Among her important moves was to launch a $10 million modernization program in 1983, and to install a new computer system in 1988. Each year, she reinvests much of the company's profits in automation. Every day, the company makes and wraps 49.5 million Tootsie Rolls and 16 million lollipops—more lollipops than anyone else produces in the world. Thanks in large part to Gordon's efforts, the company's profit margins are as sweet as the candy it produces. The company has net profit margins of 17 percent, compared to chewing gum maker Wm. Wrigley Jr. at 15 percent and Hershey Foods at 12 percent.[11]

"The company has gotten much more sophisticated with greater financial discipline once I came on board," she recalls. "Our goals and how to get there have become much clearer now that I am here. We've gotten smarter and more sophisticated, and avoid the temptation for a quick buck. All these things weren't priorities until I got here. Today, being a leader is about being persistent and learning to adapt."

Like Pat Russo, Orit Gadiesh, and other new paradigm leaders, Ellen Gordon has bucked conventional wisdom throughout her career and used her business acumen and team approach to management to turn around the company she leads. At sixty-eight, she is one of a few women of her generation to preside over a thriving business. She credits the dynamics of thirty-year-olds working alongside others in their sixties as one reason for Tootsie Roll's success. She works like a thirty-year-old—usually putting in an eighty-hour week.

A PASSION FOR CANDY

On a tour of the plant, she looks like a grandmother in a candy store, except it's hers. Her blond hair is short and neatly coifed, and she wears a traditional navy suit with a cream silk cowl neck blouse. She wears no jewelry—it's not allowed in the factory for sanitary reasons. Her deep blue eyes have a warm glow, and Gordon smiles broadly as she puts on a shower cap, a requirement for entering her 2.2-million-square-foot Chicago plant that spans fifty football fields. Addressing them by first names, she greets each employee she passes, and knows every one of the 900 staffers at the Chicago plant. She also knows something about their families. She learns this information because she views the company as a large family. And Gordon likes to get close to the action. She watches closely as a gooey slab of the luscious cocoa confection travels along high-speed conveyer belts before being shaped and spliced into those familiar logs. She can't help dipping her fingers in for a taste. "There's nothing like a hot Tootsie Roll," she says with a laugh. She takes a sample of the Tootsie Roll Pops, Mason Dots, and Charms pops produced at the site as she travels around the vast and sweet-smelling factory.

Candy is this woman's life. Her windowless office at the facility resembles a convenience store with its brown linoleum tile floors, fluorescent lights, and shelves of sweets lining the wall. The colorful candy wrappers brighten an otherwise dark and dingy room. Black and white photographs of Tootsie Roll advertisements dating from the early twentieth century cover another wall. A shot of her with a big grin appears in one, dating from 1950, that graced the pages of *Life* magazine. She devotes one entire area to wartime Tootsie Roll pictures. Soldiers from conflicts including World War II, Korea, Vietnam, and Desert Storm are pictured gobbling up the chewy cocoa candies. Her traditional dark brown wooden desk is clear except for a Tootsie Roll bank she uses as a pen and pencil holder, her trusty Dell computer, and her small candy plate filled with a caramel apple lollipop, four Tootsie Rolls, two Tootsie Pops, and a box of Mason Dots. She proudly points out one of her newest lollipop varieties—Extreme Lemonade.

When Gordon launched her business career, she focused on the fun of the business and did not allow prevailing attitudes against women stop her. In the early 1970s, for instance, Gordon discovered the door to the executive suite literally bolted when she tried to go to a business meeting at a men's club in Virginia. Her male colleagues had to sneak her in the back door. "It was an important meeting, and in fact, I was leading it," she recalls. "When I began, there weren't many women heading companies. Women were just beginning to come into the executive suite. I used to get letters addressed to Mr. Ellen Gordon, or the salutation, 'Dear Mr. Gordon.' Of course, that has changed now."

COMING INTO HER OWN

Born in 1931, Ellen Gordon grew up in a privileged home as the private school–educated daughter of a successful manufacturer. Her family has controlled Tootsie Roll for over sixty-five years. In the nineteenth century, her grandfather manufactured paper. He sold his product to customers like Macy's and Tootsie Roll, who used it for packaging. He noticed that the management at the confectioner was weak, and the firm always had difficulty paying its bills on time. Meanwhile, her mother became the first Tootsie Roll stockholder in the family. A schoolteacher, she always squirreled away a little of her salary to buy shares. She advised other family members to do the same. Her late father eventually purchased the majority of Tootsie Roll shares following the Depression, and ran the company from then until 1962, when he passed it on in the traditional manner to Ellen Gordon's husband. "We avoid debt as a company because my parents went through the Depression and learned a valuable lesson about leveraging companies," she says. "That was a good lesson my parents taught me."

Gordon's father taught her other lessons about business. He brought her to the office frequently, and helped spark her interest in business. "My father had mixed feelings," said Gordon. "He loved to talk about his work and every night he would come home and tell me about his day—what he did, what kind of letters he received, who he talked to, and the types of meetings he had. So he wanted me to learn because, he said, 'You have a responsibility,' but on the other hand he also felt I should marry and have children and take care of them and my husband."

Ellen Gordon was a spirited young woman who did not follow the conventions that bound most of the women of her generation to a life without a career. "When I graduated from high school, I wrote a paper about what I really wanted to be—a businesswoman," she says. "At the end, I wrote, 'Of course, this is just a joke. I'm going to get married and have children and be very happy to do that.' I wrote the last part to be a good girl, and to get a good grade. My history teacher thought it was very amusing that I thought I'd ever be a businesswoman."

The joke continued through college. She majored in mathematics at Vassar. "Unusual? Very. There were only a few math majors in the whole college," she remembers. "But when I was very little and went to the office with my father, I always added up the numbers in the telephone directory. I always wondered if I shouldn't be majoring in something like French literature or history. It was a little scary, especially to the boys."

Her pursuits didn't bother Melvin Gordon, a Harvard alumnus whom she met while a sophomore at Vassar. She married him in 1950, then transferred to Wellesley before becoming pregnant with her first of four daughters. "So I left Wellesley, and had my children," she recalls. "But after the third one was born I went back to school." She finished her undergraduate studies at Brandeis. By then, it was the early 1960s. She would take her third daughter to nursery school, before going to class herself. Like Martha Ingram, she also learned negotiating skills helpful for business from raising children. Her kids helped prepare her—after all, children between the ages of three and twelve are her biggest customers.

A HIGH ROLLER

By 1968, Ellen's career was beckoning. That year, she gave up her graduate studies at Harvard in Slavic linguistics and joined Tootsie Roll as a director. Long before career and family became a national issue, she was a working mother who took her daughters on business trips in 1969. She quickly took on the financial role at the company, and strengthened the business through innovation.

It's an old-fashioned company, but there's nothing retro about the way the Gordons make their candy. Ellen Gordon has been investing in automation since the early 1980s after seeing companies in other capital-intensive industries, such as U.S. Steel and General Motors, lose market share to competitors because they lagged in terms of innovation and technology. High-speed machines controlled by microprocessors produce, sort, and wrap candy. Robotics allow for fast packing and bagging. Gordon installed advanced computer systems so she could receive figures from retail stores to measure sales immediately. When considering new technology for the company, she consults with customers and staffers who will be using the machinery before making a choice.

"My father ran things in a different era. I've had to learn more about information technology, manufacturing technology, and engineering," she says. "We don't just want to add sales, but profitable sales. We are dedicated to technology, and feel strongly about reinvesting in our company. Making candy is not a high-margin business, so we have to run a very lean operation. We rely on using state-of-the-art production and information systems to make the most efficient and best product."

A DEVOTION TO BRANDS

Like Shelly Lazarus and other new paradigm leaders, Ellen Gordon takes risks in business. Unlike competitors, such as Brach, that produce generic candies, she is dedicated to brands and grows the company with that concern in mind. When making acquisitions, she seeks to purchase other established brands that will enhance the Tootsie Roll name, such as Mason Dots, Junior Mints, and Charms. "She is growing the company through acquisitions, but in a carefully planned way," says Pat Magee, editor of *Candy Industry* magazine. "She buys companies that fit well into the Gordons' philosophy of candy making. They have high standards, but they do add snap and pizzazz to the companies they buy."

Gordon also tries to mirror changing customer tastes by producing different sizes, and accommodate various retail outlets from 7-Eleven to Wal-Mart with new packaging. She also relies on brand extensions such as adding new lollipop flavors like Black Cherry and Blue Razz. But she believes that a devotion to branding is a vital ingredient in her candy company's success because it draws customers. She hopes that if she maintains her focus on brands, the company will continue for another century. "People always ask, 'Why don't you produce generic brands to boost sales when you have all the equipment?'" she says. "But we really are a branded company and our commitment to them is paramount. We make sure that any actions we take will not jeopardize or pollute our brand. We are not interested in any immediate return that might affect our ability to be around for the next 103 years."

Gordon involves employees in decision making and believes, like leading travel executive Marilyn Carlson Nelson and advertising giant Shelly Lazarus, that the best leaders attract good teams. She tries to foster a family atmosphere in her public company. She has an open-door policy so anyone in the company with a question or concern can come see her or stop her in the hall to discuss it. The company employs 1,750 people. Although she does not collect data on turnover rates, she claims that the turnover figure is low by industry standards. She points out that the average tenure for each employee is over twenty years. She interviews all office staff applicants and managerial candidates before hiring.

"As a manager, you really don't know all the answers, and it's important to bring in staff of different levels to help solve a problem," she says. "You haven't worked at all the jobs. So you've got to get people to contribute. I don't just dictate from above. We get everybody's input to make the best decisions because people who can help shape ideas are not always at the top. Most of our people stay here for their entire careers. We cross-train our people so they can participate in decisions and feel good about their work. And their input is most helpful. We find that in our meetings, we have chairs being dragged from one office to another as the meetings get larger and larger. That's why my chairs have wheels on them. As a leader, you have to adapt."

FUELED BY CHALLENGES

Like Martha Ingram and other new paradigm leaders, Gordon is fueled by the challenges of her work rather than by a powerful title.

She has no plans for retirement, but hopes to pass the company on to one of her top managers or to one of her daughters some day. Succession plans are still unclear at the company, and some analysts worry about the next generation of leaders at Tootsie Roll. Both Gordons are over sixty-five, and their daughters have yet to become active in the company. "I am always learning," she says. "When one of my daughters was little, she had a latex doll. You could stretch it, and the doll would pop back into place. But if you kept on stretching, it never popped back all the way. I always feel like that. I'm being stretched, and afterward, I'm just a little different. I like that. That's the fun. There are new issues all the time—a customer has a problem or commodity prices go up. I love the game."

Looking back on her career, Gordon doesn't attribute her success to inheritance. "With my energy, I would have been able to achieve elsewhere what I have here," she says with a laugh. "I still get calls from headhunters with proposals I have to turn down."

7

AN OBSESSION WITH CUSTOMER PREFERENCES

I look at how the audience is being served and think whether there is something that will break through and attract their attention. It's about identifying a need, then going with your gut to serve it.

— PATRICIA FILI-KRUSHEL

For Patricia Fili-Krushel, former president of the ABC Television Network, giving the people what they want is not just idle talk. She's made a career of it. In 1996, when Fili-Krushel ran the alphabet network's daytime programming, she turned what had been a dead zone into a hot property by giving the audience what it craved: a chatty show about women for women. Although executive producer Barbara Walters conceived of the program, which features four women hosts with diverse backgrounds ranging in age from their mid-twenties through their mid-fifties, Fili-Krushel put it on the air. In kaffeeklatsch style, the group dishes about the behinds of baseball players like the Atlanta Braves' Greg Maddux, peppers a gynecologist with questions about the origin of yeast infections, and raps with celebrity Peter Fonda about his recent movie. "You gals are great," remarked Fonda on the show. The audience seems to agree: ratings for the program Fili-Krushel launched, *The View*, have risen more than 50 percent for the segment of women aged eighteen to forty-nine that advertisers covet. In fact, *The View* is one of the few successful new daytime shows in recent years and a star performer for the network. The show's popularity helped her keep ABC's daytime lineup in first place during the five years she led the unit.

Because she was attuned to the tastes of her customers, in this case viewers, Fili-Krushel was able to score a winner that boosted the network as well as her career. This careful attention to customer preferences allows executives to best plan future business strategies because they can anticipate the direction of the market, giving them a critical edge. When Fili-Krushel picked up on just how big an appetite TV-land had for the game show *Who Wants to Be a Millionaire*, she made sure the network would maximize the mileage on this huge cash vehicle by expanding the show's reach. Her aggressive approach of putting *Millionaire* on the air three times a week starting in January 2000 not only inspired knockoffs on other networks, but also scooped ABC out of the ratings dumps, and made the network number one in the country for the first time in five years.

At the peak of her success, Fili-Krushel, forty-six, resigned from ABC to accept a job where she would reach out to a new audience. In April 2000, she became president and chief executive officer of Healtheon/WebMD's consumer health division. Healtheon is the largest company providing links between consumers, doctors, hospitals, and health plans via the Internet. At Healtheon, she is working to deliver information and programming that will draw customers to its Web site and cable channel. "We are relying on Pat to help us determine the right programming to draw customers to our Web site and to our cable network," says Jeffrey T. Arnold, chief executive officer of Healtheon/WebMD Corporation, who hired Fili-Krushel. "Her superior financial skills and her success in driving viewers to ABC made her the perfect choice for us. And women make eighty percent of health-care decisions. Her experience of connecting with viewers at ABC Daytime and Lifetime is key. She will help us to understand how we can reach out and touch our female viewers. We are relying on her to help us provide information that will be relevant to them."

Fili-Krushel's talent for understanding the changing likes and dislikes of her audience sets her apart. In 1998, *Fortune* magazine ranked her the thirty-eighth most powerful woman in American business, and in 1999, *Entertainment Weekly* labeled her the thirty-third most powerful player in the entertainment industry. A knack for not only keeping abreast of customer likes and dislikes but also for predicting the direction of these preferences in the future is a key new paradigm trait. It enables these leaders to anticipate needs that might be overlooked by traditional customer surveys and to think beyond assumptions that are common in the industry.

"I noticed her strong passion for and understanding of the audience when she was president of ABC Daytime," said Robert Iger, president and chief executive officer of the Walt Disney Company, ABC's parent corporation, who promoted Fili-Krushel to her current position. "Her entire management of [ABC Daytime] was done with the consumer in mind. She took a much more aggressive approach to getting into the minds of consumers than anyone we had in that position before. She personally attended focus groups in different parts of the country to listen to viewers. That was unique."

Fili-Krushel's keen insight into customer needs powered her rise to the presidency of the ABC Television Network in 1998. The new title made her the highest-ranking woman in network television, and the first female president of one of the big four broadcasters (ABC, NBC, CBS, and Fox). When she got the promotion, ABC brass gave her broader duties than her male predecessor in the post, Preston Padden. His responsibilities were centered mainly on the business side of the network, including ABC sales and affiliate relations, but Fili-Krushel's job description included programming, with oversight of ABC's news and entertainment divisions.

"I decided that she is more capable at this job," said Iger, who redesigned the post to suit her skills. "She had a wide range of experience in television, and I felt she combined good business judgment with great creative instincts that are vital for programming."

CUSTOMERS RULE

New paradigm leaders like Fili-Krushel understand the increased role customers play in the Information Age because of the myriad of choices available to them as consumers. In television, the loyalty of the customer has never been harder to secure with more and more edgy new cable channels going live every day to compete for viewers with the four major networks. Mindful of increasing competition in every field with the Internet boom, new paradigm leaders view clients not just as sources of income but as sources of creative ideas for services that can fuel business growth. These leaders respect the "new authority" James Champy writes of in *Reengineering Management:* "In the Rough Weather we're sailing in today, a culture of obedience is still called for, but the authority we must obey is totally different. It is no longer anything so simple, stable and rational as a hierarchy of corporate powers or the specifics of a job description. The new authority lives in our markets and usually appears in the form of our customers."[1]

Respecting the new authority of the customer is a penchant all new paradigm leaders share with Fili-Krushel. The close relationships they form with clients and the priority they place on responding to customer needs allows them to develop keen insights into their demands. Marcy Carsey has produced a string of hit television series because she makes no distinction between herself and the audience, but counts herself as one of its members. In a move that signals the supremacy of the customer at her consultancy, Orit Gadiesh pays her associates according to how well her clients perform after using Bain's consulting services. Ellen Gordon works to keep the time-honored Tootsie Roll brand current by altering packaging and diversifying her product line to suit the changing tastes of consumers. Shelly Lazarus's attention to her advertising customers has helped her agency become the firm of choice of some of America's biggest corporate giants including IBM, American Express, and Kodak. Rebecca Mark traveled the globe to build relationships with customers, and her efforts were key to the growth of her business, especially in the India deal. The technology that travel maven Marilyn Carlson Nelson added allows her company to register customer preferences throughout the system, so that Radisson hotels from Denver to Dubai, for example, will have a hyperallergenic pillow waiting for a guest before that traveler even requests one. Another new paradigm leader featured here is Kim Polese, who is trying to service customer needs now and in the future with her own technology start-up, Marimba, Inc.

FIGHTING BACK

When Fili-Krushel took on her senior post at ABC, the broadcaster was in deep trouble. The network's prime-time ratings for its eighteen- to forty-nine-year-old target demographic group were in third place behind NBC and Fox. She faced the tough task of revitalizing the entire network. Even oft-revered Walt Disney chairman Michael Eisner was criticized in the press at the time for his company's faltering performance and falling stock price. Deepening her woes, the industry was under siege by brash new upstarts who were luring away advertisers and viewers. Collectively, the more than 200 cable stations that have emerged since 1978 had smashed the profitable oligopoly the major networks once held. As cable channels gained viewers, the main networks were losing ground.

But the true test of a new paradigm leader's abilities may, in fact, come when her company is under attack. Like Pat Russo and the other women featured in this book, Fili-Krushel worked to turn challenges into promising opportunities. She helped ABC fight back with hot shows that appealed to audiences. She scored huge programming wins, particularly *Millionaire,* the game show Regis Philbin hosts. Her efforts put the network back on top.

DEFINING A NEW ROLE FOR LEADERS

Leaders who succeed today must "get inside their customers' hearts as well as their heads," writes Tom Petzinger in *The New Pioneers.*[2] To achieve this goal, new paradigm leaders draw on the natural talent women possess for achieving cooperation with customers. According to psychiatrist Dr. Jean Baker Miller, "Cooperativeness may appear to men as if it were somehow detracting from themselves. . . . To women . . . cooperativeness does not have the same quality of loss. . . . Women . . . seek out and enjoy situations that require that quality."[3] New paradigm leaders like Patricia Fili-Krushel, Kim Polese, Shelly Lazarus, and Patricia Russo take their cues from customers in redirecting their business strategy. They lead customer-focused organizations and devise future business plans by quickly responding to changing customer needs as a way to get an edge over the competition.

All companies are clamoring for executives with these skills now. Regardless of the industry, intensified competition in the new economy calls for companies to expand rapidly around the globe. Shareholders have scant patience for executives who lose touch with the needs of key clients. They demand that chief executives play a vital role in winning new multinational customers and cherishing old ones by anticipating and accommodating shifting consumer tastes. Staying in touch with customers' needs cannot be done by simply having staff members conduct an occasional marketing survey or a focus group. Business leaders must spur creativity among their associates by offering wider services and striking a chord with viewers and clients through innovation. A passion for understanding and connecting with consumers helps such executives play that part.

Smart managers also learn from their own failures and make changes to address customer concerns. Shelly Lazarus, for instance, led the charge to win back the American Express account by paying close attention to this important client, which had canned her advertising firm. She put her best people on the account, then produced a campaign that wowed the client and regained the business. Ann Winblad's investment in Slate, a software start-up geared toward pen-based computing, failed. The pen computing market never materialized, preventing the business from getting off the ground. From then on, she invested in large markets only.

An obsession with service to customers is not only a basic leadership quality but integral to a company's progress. When this feature is absent, a chief executive's job is at risk. Gil Amelio grappled with his own inability to connect with customers when he was chief executive officer of Apple Computer from 1996 through 1997. The press labeled him incapable of relating both to customers and to Apple's rank and file.[4] The company was plagued by employee departures during his tenure, in which he cut staff and lost nearly $2 billion.[5] As a result, Apple's market share eroded as major accounts defected to other vendors, and the company was criticized in the press for a "lack of direction." The company's sales languished until cofounder Steve Jobs returned and reportedly engineered Amelio's ouster.

A HEIGHTENED FOCUS ON CUSTOMERS

An obsession with understanding customer preferences, a classic new paradigm trait, helped Fili-Krushel ignite her company's potential for profit. *Millionaire* was crushing its competition in the fall of 1999 when it was launched, even winning more viewers than top-rated comedies like *Frazier*. It was the first time an ABC series had beaten an original episode of an NBC comedy on Thursday night at 9 P.M. since 1983.[6] The show captivated a nation. At the time, more than half the population with TVs[7] were glued to the set for *Millionaire*. By January 2000, each episode was pulling in 28 million fans, making it the most popular show in the country, and defeating other hit shows like *ER* and *Friends*. And other networks were copying *Millionaire* with shows like Fox's *Greed*, CBS's *Winning Lines*, and NBC's *Twenty-One*. By March 2000, *Millionaire* was still leading the pack with ratings at or near the top of the Nielsen rankings each time it aired. ABC charged $400,000 and up for a thirty-second commercial during the show.

"*Millionaire* is so brilliant not just because it's a game show but because there is nothing in prime-time television like it," Fili-Krushel says. "I look at how the audience is being served and think whether there is something that will break through and attract their attention. It's about identifying a need, then going with your gut to serve it."

Thanks to their accurate read of viewers, Fili-Krushel and other leading executives at ABC bucked convention by championing this quiz show. Top brass at the network saw that the British version of the show, which started in 1997, was a huge hit that attracted 73 percent of those watching television when it aired, and wanted to duplicate the program and its success in the United States. But prevailing wisdom at the time went against the program. Quiz shows were considered an outdated concept that would appeal only to older viewers. Game shows had already reached a height of popularity in this country back in the 1950s, and were tarnished by scandal. Back then, network executives from CBS pulled five shows off the air after word leaked that questions and answers were rigged. For more than four decades, the prime-time network quiz show was thought to be a television has-been in an age of sophisticated dramas and niche-oriented programming. Making matters worse, a game show geared toward a mass audience seemed particularly hopeless in our era of "narrowcasting," when television executives tailor nearly all programs toward specific age groups. Despite these concerns, Fili-Krushel and other senior ABC executives believed viewers would watch *Millionaire*. The surprise hit defied all of these stereotypes by capturing every demographic group from adults aged eighteen to over fifty, to kids and teens.

What distinguishes the program from game shows in the past, and how does it lure such a broad audience? Contestants are likely the first in game-show history to receive multiple choice questions. And they can solicit help from the audience, family, or friends, whom they can call at home while on the air, to answer questions like, What is the capital of Australia? The format has struck a chord with viewers.

"As one of my colleagues said in a rather unfortunate choice of words, the show is like crack, because we are all so addicted to it," she explains. "It's a cultural phenomenon. We put it on so frequently because we talked to viewers, and they said they would like the drama to carry over a few nights a week. The other networks are extremely jealous because this show knocks out anything it's up against, and serves as a formidable launchpad for shows that come before and after it. I'm not afraid to take risks, and I'm a good listener."

By airing the show three times a week, Fili-Krushel risked oversaturating the market, but she felt confident that *Millionaire* would continue to attract audiences. So far, with the 1999–2000 season nearly over, results have confirmed that she made the right choice. The gutsy move not only catapulted the network into first place for the first time in more than five years, it was heralded in the press as one that was likely to "transform the competitive landscape of prime-time television."[8] And *Millionaire* strongly improved ABC's economic position, with co-chairman of ABC Entertainment Stuart Bloomberg predicting that the program would add at least $50 million to network profits this season.[9]

"I have often felt that this business is inequitable, and that women have to work harder to prove they are better, smarter, more flexible and more willing to take risks. You have to be a better minority, no matter what your minority is," she says. "But television, for the most part, is a female vehicle. Just like twelve- to seventeen-year-old boys define a hit in theatrical releases, sixty percent of TV viewers are women. We'd better reflect our viewers' interests."

While at the network, Fili-Krushel took steps to reflect those interests. "She met with me once a week to go over ratings so she understood the audience, and got the daily nuances that [she] would miss otherwise," says Larry Hyams, vice president of audience analysis at ABC. "Before she became president of the networks we met with someone at her level maybe twice a year. In the past, we only wrote memos if there was something of note, then sent them out. Meeting weekly was a new feature she requested."

FINDING HER OWN WAY

Fili-Krushel's natural ability to connect with customers and parlay this talent into measurable success has helped her climb the corporate ladder in a mercurial industry where only a handful of women have attained top levels. Among Fortune 500 entertainment firms, a category that includes Walt Disney, only 10 percent of the most senior corporate officers in 1999 were women, according to Catalyst.

But Fili-Krushel stood out at a major broadcast network because she rose to become the highest-ranking woman. Other women who have managed to get ahead in the television industry have risen in the more free-flowing world of cable, including Geraldine Laybourne, who earned her reputation at Viacom Inc.'s Nickelodeon; Anne Sweeney, who is chief of Disney's cable networks; and Kay Koplovitz, who led USA Networks. "I started as a secretary, but I'm a survivor," says Fili-Krushel. "Programming is what I've done the most and what excites me the most, but I feel I can handle the business side equally well. I am comfortable in both arenas while most people are comfortable in one or the other."

WIRED FOR SUCCESS

As Fili-Krushel squeezes in an interview between meetings, her brown hair cascades in big curls down to her shoulders, and her large green eyes demand attention. She's clad for the occasion in olive pants, with a black blazer over a cream blouse. A beige scarf gives the outfit a simple elegance. Her spacious tenth-floor office with views overlooking Manhattan's bustling Upper West Side hums with the sounds of four different television sets. While one large set flashes scenes from ABC's longtime popular soap opera *General Hospital*, CNN reporters rush to cover the Columbine High School murders on another. *Power Rangers Playback* is on Fox, and soap rival *Guiding Light* appears on CBS. She's placed a photograph of her husband, Kenneth B. Krushel, chief executive of CEI, an on-line software publishing company, and two children—Jacob, nine, and Kara, eight—on her light maple desk. But in a sign that television also plays a big role in her life, a wedding album from ABC's various soap operas rests on a side table. Posters of a few of the network's celebrities, Bill Maher and Michael J. Fox, hang outside her door.

MOVIN' ON UP

Fili-Krushel always wanted to work in media. A communications major at St. John's University in New York, she landed her first job after college at a small company selling television time to advertisers. But after nine months, she was bored because she wanted to work at a television station rather than on the periphery. She trekked back to her college placement office. There she found a fortuitous posting— an opening at ABC Television. She took an entry-level job at the network as a secretary for fourteen sports production managers, and rose through the ranks at the division.

"It was really exciting. First of all, it was a lot of live television, and sports in the seventies at ABC was the place to be. You know, 'the thrill of victory and the agony of defeat.' It was a dynamic, hands-on, people-oriented business. But it was difficult being a woman because it was such a man's world. I just didn't see where I was going to go at ABC Sports. That is why I ultimately left. I was usually the only woman on the road at a sporting event, and the guys stuck with the guys. When they did speak to me they'd start talking about statistics. I remember sitting at a dinner and listening for three hours to all this sports and jock stuff, while I kept thinking I'd like to work in something that I found enthralling."

Like Pat Russo, Darla Moore, and other new paradigm leaders, Fili-Krushel found a back route to success. In 1979, she ditched her high-profile job at ABC for the new frontier: the then-fledgling cable network, Home Box Office (HBO). The cable station had been launched just one year earlier, and few expected such channels to one day sap profits from the major networks. Fili-Krushel moved up quickly in the scrappy world of cable television and helped build up for the company programming that would appeal to viewers. "When I left for HBO, no one even knew what it was," she remembers. "That was when HBO was first on the map, and was growing by leaps and bounds. I saw a big opportunity there. Within a year, I shifted from head of production of HBO Sports to head of production for the entire company. I oversaw production of original movies and original comedy specials in addition to boxing events. It was much more fun for me to put together a Cher concert than a boxing match."

In 1987, Fili-Krushel moved to the Lifetime Cable Network to become a group vice president, focusing on reeling in viewers. At Lifetime, she joined in that network's switch to an all-women's programming format and helped the network grow. She stayed at Lifetime for five years and introduced such original series as *The Life and Times of Molly Dodd*, as well as original movies that resonated with the predominantly female audiences.

"I left HBO as head of business affairs and production because

I was really executing a lot of other people's visions," she says. "When I went to Lifetime, it was my vision because I was head of programming."

In 1993, after her tour of duty in the cable world, Fili-Krushel reenlisted at ABC as president of its daytime division with a fuller understanding of delivering shows that viewers would tune in to watch. Back at the big network, she learned a key lesson about customer preferences that would shape the rest of her career. In a bid to lure a new audience, she sliced and diced characters from an existing daytime drama, *Loving*, into a new and hipper soap called *The City*. Despite an initial 40 percent ratings surge when she killed off many favorite characters, the new show failed to attract viewers. In fact, ratings dropped so sharply after a year that the network had to cancel the show.

"What I ultimately learned, was that I had created a revolution, not an evolution," she says. "I had brought the genre into the nineties with a new look, a big star [Morgan Fairchild], and a serial killer, but viewers were happy where it was. I didn't pay enough attention to the viewer, and that was the most important lesson for me. So I took all of that learning, and tried again."

Fili-Krushel's next effort was the daytime drama *Port Charles*, a spin-off of an existing show, the long-running soap *General Hospital*. This time she got rave reviews for the series, which proved a popular new edition to the network's lineup. What she learned from *The City's* flop and the success of *Port Charles* was that audiences were not content simply with a racy plot, they also wanted to see characters on the screen who were complex and layered. "I took anchored characters who had depth and meaning to viewers," she says. "We did a much more traditional-looking soap opera that was just a little bit more nineties than it had been. It was a valuable lesson."

VIEWER INSIGHT PAYS OFF

Fili-Krushel's strong performance in daytime, underpinned by her close attention to what was resonating with viewers, paid off. The knowledge of fickle audiences she's gained during her twenty-three years in televi-sion has paved the way for her success since she rose to the presidency of the network in 1998. Fili-Krushel has relied on her understanding that evolution, not revolution, appeals to viewers. That insight enabled her to strengthen existing shows and to bring on new ones. She has already revamped the slumping *Good Morning America* morning program by adding ABC big gun Diane Sawyer as a cohost along with the show's for-mer talent Charles Gibson. The move resulted in a 31 percent ratings boost for adults aged twenty-five to fifty-four.

Also on her to-do list was finding a way to shore up ABC's sagging prime-time schedule. With this in mind, the network committed to *Monday Night Football,* a longtime hit with viewers. One of Fili-Krushel's big wins was a deal in which she persuaded affiliates to help shoulder the burden of paying for football. Initially, local affiliate sta-tions balked. Her predecessor, Padden, had tried for over a year to seal a deal with affiliates, but failed. But less than a year after taking over his job, she ironed out a pact with them. To close that deal, like Darla Moore, Fili-Krushel had to blend shrewdness with cooperation. The payoff: In 1999, affiliates agreed to hand over $150 million during the next three years to ABC to help defray the broadcaster's $550 mil-lion annual expense for *Monday Night Football.* To boot, she also got affiliates to fork over ten ad spots that could add up to several million dollars in revenue for ABC. In exchange, Fili-Krushel gave the affili-ates an undisclosed portion of revenues from a new cable soap opera channel ABC developed despite affiliate concerns that it will draw viewers away from them. She also threw in eight additional prime-time commercial spots a week. The trade press hailed the bargain she struck as a "fundamental realignment." "I tend to put my cards on the table when negotiating," explains Fili-Krushel. "I try to get people to problem solve together."

In her quest for new revenue sources, Fili-Krushel drew on her under-standing of viewers to launch a soap-opera channel, SoapNet, in January 2000. On SoapNet, she repeated in prime time the day's 3 ½-hour soap lineup including *All My Children, General Hospital,* and other classics, to draw audiences who cannot tune in until the evening. The service represents the first time that the same television programs have appeared on a network and a basic cable channel on the same day.

"Viewers have very fond memories of soap operas. People watched them twenty or thirty years ago with their mothers or their grandmothers. They're now working, so they can't watch during the day, but would love to have it available at night. It's a link between family members who ask each other 'Did you see what Erica Kane did today?'" she says. "From the testing, we saw the channel helped us grow our audience by about a third."

Like Shelly Lazarus, Fili-Krushel collaborates in a high-touch way to get the job done. When she approached her senior staff for the first time as president of the network, she sat down with each to define objectives. As a first step, she asked them to lay out their goals for the year. Then she met with each one individually to iron them out further.

"I feel like you hire the strongest people you can find, and then you let them do their job once you've agreed on what the job is they are trying to accomplish," she says. "The only way to attract good people is to let them go. They have to make the decisions and you have to be willing to let them make mistakes. Very often, people are afraid to hire the best people because they fear for their own jobs. I just think, 'Great, let them take my job and I'll go do something else.' When I got this promotion, I had two people to choose from that worked for me to be my replacement. If you are so valuable that no one else can do your job, people don't want to promote you. I try to learn from the people I work for, and people who work for me. That's where the listening comes in and being open, not dictatorial."

COMING INTO HER OWN

Fili-Krushel is used to setting her own course. The eldest of three children, she grew up in Queens, New York. She was only seven when her parents divorced. Her mother was still pregnant with her little brother when her father, a successful architect, left. After the split, Fili-Krushel went from living in a big house to a two-bedroom apartment. She soon felt reality's bite. "My mom had been home until then, but once they got divorced, she had to go to work," recalls Fili-Krushel. "I became an adult at seven. And I was trying to meet my parents' expectations because they left me, in essence, in charge. I always wanted their love and affection, and thought I could get it by being really good at what I was left in charge of."

Making matters worse, her father was an alcoholic. Weekly visits with him were like walking into a minefield. But Fili-Krushel said the drama at home, ironically, helped prepare her for a career in television by providing her with a basis for understanding others. "Most of my adolescence was spent dealing with his drinking," she recalls. "I never knew what I was going to encounter so I had to think on my feet, and listen carefully to understand the situation and respond to it. My childhood came into play very nicely in the television industry, where you always have to adapt yourself to be more masculine or more feminine because some men just are not at ease with women."

Fili-Krushel's mother taught her about the determination she would need to succeed. After the divorce, her mother, who had few marketable skills to fall back on when she found herself entering the workplace, became an office assistant in a print shop. She used her skills in layout to serve customers. "To see her bring up three kids in the fifties and sixties by herself was a true testament to my mother's strength," adds Fili-Krushel. "We moved every two years because she was always trying to raise our standard of living. And each time she made a little more money, we improved where we lived—we went from a small apartment, to the bottom floor of a house, to renting the entire house. It was always in a different neighborhood right in that environment so that we could stay in the same school. It was just that commitment to being a hard worker, providing for the family and just being an example that ultimately showed you can do it."

Fili-Krushel's college years were not easy because she had to pay her own way. She was crushed when she realized she could not afford to go

out of state for school, but she took on three jobs to put herself
through St. John's University, where she received a partial scholarship.
She juggled her studies with working part-time as a bookkeeper at a
limousine company, a salesperson at a clothing store, and a clerk at a
tax preparation company similar to H&R Block. Later, she earned an
MBA from Fordham University. "My dad came from an old-world
Italian family and said, 'You're a girl, you just go out and get married.
What do you need a good education for?' I really had to strive to work
my way through school and to get past those difficulties. But I think
overcoming adversity enabled me to accomplish what I have today."

BETTING ON THE AUDIENCE

Accustomed to accomplishing what she sets out to do, Fili-Krushel
bet on viewers to improve ABC's fortunes and put the network on
top. She took a gamble in a bid to expand her audience by hinging
the network's future largely on the fortunes of *Millionaire*. But Fili-
Krushel relished the challenge of trying to return the network to profitability by dusting off a traditional genre. In the process, she helped
revolutionize the way the industry looks at low-cost alternative programming since the game show is relatively cheap to make.   She
achieved other programming successes during her tenure with *Once
and Again, The Practice, Dharma & Greg,* and *The Drew Carey Show.*
ABC also ranked first with kids aged two to eleven on Saturday
mornings and in daytime when she left the company. To ensure that
ABC stakes out its space on the Internet, she also worked to polish
the brand for success on-line at ABC.com.

NEW CHALLENGES

That pursuit whetted Fili-Krushel's appetite to stake out her own
space on the Internet. At the height of her career at ABC, she left to

lead Healtheon/WebMD's consumer health division. Like Meg Whitman and Marcy Carsey, Fili-Krushel is rebuilding the rules and embracing change as she moves from a traditional broadcaster to what she calls a "new media" company.

Her shift to an Internet company is part of a growing trend among influential women. Like Fili-Krushel, Meg Whitman, and Kim Polese, top female executives at traditional American corporations are increasingly turning toward the dot-com world for job opportunities. Jeanne Jackson resigned as chief of the Banana Republic division of Gap Inc. to take the helm of Wal-Mart.com, and Heidi Miller departed from her high-profile chief financial officer post at one of the country's most profitable companies, Citigroup, to become chief financial officer of a company that has yet to earn a profit, Priceline.com. Not only are Internet companies thirsty for talent, but like men, many women are taking risks to seize opportunities in the fast-paced wired world that are equal to or better than their jobs in traditional firms.

"This opportunity to build a business in such an exciting area, health, was just too interesting to pass up," says Fili-Krushel. "And as risky as dot-coms can be, this job is the least risky because the company is the gorilla of the business. The Internet feels like the future, and women like me gravitate to these new businesses because there are no established rules so we are free to lead in our own way. I have the chance to write the rules. I don't like to follow in someone else's footsteps."

Appealing to consumers is a key aspect of these Internet jobs. Like Marcy Carsey and Geraldine Laybourne at Oxygen Media, Fili-Krushel will be working to attract audience both on-line and on cable television. In her new position, at Healtheon/WebMD, she will lead the company efforts to create programs and services that will attract consumers to its Web site, WebMD Health, and to its cable channel, WebMD television. Family concerns also played a role in her decision. In her new job, she remains in New York, where she wanted to raise her children, but if she had stayed in her former post, she would have had to relocate to Los Angeles. She is again looking forward to taking on a new position at Healtheon rather than filling an existing post.

"Most of the jobs I have had have been created for me," Fili-Krushel says. "I didn't step into too many jobs that existed. I like reinventing and finding my own way, then routing people through it. My philosophy is that power is setting goals and getting people to reach those goals believing that they did it by themselves."

FORGING A PATH FOR THE FUTURE

Like entertainment executives mindful that viewers can switch channels when the first flicker of boredom sets in, technology visionaries must do what they can to hook and reel in their customers. With more and more Internet-based companies sprouting up each day peddling virtually the same electronic wares as their neighbor in the next Silicon Valley stall, competition is only intensifying. Kim Polese, cofounder and chief executive officer of Marimba, Inc., which delivers software over networks, has managed to stay ahead of the curve by gearing her company's products to the needs of businesses. How? By adhering to that hallmark of new paradigm leadership: keeping close tabs on what customers want.

"We have been unique among Internet start-up companies in having a real and substantial customer base," says Polese. "There is a very well defined need for our product in the marketplace, and it is growing. Our customers are using our product today in the real world of solving business-critical problems. And these are not little Podunk companies forking down a couple thousand; these are Fortune 1000 companies that are spending mid-six figures and even seven figures on our software."

Just how successful has Polese's company been in attracting big-name clients? Intuit, FedEx, Bear, Stearns & Co., Charles Schwab & Co., Cisco Systems, DaimlerChrysler, The Home Depot, Sears Roebuck & Co., and other leading corporations now use her company's core product, Castanet, to deliver information and software updates over the Internet or over their private corporate networks to employees and customers. Marimba has set up shop in what is expected to be a considerable market as zapping software over neworks is expected to become increasingly commonplace. Consulting firm Forrester Research estimated the commerce software market at $3 billion in 1999 and growing. Polese's company of 162 employees has attracted well over 100 clients.

Polese's accomplishments in the still male-dominated Silicon Valley has not gone unnoticed. At just thirty-eight, she is the only woman who has led a substantial technology company from its founding to its initial public offering, according to technology trade publication *Upside* magazine. In 1997, *Time* magazine named her as one of the 25 Most Influential Americans, along with prominent figures such as Madeleine Albright and George Soros. And women were CEOs in only 6 percent of Internet companies that venture capital firms funded in 1999, according to Venture One, a research firm in San Francisco.

Polese was first noticed in the mid-1990s while working at Sun Microsystems, where she helped develop and market the Java computer language, which allows Web developers to deliver programs to any computer on a network. Java became one of Sun's biggest success stories. Since Polese took Marimba public in April 1999, the company has performed on Wall Street like a typically "hot" but volatile Internet stock. After an IPO at $20 per share, Marimba stock climbed to about $74 and sank to $25 in the summer Internet sell-off before rebounding to $60 in March 2000. In fiscal 1999, she nearly doubled revenues at the company to $31 million, and is expected to steer Marimba to profitability in the third quarter of 2000. Harley Manning, research director at Forrester, sees her company doubling revenues again in 2000, and reaching about $200 million in sales within five years. She was worth $150 million on paper in March 2000.

Polese boasts so many big-name customers because she created a product for the burgeoning Internet market for corporate clients, who were looking to save money on software management. Rather than targeting individual consumers, as do pure play Internet companies, Marimba started selling her products directly to companies—where the big money is. Forrester calculated that in 1998 the business-to-business market represented $43 billion worth of goods, more than five times the retail total. That business-to-business market is growing phenomenally, and is expected to increase from $145 billion in 1999 to $7.3 trillion in 2004, according to the Gartner Group, a consulting firm.

From the start in 1996, she displayed a classic new leadership talent for listening closely to those customers, and tailoring her services to their unique needs. For instance, when Charles Schwab & Co., the nation's largest discount broker, went looking for a system that would enable its high-end clients, who make up 20 percent of its customer base, to track all their trades, Marimba was able to fill the need.

"Essentially, it's the personalized Schwab portal on your desktop," she says. "These customers trade frequently and want to be able to see all the trades they have ever done on the screen. That's not information you can get from the Web site because of the bandwidth issue. But Castanet can actually do it efficiently and it's always available. And the advantage of Schwab having its logo on the desktop in front of the customer is huge."

MOVING BEYOND HYPE

Polese's close attention to customers helped her ride out one of the roughest storms a young technology entrepreneur can face: preserving a reputation as an innovator despite the often limited life span of the latest technology. When she launched Marimba in 1996, she and her company were linked to hype over a new technology, called "push," that was touted in the press and the industry as the "next big thing." Rather than waiting to download a slew of information that could take hours, users could purchase services that would automatically send or "push" data to them. At the time, this technology seemed like a revolutionary way to deliver data over the Internet because customers would demand it.

Labeled a push company, Marimba became one of the hottest start-ups in the Valley, and Polese, too, was crowned another "superstar of the Internet age." Not only was her company in a sizzling space, but she stood out from the male-dominated computer geek crowd by virtue of her being young and female. Soon, she became something of a cover girl for technology. She graced the covers of trade magazines like *Wired* and *Red Herring*, as they rushed to print her story, and her technology was touted in *Newsweek*. With her slim build and flowing strawberry-blond curls, Polese was asked to pose for an Anne Klein fashion advertisement with other notable women, including former Texas governor Ann Richards and country singer Reba McEntire. At first, the attention helped her company gain publicity and attract investors in its nascent stages. But push technology soon fell out of favor because it proved troublesome to use. Then came the bad weather, with Polese and Marimba becoming objects of ridicule. *Fortune* charged that there was little more to the company than her pretty face.[12]

"It was all a reaction to the oddity and the novelty of a woman CEO," she says. "But it didn't really bother me at the end of the day because I knew we were going to execute, I knew we were going to be successful, and I knew we were going to kick butt. Our success depends on that of our customers, and they won't place a bet with a young company like ours unless they are assured the product will work and are pleased with the results. In a world of hype, I value substance and delivering more than ever."

Polese shrugged off the criticism. She stuck to expanding her client base because she knew that customers, not ephemeral buzz, would sustain a company. As a result of her fortitude, 70 percent of Marimba's customers came back to buy more services, building Marimba's revenues and proving that she was a chief executive officer of substance. What's more, she has recently drawn new, prominent customers such as Nasdaq, a leading electronic stock market, GTE, and NEC Electronics. "It doesn't come down to hype or how many magazine covers you were on," she says. "It comes down to do you have a product that is of value to customers in the marketplace, and the answer for us is 'yes.'"

Like Fili-Krushel, who built a career on providing programming that appealed to audiences' tastes, Polese caters to clients and creates technology to suit their needs. "Sears, for example, is one of our customers. They have a service called Appliances On Line available to consumers. I can point to their site and get information about appliances I might want to buy, warranty information, past purchases and so forth. Sears wants to synchronize and update the software and the information automatically and we help them do that."

FOLLOWING HER PASSION

Like Meg Whitman, Polese's office in Mountain View, California, is modest by CEO standards and looks much like the cookie-cutter rooms her colleagues occupy. The door to the cramped office, which fits only her desk, a couple of file cabinets, and a small table with two chairs, slides open like a Japanese screen. Fluorescent lights beam down from the ceiling onto the slate gray carpeted floor, emphasizing the dark tones of Polese's masculine office furniture. Sitting in a burgundy fabric chair, she looks up from the Compaq laptop computer that is on her modern black desk. The walls are bare. No family photographs nor any of the award plaques that are the usual trappings of CEO suites are found. Jeans abound at Marimba headquarters. For an interview, Polese dresses down in black pants, a yellow cotton Vneck sweater, and fashionable but clunky-heeled black shoes. The locks of her hair spin and curl across her shoulders.

"I've never been a CEO before," she says. "I never even rose through the managerial middle manager ranks or anything. I don't have the stripes to point to, and I'm not going to pretend that I do. But I am comfortable and confident in my own abilities, and we are building a great company here. None of us have time to waste in this whole industry right now with the way things are going. Getting results is what matters. If I don't know something, I am going to speak up and ask questions to get the answer. It's amazing how much progress you can make when you break down the barriers."

PUTTING THE CUSTOMER FIRST

Intuit is a customer that has kept coming back for more services from Marimba. After using the Marimba's technology with Quicken software in 1997, Intuit bought Castanet for its QuickBooks 2000 software as well. "Marimba's Castanet plays an integral role in our e-business strategy," says Tom Villanueva, director of QuickBooks Internet Gateway at Intuit. "It allows Intuit to efficiently and transparently provide our business customers with new innovative software features, e-finance services, and information updates via the Internet. We chose Marimba because its Castanet technology was an important component in connecting with and servicing our customers."

Polese credits putting the customer first for much of her success so far. She makes it her job to ensure that Marimba's products enable companies to perform everyday tasks. She is also bent on improving Castanet to meet client needs more efficiently. After early clients PeopleSoft Inc. and Walt Disney used Castanet, Polese polled them and used their feedback and that of other customers to help upgrade the software. Since the company's inception, she has already updated Castanet three times by March 2000. To better gather customer responses to her product, she also set up a representative group of clients she called a "customer council." "We fly in ten to twelve customers a year for a few days in California so we can get to know them and their experiences with our products," says Polese. "We like to keep it small so we can have intimate conversations, and we make sure these clients do not compete with each other. This year, for instance, we have the Navy and companies like Home Depot, Cisco Systems, and Intuit. We have changed features and plans as a result of these meetings."

Not surprisingly, the feature that clients like most about Marimba is that its service saves them money. One Marimba customer is Passport New Media, Inc., a company geared for kids formed in January 1999 to enable a computer to pull information available from the Internet without a child logging onto the Web. The product's main selling point is that it lets parents screen Internet access.

"When I saw that Marimba's product gave us more flexibility and broader features than competitors like Novadigm and Backweb, I was convinced Marimba was the best choice," says Ira Dworkin, chief technology officer of Passport New Media. "She saved us easily $300 to $400,000."

Castanet essentially provides the technology that takes information from the Web daily and delivers it to the computer's hard drive. This means young users never actually go on-line, though they seem to when they can play educational games from the Learning Company, read news articles from Time Warner's Time for Kids, and use other programs.

Like Orit Gadiesh, when Polese approaches a new client, she tries to really understand their concerns. On a typical first visit, she sits down with the company's chief technology officer or chief information officer, then listens closely as the customer explains some of the challenges his or her company faces in the marketplace. "We form a partnership," she explains. "We have lunch or dinner together so we get to know each other one on one. We gauge how our products apply to their situation. Then we do a test drive at the company, where we bring in our product and demonstrate it in their environment so they are assured that the product will work. We just did that for Nasdaq, and now eight thousand traders use our technology to receive customized and updated information automatically over the Internet. They can now use our software to seemlessly play out 'what if' scenarios on their computers."

She directs Marimba toward fulfilling customer needs and opens communication lines with staff to keep the goal of satisfying customers at the company's core. She has monthly brainstorming sessions with her management team to discuss what customers are saying and how to derive new ideas for services from those comments. "Lunch with Kim," a monthly ritual when she eats with eight to ten employees at a local restaurant, gives her another opportunity to talk about client concerns with her staff. "My role is bringing people together and getting them moving in the same direction, and making sure they know where they are going and why," she says. "I don't hand down edicts or pound my fist on the table. I always ask for feedback, and I think getting out there and talking to people is the most important thing I can do to keep the company moving forward."

BREAKING DOWN BARRIERS

A child of immigrants, Polese grew up in Berkeley, California, with the traditional first-generation American will to work hard. Her father hails from Italy, and her mother is from Denmark. Both parents wanted her and her older brother to put school first. A high achiever, she earned straight A's, learning to dance and to play piano when she wasn't hitting the books. "You didn't come home from school, turn on the TV, and open a bag of Chee-tos," she recalls. "I could not talk back or mouth off. My parents expected that my brother and I would be in the top ten percent of the class, and that we would both go to a very good and respectable university. They always taught me to work hard, and to never give up when things went wrong."

By age nine, Kim Polese decided she wanted to follow in the footsteps of her parents: She wanted to be an entrepreneur. Her father, who had worked for General Electric, left to start his own company, a machine shop. He built machinery and Polese's mother worked at the family business looking after the books. Despite her father's long hours, including weekends, Polese saw he was driven by the freedom of working for himself. "He followed his passion," she explains. "And I wanted to follow mine."

Unlike many girls her age, her passion was science. As a high school student, she helped teach kids at the Lawrence Hall of Science, a local public science museum in Berkeley. "As a kid, I loved science and was entering science fairs all the time," she says. "Then I fell in love with programming. I have a passion for computers. What I liked was the combination of science and creativity. I loved being able to communicate my passion for technology and computers to others."

LEARNING SELF-RELIANCE

The interest served her well, both in school and at work, by distinguishing her from the crowd. She got into the University of California at Berkeley where she thrived as a biophysics major, earning her bachelor of science degree in 1983. She spent the following year studying computer science at University of Washington, Seattle. After a stint in artificial intelligence, a hot field at the time, she joined Sun Microsystems in 1989. Her big break came in 1993, when Polese joined a team developing a new computing language. The language became the precursor of the now ubiquitous Java, which allows Web developers to create and automatically deliver programs, rather than just files, to any computer on the network, and became a big seller for Sun. All told, Polese spent more than seven years at the software giant, playing a pivotal role in conceiving and driving the Internet strategy for Java.

"I kept going to senior people who should have been really smart and visionary, just thinking that they must know the answers," Polese recalls. "But I quickly realized no one was going to figure this thing out for me. I had to guess, but realizing that my guess was right on or as close to right on as any of them would have gotten was a real source of confidence and belief in myself."

At Sun, Polese would develop her knack for connecting with customers, becoming a virtual one-person marketing department for Java, which she helped make a sensation. As part of her strategy, she transformed its business model, choosing its catchy new name (it was formerly called Oak), signing licensees, and creating its brand identity. She pulled off no small task: turning an obscure programming language into a common name. In addition to her marketing duties, she remained responsible for the definition of Java's technical features.

Like push technology, Java ushered in a wave of hype that hit Silicon Valley like a tsunami. The language was intended for interactive televisions of the future. But Polese had the foresight to realize the language would have wider application on personal computers. She lobbied to have the language repositioned for use on PCs because she wanted to focus on a real piece of hardware rather than a market that did not even exist. Her decision, though not well received at the time, proved vital to the future of Java. Sales began to beat expectations. In effect, she made the new programming language sexy and popular, while Sun spent very little on marketing. By the time Polese left Sun in 1996, Java had been loaded onto well over 7 million computers and licensed to over a dozen companies that were building it into their products, including IBM, Netscape, and AT&T. The language was credited with much of a $4.5 billion surge in Sun's stock price.[11]

"I remember feeling overwhelmed by the enormity of the task—it was basically my job to take this new technology and make it a commercial success with a mass audience," she recalls. "We made Java a tool for creating interactive Web browsers, and then we got Sun's blessing to put it out there for free on the Internet. Essentially from then on Java was huge, and the possibilities for people to use it became endless."

Polese's role in bringing Java to market made her a prominent public face in computing at just thirty-five. Then vice president of the United States Al Gore tapped her for a panel that meets to discuss policy issues that affect technology companies.

"What really turned me on was being able to explain and communicate my passion for technology to other people—to show them how exciting and nonthreatening technology can be," she says. "My career decisions were driven by cool technology I wanted to work on with smart teams of people who really impressed and motivated me."

SOLVING PROBLEMS FOR CUSTOMERS

Satisfied that she had been part of putting Java on the fast track, Polese set out to look for new opportunities where she could help customers use technology to build their businesses. So at the height of Java's popularity, she left the company to start her own software business.

"I could have stayed at Sun and been very comfortable watching my baby grow—that's the way I felt about Java," Polese says. "But I had been running the show in terms of marketing and development for Java, and suddenly there was going to be an entire department full of hundreds of people doing that, lots of hierarchy and decision making beyond my control. At the same time, I saw Java enabling all these new products and companies to be born that would help people solve real business problems, and I wanted to be part of that process, not just watch it happen."

She joined three computer engineers from Sun's Java team, and devised a plan for their nascent software start-up. Between Christmas and New Years in 1995, she met with partners Arthur van Hoff, Sami Shaio, and Jonathan Payne for eight hours a day at a cafe to iron out their business plan. By 1996, the foursome had formed Marimba, and each founder invested $15,000 in the company. The money helped pay the rent for headquarters—a 2,000-square-foot office on the second floor of a walk-up apartment in Palo Alto.

Polese was asked to take the helm because her technically oriented cofounders lacked the business experience she gained from overseeing marketing for Java. Through handling marketing for the popular computer language, she had built up relationships with customers, analysts, and the press that would help her connect with potential investors. And with her name linked to Java, she instantly had cachet among venture capitalists. It wasn't long before John Doerr, the star partner at top venture firm Kleiner Perkins Caufield & Byers, sent her an e-mail with an offer. But Polese waited to take the cash until she and her partners had made a prototype of Castanet that was ready to sell. Once the product was cleared for take-off, she collected $4 million in financing from Kleiner Perkins as the first company in its Java Fund.

STAYING FOCUSED

Polese credits her attention to customers for helping to keep her focused amid a changing environment. Marimba, once seen as a gold mine, underwent a rapid rise and then a steep fall, brought down by concerns about push technology. Now the company is back on a growth track, having built up a solid customer base for its software products. Of course, Marimba's future, like that of many young Internet-based companies, remains to be seen. Still very junior in age compared to most CEOs, Polese likely has a long career ahead of her. "She's come through very well," explains Harley Manning from Forrester. "I expect that we will see that story play out very many times in the future, but without a happy ending like she's had. Many entrepreneurs will jump on something that seems promising, but may also run into trouble. They will be looking to her to help them find their way through."

As a woman chief executive officer, Polese believes the pressure to succeed is even more intense. It's a bumpy road. A patent dispute with another software distribution company, Novadigm, is pending. Both companies have filed lawsuits alleging that the other is infringing their patents. Undaunted, Polese remains devoted to her work— still single and putting in well over seventy hours each week. "Women have to demonstrate they can be decisive," she says. "Women have to do this in a more demonstrative way than men because there is a built-in perception that they won't be able to do that. They won't be able to do the hard thing. People need to feel there is someone who is strong that is leading this organization."

8

COURAGE UNDER FIRE

*I have made some decisions since [Bronson's] death that no one else has
agreed with, but I don't regret them. It felt right . . . to follow my own
instincts.*

— MARTHA INGRAM

When Martha Ingram and the world learned that her husband had
died of cancer in June 1995, many feared the worst for the $10 billion
distribution powerhouse Bronson Ingram had built. Wracked with
grief, Martha Ingram, then sixty-one, had a family to consider and
the reality of facing the rest of her life without her closest ally. That's
why her friends and executives at the company were hardly prepared
for what was to come next.

Three days after she buried Bronson, she made a bold corporate decision that her husband had put off during his entire career: taking the distribution empire's fast-growing computer unit public. Equally surprising,
within six months of his death, Martha Ingram had assumed control over
the entire company, stepping over its longtime chief executive officer. As
she saw it, it was a time for demonstrating courage under fire.

"I have made some decisions since [Bronson's] death that no one
else has agreed with, but I don't regret them," says Ingram. "It felt
right and built my confidence that I have to follow my own
instincts."

Such gutsy decisions are supposed to be the province of men, but new paradigm leaders like Ingram know better. She was not just acting as a decisive leader but making daring choices in the face of powerful opponents. And all new paradigm leaders share her tenacity to withstand forceful opposition to fulfill the goals they have for the businesses they run. Rebecca Mark overcame government foes who opposed her plan for a power plant in India, and wrestled an even larger deal out of conflict. Patricia Fili-Krushel, former president of the ABC Television Network, overcame antagonism from local television station affiliates to get them to help shoulder the burden of the network's commitment to *Monday Night Football.* Marcy Carsey of Carsey-Werner convinced television studio executives to air her programs despite their unconventional flavor, and produced huge sitcom successes.

Another new paradigm leader, also featured in this chapter because of her ability to overcome rivals and take steps that differed from her predecessor's, is Loida Lewis. Following her husband's death, she unseated his handpicked successor to take over the billion-dollar food company that was once the largest African-American-owned business in the country, TLC Beatrice. One could argue that widows who inherit powerful corporate posts have no place in a book about business leadership. Yet Ingram and Lewis both overcame a powerful legacy not only by countering top management but by taking action that their very successful and much beloved husbands had not.

New paradigm leaders have a tendency to make decisions that break with tradition at the firms they run. That often involves overcoming obstacles and withstanding criticism. The very essence of courage under fire is having the smarts and the constitution not only to make a decision but to follow one's own instincts and do something counterintuitive even in the face of great resistance. The women featured here understand that their approach may be different, but that does not deter them from taking action. The high level of self-confidence each has, as well as their laser focus on achieving goals, keeps them centered and motivated to face up to their opponents and satisfy objectives that define their leadership. A company that will excel in the digital age needs that kind of commitment at the top.

Ingram did not just have to face up to internal rivals. External opposition was fierce as well. The business press had written her off as the "grande dame" of Nashville's arts scene. No matter. She helped power her distribution empire to further prominence with more than $22 billion in revenues in 1998. Ingram is the country's wealthiest active businesswoman, and the seventy-ninth richest person in the nation in 1999, worth an estimated $2.8 billion, according to *Forbes*. "I like winning," she says.

SITTING IN THE BIG CHAIR

Martha Ingram is not a typical company chairman. She eschews the chairman's office on the ninth floor of the Nashville headquarters of Ingram Industries. Her husband, Bronson, used to occupy the space, but after he died she converted it into a boardroom for conferences and meetings. His presence still looms large in the room. Now a big oil painting of this broad-shouldered man, wearing a traditional blue suit and with a serious and calculating look in his brown eyes, stares down from the wall. His seat at the head of the table remains empty.

After assuming the chairman's role, Ingram stayed in her own office, which feels more like a library than an executive suite. The scale is intimate, with a low ceiling and a plush sofa and chairs. Bookshelves line one of the mahogany-toned walls, and the room is decorated with furniture upholstered in warm earth tones of beige and brown. Soothing music of Mozart and Vivaldi drifts from the bookshelf speakers alongside her desk, while the air conditioner hums steadily. She sits calmly wearing a brown pantsuit, an elegant white blouse with widely spaced brown stripes, and stately gold jewelry. She glances occasionally at a photograph of Bronson on a side table facing her desk. The black and white picture can barely contain his frame—standing behind a desk and leaning forward with his hands outstretched across it, his eyes glaring intensely at the camera. Be it in the boardroom or in his wife's own space, Bronson's imposing image is never far from view at Ingram Industries.

It was while she was a senior at Vassar College in Poughkeepsie, New York, that Ingram met Bronson on a blind date in 1957. He was a perfect match—an intense and driven businessman who was the latest in a line of wealth that had lasted for five generations. His great grandfather had built a fortune in timber back in the late nineteenth century. The two married in October 1958, then moved to Nashville.

Even from her early days of marriage, Ingram made choices that drove her to stand up to opposition. With her rich husband ensconced in the Nashville establishment, Ingram could have spent the majority of her time swimming, golfing, and playing tennis at the local Belle Meade Country Club. She gave birth to four children in five years: Orrin, now thirty-nine; John, now thirty-eight; David, now thirty-seven; and Robin, now thirty-five. But having developed a fondness for the arts while a student at Vassar, she determined that her children would grow up in a society where they could have access to cultural events. In those days, Nashville had little to offer in that arena. Rather than raising four children who would be, as she calls it, "culturally deprived," she tackled the problem.

In 1972, Martha Ingram unearthed her competitive nature and started what would become an eight-year crusade to attract money and legislative support to build the Tennessee Performing Arts Center, or TPAC. She organized a staff of twenty-five and enlisted seventy-five women across the state to lobby local legislators to endorse the cause. She faced stiff opposition, including much skepticism from the head of the state's House Ways and Means Committee, John Bragg, who she says balked at the proposal for a place where Tennesseans could go to take in a play or a concert: "I'm like this country boy whose wife took him to Atlanta to see the ballet," she recalls Bragg telling her. "I said, 'Honey, why are all those girls running around on their toes? If they want those girls to look so tall, why don't they just hire taller girls in the first place?'"

Undaunted, Ingram continued to work toward her goal. Each day for the next two years she traveled the state, made efforts to raise money, and lobbied legislators until the state finally relented. The building was under construction for the following six years before the doors finally opened. "You can see that this project was a hard sell," she said. "I knew it was going to be difficult, but I just kept right on. To me, the big payoff is just watching kids file into the center today, and knowing they would never have had that experience if we hadn't slugged it out for those eight years."

In 1979, after Martha completed raising a $5 million endowment for TPAC, her husband discovered a key asset within his own nuclear family. He noted her diligence in the face of opposition and wanted to put her skills to work at the family business. "Bronson said why don't you come to work for me, because we don't really have any family involved, and if something were to happen to me, you would need to know as much about our company as possible," recalls Ingram. "I decided to come just one day a week. Well, I went one day, and never left."

Martha Ingram was instantly fascinated by the company, a giant distributor of computer components, books, movies, and video games that her husband had built. Instead of manufacturing these items, Ingram acts as a middle man between producer and seller. Bronson's strategy was to enter sleepy industries, such as book distribution, then invest in new technology while buying up tiny wholesalers quickly to bring his company to scale and fend off entry by a powerful rival. The efficiencies her husband incorporated into the business by updating systems enabled Ingram to surpass competitors in customer service and offer speedy, accurate delivery in a capital-intensive industry of minuscule margins. After growing the book division in this manner, he applied the same approach to dominate distribution of computer software and hardware, videocassettes, and video games. In addition, the conglomerate pushes inland river barges and provides auto insurance.

Martha Ingram learned the company's intricacies and did her homework—sitting in on board meetings, touring distribution centers nationwide, chatting with workers—before joining the board in 1981. "I realized right away that there were things I could do for Bronson that he could not do for himself, such as interact with the employees other than the top lieutenants who reported to him," she said. "The company needed me."

Despite serving as director of public affairs, she worked alongside her husband. It was evident to other company directors that she was knowledgeable about all aspects of the business. Besides supervising corporate giving—Ingram donates 2 percent of its pretax profit to charity—she became a link between management and the company's 12,000 employees. She set up a toll-free harassment hotline in her office for personnel who want to talk about their concerns but feel uneasy telling their supervisors. That line still rings at least twice a week. "I knew that I was a part of a team with Bronson. He involved me in all of his decisions," says Ingram. "I definitely shared with my husband the sense of wanting to accomplish whatever we set out to do. And whenever we talked about succession, he always said nobody will look after our resources as well as you will."

OVERCOMING A POWERFUL LEGACY

When Ingram took over the company following Bronson's death in May 1995, just six months after doctors diagnosed him with cancer, she showed courage under fire right from the start. Her first move was to assert herself, and that meant standing up to chief executive officer of Ingram Industries, Linwood (Chip) Lacy, who also ran the company's most vibrant business, Ingram Micro. Micro is the world's largest computer distributor, working for the majority of computer hardware and software manufacturers, such as Compaq, IBM, Microsoft, and Sun Microsystems, as well as e-tailers, resellers, and retailers, including Buy.com, Amazon.com, MicroWarehouse, and CompUSA. By 1995, the unit served as the middle man for 20 percent of all computer products sold in the United States. Lacy was a legend just as Bronson had been. But that didn't prevent Ingram from deciding that she was the best person to run Ingram Industries because she felt she would have her family's best interests at heart.

"After Bronson's death, it was kind of like who's in charge here?" Ingram recalls. "And actually Chip was his heir apparent and quickly made CEO, but I said to Chip and to the board that Bronson told me to make myself chairman. Some people were reluctant, but my stepping in as chairman gave a sense of continuity to people. Doing my best to make what my husband started soar—and making sure there's opportunity for my sons and the other people who devoted their lives to this company is my passion."

Many doubted Ingram could succeed at running the company. But like Darla Moore and Rebecca Mark, Martha Ingram had a will to win and wasn't afraid of taking risks, even if that meant running her husband's company differently than in the past. Bronson had been an industry baron who was loved by his loyal employees and feared for his fiery temper. Respected immensely, he was also known as the "king of global distribution" because of the thriving empire he built, which included many of the most popular products of the Information Age. He had planned to take the conglomerate public upon his retirement. "Bronson did not want to have to deal with analysts and looking from quarter to quarter at his earnings," explains Ingram. "He would have had a hard time spinning off any of them because each business was very much like his family to him."

But that is precisely what she chose to do, along with her family and the board of Ingram Industries. Still reeling from Bronson's death, Martha Ingram and the couple's three sons, who also worked in the business, met with other board members to determine the fate of the company in June 1995. At that meeting, she made some bold and unprecedented choices about the company's structure and the future of Ingram Micro. The rapid expansion of Ingram Micro, the company's largest and fastest-growing unit, was beginning to drain its parent company. Lacy had developed the computer distributor into an $8 billion behemoth in just eleven years. "Micro was growing so fast that it was not going to be too much longer before it started milking all of the lines of credit that we had. Just the operating capital that it was going to take to support its growth was going to make it hard to expand any of our other businesses," says Martha Ingram. "So we decided to alter things."

Martha Ingram's tenacity drove her to take, just three days after his funeral, a bold step her husband did not dare take during his lifetime. While Bronson had avoided the public scrutiny that comes with public ownership, she embraced it. She led her sons out of the room to "huddle" about the future of the family business. After just thirty minutes, they returned. Then Ingram convinced the board to pursue a new plan—spin off Ingram Micro as a public company by selling 20 percent of it in an IPO to fund its growth, while allowing the family to run the rest of the conglomerate as a private business. Jaws dropped as board members outside the family were stunned. Some directors labeled it "Operation U-Turn."[1] "I learned from Bronson how to be decisive, to listen to everybody, but make up your own mind and stick with it," says Ingram. "One board member suggested we take a couple of weeks for the family to decide what to do, but I said, 'No.' We talked about the matter, and I had already made up my mind."

But Martha Ingram would need to marshal even more courage for her next bold gamble. She had another equally daunting problem to face, and that was Lacy himself. He had built Ingram Micro into the leading computer wholesaler in the United States and, in the process, had become one of the most recognizable and respected names in the business. But however famous he had become, he was at once an able and headstrong manager labeled "the Tasmanian Devil" by a trade journal because of his intensity.

Now, three months into the process, as the public offering of Ingram Micro neared, he wanted greater authority than she was willing to cede. Both parties decline to discuss specifics of the negotiations, but Lacy reportedly ordered Martha Ingram to deposit her and her children's holdings, then about 60 percent of the company, in trust to be voted by the management.[2] Rather than give in on something as important to her as family ownership, she refused. Instead, she asked for and received Lacy's resignation in May 1996. Ingram had effectively let go her strongest superstar when she needed him most—something akin to discarding Michael Jordan in the middle of the NBA playoffs. "She combines a soft heart with an iron will," says son Orrin Ingram, now chief executive officer of Ingram Industries. "She pleasantly looks you in the eye and feels your pain, while telling you, 'No.'"

How would Ingram Micro proceed with the IPO? The industry was aghast that Martha had, in effect, removed the chief executive officer of Ingram Micro in the midst of its IPO road show. She remembers that underwriters were concerned that investors would not even want to buy the company's stock without Lacy on board, so much had he become synonymous with its startling success. Employees, too, were concerned about their own jobs, and feared that his departure would dash their hopes of IPO riches.

Even before Lacey announced his decision to his staff, Ingram's first thought was to placate Micro's employees. She wanted to communicate face-to-face with associates to reassure them that their jobs were secure, and that the change would be an advantage, not a disadvantage, for Ingram Micro. Ingram immediately boarded a plane to Santa Ana, California, where the company is based, and gathered the troops around her. "I can still remember flying to California and standing before an assembled crowd of hundreds who had no idea why they were there," she says. "I told them that Chip Lacy had just resigned. The gasps were audible, but I said, 'Trust me, we will have another leader here just as soon as we can.' I think I basically reassured people that the company would go on and their jobs were secure. I committed to them . . . which at that point was all part of being a good communicator."

Martha Ingram was determined to choose a strong candidate to prove the virtue of her audacious decision. As soon as she sensed trouble—several weeks before Lacy left and she visited Santa Ana—she trusted her own instincts and hired a headhunter to seek his replacement. She had already begun to sift through résumés. By August, she had hired Jerre Stead, former chief executive officer of AT&T Global Information Systems. Stead had the international business experience and leadership skills Ingram sought to lead the company to greater global dominance. Stead even agreed to a pay package that did not include a salary or a bonus. Instead, his pay rested entirely on stock options, tying his compensation directly to the fortunes of Ingram stock. In 1999, the firm ranked number thirty among the 100 largest U.S. multinationals in *Forbes*. The Ingram family retains about 84 percent of the voting power in the company, and 48 percent of its stock.

Ingram's intuition about Stead proved to be correct, and her actions showed that she was firmly in charge of the business. Her courage under fire buoyed the company through an important transition period. The IPO proceeded on schedule that November, selling 20 million shares of stock and raising $360 million. Stead's intense focus on servicing customers led to strong sales and profit gains. The price at the IPO was $18, and the stock rose to $54 under his leadership. In 1998, the company earned $245 million on revenues that grew 52 percent over the prior year to $22 billion. Stead more than doubled sales at the unit, and made Ingram Micro the world's leading distributor of computer hardware and software. The company's success validated her actions, and she even mended fences with Chip Lacy so that he has remained on Ingram Industries' board of directors. She says he offers creative ideas in that capacity, and is one of the company's best directors.

Today, Ingram faces new challenges with her computer distribution business. Stead guided the company to a height of profitability before an industrywide price war hurt the business.[3] Recently, Ingram Micro and other computer distributors have suffered from eroding profit margins, in the face of tough competition from Dell and manufacturers shipping directly to customers who purchased machines on the Internet. Stead resigned, and Martha Ingram tapped former GTE Corporation president Kent Foster as CEO for the unit; she is hopeful about Micro's prospects. After all, the company reported revenues of $28 billion in 1999, and ranked forty-one among *Fortune*'s top fifty U.S. companies, a fourteen-point jump over 1998's ranking of fifty-five.

LOOKING OUT FOR THE FAMILY INTEREST

Ingram also took a third bold step, the goal of which was to keep peace in her family. David, the youngest of her three sons in the business, wanted his independence. Since 1994, he had been president of Ingram Entertainment, the video distribution portion of Ingram that was the smallest of the five companies in the family empire. Rather than compete with his brothers for resources, he felt he needed to buy the business outright and go it alone. Because her three boys were all competitive with one another, she wanted to make sure they would not butt heads while working together. When David suggested the idea, she and his two older brothers immediately agreed. In 1997, she decided to let him buy control of Ingram Entertainment in exchange for his entire 8.5 percent stake in Ingram Industries.

"My mother filled a big void after my father died, and she's kept the family coming over for Sunday night dinner ever since," son Orrin explains. "I can't stress how rare that is for large family businesses like ours. She is really good at stopping problems before they turn into battles by getting people to give a little to get a lot. My dad trained her on that because he had very little give. She was well practiced in getting him to come around."

But Ingram, like Shelly Lazarus and Orit Gadiesh, was making a counterintuitive move. She opted for a choice that would disadvantage both the book and entertainment units to quell dissension in the family. The two divisions could not operate as efficiently separately as they could jointly, and individually they would lack power in negotiating with Internet customers like Amazon.com, huge content providers including Walt Disney, and massive retailers such as Barnes & Noble.

Even in the face of this information, Ingram made the choice to follow her instincts, which has preserved harmony in her family and turned out to be a smart move. Ingram Book Group is the nation's largest book distributor with nearly $2 billion in revenue in 1998, and Ingram Entertainment is the country's biggest distributor of movie video rentals, DVD hardware and software, video games, and CD-ROMs, with 1998 revenues of $1 billion.

"Of course, I could have been wrong," she says. "But we have seen so many families that have had terrible acrimony as a result of family members working in a family business, even Bronson and his own brother. I did not want to see that happen to our three boys. The advantage of having these different lines of business is that at some point, we can break the company into pieces if our sons decide to stay, and hopefully avoid the kind of family clashes we have all seen. It's important to be flexible, and do what seems to be right."

NO ORDINARY SOUTHERN BELLE

Martha Ingram's devotion to family was instilled at an early age. She treasured her relationship with her own father, and he helped prime her for business. She grew up in Charleston, South Carolina. Her father owned a radio broadcasting company, and in 1953 built the first television station in South Carolina. The eldest of three children, she was long awaited. "I came after they had been married for six years, and wanted children for most of that period," she says. "I always felt very cherished growing up. They reassured me from birth that I was special. I never even remember being punished. They were very supportive and nurturing."

Her mother and father also placed a lot of responsibility on her shoulders. Because her father lived through the Depression as a young adult, he feared that misfortune could strike again at any time. "Although I grew up in a very privileged home, there was always a specter hanging over us. My father said if something should happen, that if the world should fall apart again or if he should lose his health, I would be the one who would have to look after the family. With that in mind, he talked business with me and wanted me to understand his business," she recalls. "My father never said anything to me about being a woman or how odd it would be in the business world."

Martha Ingram's parents encouraged her to seek out the finest education so she could take over the family business if necessary. Every time she got an A in school, she got a quarter from her parents. She made the honor roll regularly. "It was never a question of whether you were going to do something or not, but how good you could be at it and how far you could take yourself," she adds. "My father said that with a good education I would never have to be dependent on anybody else. I would be able to row my own boat. I was always afraid that I would not live up to all their expectations."

Despite her concerns, young Martha Ingram set lofty goals and met them. In high school, she aspired to go to the college she considered the best in the country—Vassar. She was accepted, and went on to earn a B.A. in history. "Vassar really opened my eyes to the world, and I guess, more importantly, really taught me how to learn," she says. "[It also] built my confidence because it was so difficult. Although I went to a girls' prep school, it was not as fine as some of the Eastern preparatory schools and it took me a while to understand what was expected. It was sort of like if you could survive Vassar, you could survive anywhere. There were so many bright young women there."

Early on, Ingram showed courage under fire. Before going off to college, she got engaged to a cadet from the Citadel, the fabled military school in Charleston. But six weeks before the big day she decided to call off the June wedding. "I just remember being so thrilled with what I was learning at Vassar that I just did not want to leave that environment to be married to anyone," she remembers. "It was then that I realized that I no longer had to do everything to accommodate somebody else, but I had to be sure that I was accommodating me."

After college, Ingram again showed professional bravery, this time in her first job. She came to work for her father as his assistant at his radio and television station. Even there she found ways to go out on a limb, and make the most of the opportunity. She quickly learned how to read a balance sheet and a profit-and-loss statement, but hungered for more responsibility. "I literally learned at my father's knee everything he could teach me about business, but in all honesty, he was having all the fun and I was doing all the [grunt work]," recalls Ingram. "So I asked him if I could take over the FM station from 7 to 11 P.M. in the evenings and have a classical music radio show. I lowered my voice and changed my name to 'Elizabeth Crawford' because I didn't want to be my father's little darling daughter running around on the air. And I wrote the programs, then sold the ads. It was like running a small business, and I learned that I liked creating something of my own, especially after I was told that it was probably not going to work."

RESPECT FOR ASSOCIATES

Later in life she would move well beyond small business. Through her sixteen years of experience at Ingram Industries, Martha Ingram learned how to run a huge concern. One of her top priorities throughout has been her employees, whom she calls associates. In today's tight labor market, rewarding personnel is a key aspect of the company chief's job. She has always followed the golden rule: "I believe that if we treat people well, they will treat the company well," says Ingram. "And once you get large, there is no way that you can see everything, so you hope to establish a company culture that encourages people to do the right thing."

Ingram showed courage under fire once again when she followed through on a verbal pledge to give employees stock options at a strike price of just $7 for Ingram Micro shares. This time, her sons and her advisers disagreed with her. Although management expected the IPO price to be $10 or $12, it had shot up to $18. They argued that because the stock price was going up so much higher than anticipated, the options should reflect that change. In another bold stance, Ingram followed her gut. Now 200 staffers both at Ingram Micro and Ingram Industries, including her secretary, are option millionaires as a result.

"Keeping those options at such a low price was the loneliest decision I ever had to make because everyone on the board opposed me on that issue," she recalls. "There was every justification for raising that price, but I just felt we had a moral obligation to do what we'd originally said we were going to do. Just because the markets were hungrier for our kind of stock than we thought originally, there was no reason to deprive the people who really made the company so valuable. Then after Chip Lacy left, our competitors tried to pick our people off, and nobody left. The decision to leave those options at that price was one of the reasons."

Ingram's respect for employees permeates her management style. While she focuses on providing the vision to lead the company, she trusts her top managers to handle daily tasks, and gives them the autonomy they need to take risks. Most say her son, David, would not have been able to split off Ingram Entertainment if his father had been the one in charge of the family empire. But Martha Ingram has a hands-off management style that she believes helps her attract and develop stronger management talent. "I'm able to turn things over to others, and I don't like to check up on people," she says. "I want to trust them to do the right thing, but if they have a problem I want to hear about it before anyone else does. Our family has always believed in surrounding ourselves with the best people."

A WOMAN'S TOUCH

The courage under fire that Martha Ingram has shown in her leadership of Ingram Industries has helped her excel in a field—distribution—where women are virtually nonexistent. Her passion for protecting her family has often driven her bold actions. "I'm often asked how do I manage in a male-dominated world," she says. "But I look at it as an advantage because I never felt diminished because I was a woman. My husband used to say, 'You could do anything I can do if you had not taken the time off to have the children.'" Now she's proving him right.

WHY SHOULD MEN HAVE ALL THE FUN

As with Martha Ingram, the deck seemed stacked against Loida Lewis, a native of the Philippines. In 1993, her husband, Reginald Lewis, who had been one of the most successful African-American businessmen in U.S. history,[4] died suddenly of brain cancer. And his once illustrious nearly $2 billion food conglomerate, TLC Beatrice International Holdings, was struggling. With debt piling up and profits sagging, the private company that *Time* magazine had labeled America's largest minority-owned enterprise was in trouble. With no business experience to speak of, and a pack of sharklike shareholders circling, Lewis hardly seemed the ideal candidate to whip TLC into shape in a male-dominated industry. What's more, she was not even on her husband's radar screen for the job.

But thanks to her courage under fire, Lewis was able to achieve something her legendary husband had not accomplished. Now fifty-six, she withstood opposition and engineered the turnaround of this failing global food manufacturer, distributor, and retailer, added value to underperforming assets, then sold them at a premium. Like Martha Ingram, she showed determination and grit to trust her instincts in the face of resistance to carry out her goals for the company. "I always wanted to be number one and just excel," she says with a grin. "My husband wrote the book *Why Should White Guys Have All the Fun*, but I believe this: Why should guys have all the fun?"

TAKING CHARGE

Like Ingram, Lewis had to affirm that she was the one in charge of the company after her husband's death. Someone had to take action to help the deeply troubled $1.7 billion (1993 revenues) company that was saddled with cash flow problems and debt. Deep recession in Europe, where the company's food operations were based, was hurting its sales. Profits under her spouse's leadership had been erratic, and had plunged more than 50 percent in both 1990 and 1992. And Reginald Lewis's pay was at issue. Despite the company's poor performance in 1992, he had received more than $40 million in salary and compensation that year alone. A prominent shareholder, Carlton Investments, which held 22 percent of TLC Beatrice, filed a lawsuit in May 1994 asserting that his compensation was "in flagrant violation" of the stockholders' agreement. To make matters worse, Reginald Lewis had chosen a successor who was hardly up to the task—his half brother, Jean Fuggett, Jr. A former National Football League player for the Washington Redskins and the Dallas Cowboys, Fuggett responded to the company's distress by trying to make an unrelated acquisition. In 1993, he attempted to buy the Baltimore

Orioles baseball team, but when he opened TLC's books in an effort to hold a bond offering to finance the purchase, investors found out that the company was losing money.

Lewis marshaled her courage under fire to unseat her husband's handpicked successor in the face of opposition. While minority shareholders of the company searched for a high-profile executive to succeed Fuggett, Loida Lewis made herself chairman in January 1994. To the further amazement of shareholders, she took on the additional role of chief executive officer six months later. Whether Fuggett left voluntarily or not, she won't say: "I told him, 'Jean, I'm ready now,'" she says. "And that was it."

Like Martha Ingram, Loida Lewis was determined to protect her family's interests, and that goal powered her career ambitions. She and her daughters, Leslie and Christina, owned 51 percent of the business. "Here is the company that he left us," she says. "Am I going to rely on someone else to take care of the company, and then, if it fails, have no one to blame but myself? I was ready to take over."

But shareholders outside of the family were not ready for Loida Lewis. Members of Carlton Investments and other prominent stakeholders were skeptical about her lack of business skills and experience. They feared that this woman, who liked to hug employees and start board meetings with a prayer, was out of her depth in managing a company in the midst of a financial crisis. The lawsuit from Carlton Investments, which originally included Michael Milken and other former investment bankers from Drexel Burnham Lambert who were involved in her husband's initial buyout of TLC Beatrice, added to her woes. Carlton sought $22 million, but she settled the suit in 1997 for a reported $15 million. "They were trying to pressure me to follow what they wanted for their exit strategy," she says. "We have tried several times to come to common ground, but it was always no go."

DRIVING A TURNAROUND

Undaunted, she grabbed the reins of power, and again showed her resolve in the face of opponents. To get the company out of the red, she slashed costs. She immediately distinguished herself from her husband, who was renowned for his extravagance. He was particularly proud of his multimillion-dollar corporate jet, a Challenger, which was custom-built to his specifications and emblazoned with his initials on its tail. Among the first of her decisions was to sell her husband's beloved airplane and the company's two limousines. She also cut staff from 5,000 to 4,500, and got rid of several underperforming subsidiaries, hired a new chief financial officer, halved the number of employees at its New York headquarters from forty to twenty, and pared down the corporate offices. She relocated from his sprawling 4,000-square-foot, forty-eighth-floor office suite to sparse headquarters that were one-third the size on the thirty-ninth floor of the same building. While her husband took in breathtaking views of Central Park from his window that stretched from floor to ceiling, her view of the park is mostly obscured by a forest of midtown skyscrapers. Her efforts helped her cut the company's administrative overhead in half in fiscal 1995. "My goal has always been to create value for shareholders and that includes the Lewis family," she says of her new role. "Having gone through the fire of Reginald's death, I had great confidence to tackle whatever came my way in business."

After taking the helm, Loida Lewis brought in good financial results for the company. She raked in $11.3 million in net profits on revenues of $1.9 billion during her first fiscal year, 1994. That was up from net profits of $1 million in 1993, and a loss of $16.6 million in 1992. Lewis continued to drive growth over the next two years, and reached profits of $59 million on sales of $2.2 billion in 1996. *BusinessWeek* magazine selected her as a "manager to watch in 1995," and she ranked first on *Working Woman* magazine's list of the top fifty female business owners that year. "My husband was trying to disprove the lie that a person of color cannot make it in this country," she says. "I am finishing his work."

But one of her most important choices that tested Lewis's courage even further and defined her leadership was yet to come. She had to overcome her husband's legacy. By engineering a $985 million LBO to form TLC Beatrice in 1987, Reginald Lewis became one of the wealthiest African Americans in the country, and earned accolades for breaking the color barrier of high finance. He was a consummate deal maker, worth $400 million according to *Forbes* just before his death,[5] who was always on the lookout for new and larger acquisitions. But Loida Lewis wanted to focus on running a company rather than looking for new investments.

So she opted to close down TLC Capital, the unit her husband had established to pursue potential takeover targets. She remembers that Fred Grant, a close friend of her husband's who ran TLC Capital, was constantly badgering her about her decisions, saying, "Reg would not do it this way."

Weary of his criticisms, she fired not only Grant but his entire department. "My husband set up TLC Capital to go out looking for deals, but TLC Beatrice was a big project that required my full attention," explains Loida Lewis. "I know my talents and my own capabilities, and it just was not logical for me to go looking for businesses to buy and sell."

Like eBay chief executive Meg Whitman, she also reinvented the rules at her company by shedding its former acquisition-oriented focus, and concentrating instead on TLC Beatrice's own future. Her efforts to hire, fire, and restructure the company set the business on a solid foundation. She essentially saved her husband's creation and her family fortune. *Forbes* magazine even dubbed her "a better manager than her flamboyant husband was."

"My husband and I are two different people," she explains. "I cannot be him. A colleague of mine who had introduced me to Mr. Lewis long ago told me, 'It's your rocket ship and you have to fly it now, Loida.' That really freed me to just be myself, and I realized that I didn't have to follow the way he wanted it run."

PROVING THEM WRONG

Lewis is a proven winner, but her style is understated. Slim and petite, she wears a simple navy blue Chanel suit, with a strand of pearls around her neck, matching pearl earrings, and a diamond engagement ring. The walls in her office are plain white and adorned with family photographs and a picture of her husband's pride and joy—the Challenger corporate jet that she sold. She points to a picture frame on her wall that is one of her most prized possessions. It holds nine $10 bills—her spoils from bets she has won against associates who doubted her since she began running the company in 1994. "This one is for a lower lease I negotiated," she explains, pointing to one of the bills. "This is for the sale of the airplane. They all second-guessed me, but I hardly ever lose a bet."

CHARTING A COURSE OF HER OWN

Like Shelly Lazarus and Marilyn Carlson Nelson of Carlson Companies, Lewis was adept at collaborating with her employees to get results. Although she made tough choices on her own to cut costs, she worked closely with employees and motivated them to help the company rebound. She took a different approach with personnel than her husband, who was renowned for having a vitriolic temper and issuing orders. Her ability to speak five languages, including French, Spanish, English, Tagalog, and Chinese, was an asset at her global business with the majority of its operations located in France. She traveled to Europe to meet managers on their home turf at least twice a year. She earned a reputation for asking insightful questions and then listening closely to answers in those meetings. She used this opportunity to set performance goals jointly with those individuals, and would then hold them accountable to those standards. She also took the time to walk the factory floors with managers in TLC Beatrice subsidiaries across the continent to greet employees and let them know she was interested in their various businesses. "It's not like I am here with a scepter and throne, and I bang the gong and that's it," she says. "Invariably [employees] rise to the level you expect from them, if you respect them as human beings."

Unlike her husband, Lewis took the important step of extending stock options to all her managers, and linking them to profit levels. Only in 1991, two years before he died, did Reginald give some options to board members and a few senior executives, but he did not link them to performance. She even offered a limited edition BMW to the manager who achieved the best results. She also tied year-end bonuses to performance of managers, and laid these out for employees at the start of each year so there were no surprises. Lewis made things clear: If managers did not meet their performance goals, she would have to replace them. But rather than motivating employees through fear as her husband did, she gave employees positive incentives to perform well. "My managers have almost full authority, as long as they produce results. They are the experts. That's why I hired them," she explains. "My husband had a strong temper that was like a whiplash. Fear was a main motivation for employees. I am finishing my husband's work, not following in his footsteps. For one thing, my feet are not a size thirteen!"

LESSONS FROM A FAMILY BUSINESS

Loida Lewis picked up lessons as a child that would later help her in her efforts to fill her husband's big shoes. Like Martha Ingram, she was intrigued by her father's business. He was an entrepreneur who founded a furniture company, Nicfur, in 1937. He made Nicfur one of the largest furniture retail chains in the Philippines. Her mother was a pharmacist who owned a drugstore in the small, affluent town in southern Luzon where the family lived. Watching both her mother and father working in business helped Loida develop an appreciation for entrepreneurs. "My mother would be very harsh and perfunctory in dealing with people, but my father was more humane and compassionate," she explains. "People wanted to work harder for him."

From the tender age of three, she recalls being interested in deals and paying attention to how they were made. Apart from his ability to work with others, her father was a shrewd negotiator, and she noted his methods. "With my father, we ate 'deals' for breakfast," she recalls. "First thing in the morning, he would go out to the beach and confront all the fishermen bringing in their catch. It was just fun to watch him haggle over fish. He always got a great price. I learned early on, you make deals."

Like many other new paradigm leaders, Loida Lewis had a close bond with her father, and she credits him with helping her build the self-confidence she needed to achieve. He had high hopes for his daughter's future, and often talked with her about what she needed to do to be successful. He counseled her that working hard, setting lofty aspirations, and being determined not to fail were the vital tools for success. She was also devoted to the Catholic faith her family followed. The third of four children in her family, she had two older brothers who worked for their father's company. "My father saw a little bit of himself in me and wanted his dreams to be realized in me," remembers Lewis. "He wanted to be a lawyer, but he needed to make money so he went into business. Being a lawyer was his ambition for me. There was never, 'Oh, you're a girl, you can't do that.' My sister and I exceeded our brothers. He would always tell me, 'You can do anything you want, even become a governor.' He wanted me to have big dreams and rise higher."

Fueled in part by her father's aspirations, Loida Lewis was determined to build a career of her own. She went to a Catholic college in Manila, then earned a law degree from the University of the Philippines. After she passed the bar examination in her home country, her father gave her a round-the-world trip as a graduation present. It was while visiting New York that she met Reginald Lewis on a blind date in 1968. The couple married nine months later in Manila. After settling in Manhattan, she passed the notoriously difficult New York bar exam on the first try without ever attending an American law school, and became an attorney in the city. She specialized in immigration law, and in 1972 began publishing a monthly magazine for the Filipino-American community. The magazine featured articles about the ways in which former president Ferdinand Marcos was violating the human rights of Filipinos.

Like Martha Ingram, Loida Lewis took time out to focus on her marriage and children. She has two daughters, and spent a lot of time at home with them when the two were very young. But her career beckoned. In 1974, she applied for a job in the New York office of the Immigration and Naturalization Service. She was turned down. Later she discovered that her qualifications surpassed those of the applicants hired, and sued the agency. In 1979, she won a discrimination suit against the Immigration and Naturalization Service. They not only gave her a job, but added five years' back pay for the time she had missed. She stayed on for the next eleven years, until 1990. During that period, she wrote three books on immigration law, including *How to Get a Green Card.* At the same time, she was her husband's sounding board, advising him throughout his career. She picked up a great deal about his businesses dealings in the process. Growing up in an entrepreneurial family also primed her for a career in business, yet her husband never considered her successor material when he got sick. "That was never even discussed," she says. "I was always his wife."

GOING OUT ON TOP

Although her husband hadn't chosen her as his replacement, Loida Lewis's courage under fire helped her take on that role and achieve his ultimate goal—selling TLC assets at a premium. By the close of 1996, the company was at its peak in terms of revenues and profits, but Lewis had no clear successor in the family. Her elder daughter, Leslie, twenty-five, was a member of the board of directors, but was pursuing an acting career. Her other daughter, Christina, eighteen, hoped to become a doctor. Neither daughter wanted to run the business. A change in French laws to limit the size of future grocery stores and consolidation in the industry were other potent factors driving her motivation to sell.

Rather than rushing to unload assets to placate company investors who were hungry for quick returns, Loida developed and grew the various businesses so that she could obtain higher prices when she chose to put these components on the market. In one of the largest transactions ever in the French food sector, she sold its food distribution business to Groupe Casino for a generous $576 million in 1997. "The French supermarket multiple was double [that of] the United States," says Lewis, when explaining the lure of the deal. Lewis continued to dismantle the company. A year later, she divested the company's interests in its European beverage group for $44 million, and in 1999, she dealt its stake in a Spanish ice cream business for $191 million.

Lewis's courage under fire paved her way, and she cashed out at the height of her success. "I kid the men I know who run companies that they keep it all to themselves," she says. "But it's fun to run a business and very challenging. There's a problem, you solve it. You set goals, and you meet them. But there is so much satisfaction when you meet those goals, not to mention the material reward. I tell my daughter, 'You want to be an actress? That's great. But why not run the movie company?'"

9

CONCLUSION: APPLYING THE LESSONS OF NEW PARADIGM LEADERSHIP

Once upon a time power was in patriarchy, a key motivator. It created great profits and efficient systems. The subordination of women made for success. Now the opposite is true.

— HARRIET RUBIN, AUTHOR OF *THE PRINCESSA* AND *SOLOING*

Running America's biggest companies used to be an all-male activity. Some captains of industry rode to power as scions of the nation's first families, who studied at prestigious universities like Princeton, Harvard, and Yale. Others, like Henry Ford, Ray Kroc, and Jack Welch, made it into hallowed senior executive suites because of their revolutionary ideas. In the past, such leaders could command others simply by the power of their bold convictions and their forceful personalities.

But something happened after a few women actually managed to break into the management clubhouse and get a crack at running things. Outsiders to corporate power, female executives began to lead from the ground up—strengthening their businesses by strengthening those around them. And people started noticing that once in the club, these women could get things done. Slowly, more and more women are actually being tapped to come on inside.

Not only are these women rewriting the rules, but the old rules are changing for men, too. In the Information Age, the rules call for leaders who develop teams and partners, rather than those who command decisions and wield absolute authority. Mindful of the new business regime, the fourteen female business leaders profiled in this book have achieved striking success. In fact, the seven common traits these women display present a new paradigm of leadership for the new millennium. To navigate today's knowledge economy, business leaders, whether male or female, increasingly need to pack the skills they exhibit: the ability to sell a vision; a readiness to reinvent the rules; a laser focus to achieve; an accent on maximizing high touch in an era of high tech; a knack for turning challenge into opportunity; an obsession with customer preferences; and the capacity to show courage under fire. Without these traits, leaders will at best find that the companies they run will fall out of step with the competition. At worst, executives lacking these skills will be lining up for an unemployment check.

This transformation does not necessarily mean that the number of women in top management slots will spike in the next few years as new paradigm leadership gains currency. Male leaders are quickly catching on that their professional survival increasingly depends on developing such skills. But it does mean that in the new economy, women will help define how companies are run. New paradigm leaders will continue to set the standard for how to lead a business so that it will thrive in a market characterized by fierce competition around the globe as well as a battle for the ever-fickle hearts and minds of the modern consumer.

The women on these pages have a lot going for them, not least of which is the fact that gender-based characteristics for which they were once ridiculed—a penchant for collaboration and fostering relationships—have become clear advantages at the office. With a distinct sense of the goals they want to accomplish, they overcame daunting obstacles and punishing odds to excel, and to inspire those around them to achieve as well. They found opportunity where others saw a conventional dead end. And they are not the only ones.

Women are setting the pace for new leadership. Just look at Carly Fiorina. As chief executive officer of Hewlett-Packard, she is one of the most prominent new paradigm leaders today, and is at the forefront of change. She is relying on her ability to sell a vision to invigorate this venerable Dow 30 company, and reposition the firm as a player in the Internet age. Her challenge is to communicate a new strategy for the company that will revamp its staid image and ignite the inventiveness among its employees that helped make the company the world's second-largest producer of computers. The skills she offers—her marketing savvy and salesmanship, along with her abilities to form bonds with customers, strike a chord with consumers, and rally employees—come at a premium. Not only did she win the position over 100 candidates, but she commands a hefty salary of close to $100 million.

HP's search committee selected Fiorina because of her strong record at Lucent Technologies, where her new paradigm skills helped her excel. She sold a vision of the company that resonated with investors, and enabled her to lead a highly successful spin-off of Lucent in 1996. Then she launched a bold $90 million marketing campaign where she again sold a vision that attracted customers by recasting the company image from a stodgy maker of phone equipment into an Internet force supplying tools for the new economy. And in 1998, she helped boost innovation by Bell Labs employees to make her global service-provider business a $20 billion enterprise, contributing 60 percent of the company revenues.

The first outsider to run the Silicon Valley institution in its more than sixty-year history, Fiorina, forty-five, is now selling a new vision for HP by acting as the company's chief salesperson. What she's pitching are HP's "e-services" in an effort to become a strong Internet player. She is reorganizing management around this theme to draw better results from colleagues and generate value for investors. Fiorina is also working to win new customers for her company in one of its most critical markets—servers that run networks of computers, phone systems, on-line shopping sites, Internet search services, and corporate databases. HP used to lead that business between 1996 and 1998, but fell behind Sun Microsystems.[1] Huge companies from retailer Wal-Mart Stores, Inc., to on-line department store Amazon.com are buying servers in vast quantities, and she is making her pitch. She recently won over Amazon, which bought twenty HP servers. And she is working to capture eBay's business. She is also searching for the next Amazon in the hopes of selling it servers, too.

Despite the spotlight placed on the fourteen women in this book, it is obvious that these are hardly the only new paradigm leaders filling executive suites these days. Actually, such leaders are present in virtually every industry, and fresh ones are coming to the fore all the time.

ONES TO WATCH

Other up-and-coming executives who possess new paradigm skills abound. Consider Jenny Ming, president of Gap, Inc.'s Old Navy chain. Like Patricia Fili-Krushel and Kim Polese, her obsession with customer preferences has helped Ming improve her results and distinguishes her from rivals in her industry. Her knowledge of customers enabled her to make the Gap's budget-priced chain one of the fastest-growing retailers in the country just five years after Old Navy was launched. She has struck a chord with discount shoppers of all ages, particularly teens. Her trick? Offering casual jeans, khakis, T-shirts, striped knits, and dresses that play well with the urban chic but are not so fashionista as to scare away the mall shoppers of Peoria. With only 16 percent of the company's total stores, Old Navy is expected to account for 35 percent of Gap's projected overall sales of $11.5 billion in 1999.[2] In 2000, *BusinessWeek* rated her one of the twenty-five top managers of the year.

Ming, forty-four, has displayed a finely honed ability for predicting hot clothing trends that will appeal to a broad base of consumers, then has taken big production risks to lay out the huge quantities necessary to supply her chain with a potent string of merchandise hits. She picks up many of her fashion ideas from her three teenage children, and flips through the pages of *Seventeen* magazine with them to search out trends. She keeps up on the latest from American designers like Ralph Lauren and Tom Ford as well. Like many retailers, she also hits the streets of London and Paris for clues on where American fashion may be headed next. Cafes, clubs, and other student hangouts—Ming checks them all out to see what the kids are wearing. She leans as well on her New York–based design staff of eighty-five people, who are also searching for up-and-coming looks. Her intuition for fleece tops and vests, and cargo pants with monster-sized pockets, have been particular standout successes that have helped drive her chain's growth. She opened 135 new Old Navy stores in 1999, taking the total to over 500 across the nation.

A native of Macao, the formerly Portuguese colony near Hong Kong that recently reverted to Chinese rule, Ming has exhibited a will to achieve that helped her rise from a modest upbringing. She came to America when she was nine and grew up in San Francisco's North Beach neighborhood as the middle child of five. When she was a teen, she worked on weekends as a bank teller, a salesclerk at Macy's, and her favorite job—a seamstress. She went on to attend San Jose State University and earned a degree in home economics. After college, she worked at Dayton Hudson Corporation's Mervyn's unit. She rose from a management trainee at the retailer to become a buyer in linens and junior sportswear. In 1986, she was recruited by Gap's chief executive officer, Millard (Mickey) Drexler, to become a buyer at his company. After three years, he promoted her to a vice presidentship of Gap, Inc., then he selected her to help launch Old Navy in 1994. She led its merchandising division for four years before being elevated to president of the unit in April 1999.

Ming's ability to determine what customers want and will buy has spurred her sprint up the corporate ladder at Old Navy. To stay close to consumers, she routinely travels across the country to check out shoppers at various store locations. Thanks in part to her leadership, the stores have a current and eye-catching look. Bouncy pop music blares from the speakers, sale "Items of the Week" are marked by flashing signs, and a toy version of Magic the dog, the chain's mascot, rides in a prominently displayed 1950s pickup truck. On a visit to Staten Island, New York, Ming spied a man in his mid-forties buying three pairs of cargo pants. In a sign of her dead-on intuition, Ming reasoned that if this forty-something guy was gaga for cargoes, the trend would spread well beyond the teenage crowd. She packed her stores with cargo pants up to the ceiling. Needless to say, those pants flew out of Old Navy. Ming is well positioned to become CEO of a big retailer, perhaps even Gap, Inc. someday.

Another new paradigm leader making some waves is Ann Fudge, the forty-eight-year-old executive vice president of Kraft Foods, Inc., and president of its Maxwell House Coffee and Post Cereals divisions. Like Shelly Lazarus and Marilyn Carlson Nelson, Fudge maximizes high touch in an era of high tech. Her skill in working with associates and relating to customers in a way that puts the accent on personal interaction gives her an edge and separates her from the pack. Her ability to connect with employees has helped her become an innovative force at Kraft, the nation's largest food company, and has made her a strong candidate to become chief executive officer of a leading company.

When she took over Maxwell House Coffee company in 1994, the mature company was losing market share and struggling to wake up in the morning.[3] Her first move was to ask workers at all levels for their ideas on how to revamp the product. In her words, she "unleashed the talent" at her company, then drew on those new concepts to revive the flagging business and increase market share. Conventional wisdom at the time held that price alone sold coffee, and to increase volume, a company needed to offer coupons and discounts. Instead, Fudge aimed at creating brand awareness through advertising. Refusing to cave in to naysayers, she showed courage under fire and forged ahead. Her approach paid off, and she improved market share dramatically. "We updated the old, 'good to the last drop' campaign into, 'Make every day good to the last drop' to attract a whole new group of young consumers," she recalls. "I thought it was the right thing to do."

A native of Washington, D.C., Fudge was determined from an early age to excel. She thrived in the middle-class neighborhood where she grew up, and turned challenge into opportunity as a young African-American woman. The elder of two children, she did well in school. After attending a Catholic all-girls private school, she earned strong academic credentials including a bachelor's degree from Simmons College in 1973, and an MBA from Harvard in 1977. To reach her current job, she had to shatter not merely a proverbial glass ceiling that stymies numerous white women, but a virtual "concrete wall" that prevents many women of color from reaching the top echelons of leading companies. Now she is on the corporate boards of Allied Signal and Liz Claiborne.

Fudge has been credited with invigorating a dreary division by developing premium coffees to compete with Starbucks, and introducing Honey Nut Cheerios. When she hires people from top business schools, she looks for dedication, motivation, and an ability to work as a team player. She makes it a priority to keep employees at her Rye Brook, New York–based company involved by delegating tasks and requesting input. Most of all, she is always asking colleagues for their thoughts. She invented a "Blue Sky Room" where employees can brainstorm and an awards program to reward new ideas. To encourage new approaches, Fudge has established problem-solving meetings including numerous employees from secretaries to technology experts. She likes to throw out counterintuitive concepts just to see where they go. After Meg Whitman of eBay purchased art auctioneer Butterfield & Butterfield, Fudge asked staffers to devise a hypothetical marketing plan for a Kraft product that would be sold only on the Internet. Of course, that is highly unlikely for a bricks-and-mortar player like Kraft, but she used the exercise to encourage employees to think creatively. That's how Fudge initiated special seasonal items like Maxwell House Holiday Roast, for instance, and another novel idea taking up shelf space at grocery stores, "mix your own" cereal that lets kids mix and match from an array of Post items to create their own breakfast.

Another white-hot new paradigm leader on the front lines is Judith Estrin. One of America's most successful entrepreneurs, she has already launched three successful software start-ups by the age of forty-five. Like Meg Whitman and Marcy Carsey, she is reinventing the rules in her current role as senior vice president and chief technology officer of Cisco Systems, Inc., the world's top maker of computer networking equipment and a key player in the Internet gold rush. Estrin's résumé qualified her for *Forbes*'s list of "leading women" of Silicon Valley in 1996.[4]

A bold innovator, she is reinventing the rules by blending technical skill with the ability to run a business—a rare combination in the fast-paced field of information technology. Estrin's stellar credentials stand out and illustrate her ability to rewrite the rules in technology. The middle child of three daughters, Estrin is a Stanford graduate who earned master's degrees in both electrical engineering and computer science. She is also married and a mother of one child. She was just twenty-six when she and her husband, William Carrico, founded the first of her three start-ups, Bridge Communications, in 1981. The company merged with 3Com in 1987 for stock worth $235 million. Next she launched Network Computing Devices in 1988, and took it public four years later. By the time she left the business in 1994, Network Computing Devices had achieved revenues of $144 million. In 1998, she sold Precept Software, a multimedia company she kicked off in 1995, to Cisco for $84 million.

Rather than departing for a new start-up, Estrin was part of the package.

At Cisco, she is depending on her independent and entrepreneurial savvy to oversee a $1 billion R&D budget and a bold acquisitions strategy. She is helping Cisco expand its computer networking business into telephone networks at a rapid pace. A company that makes routers and switches that allow computers to talk to one another, Cisco is trying to move from the Internet into the related business of directing voice and data traffic over the world's telephone networks, where Lucent Technologies and Nortel Networks are already powerful players.

Whether she launches a new start-up or stays with Cisco, Estrin will be renowned for forming close relationships with customers to help her develop ideas for innovations and new companies. As a sign of her power in the field and professional acumen, she sits on the boards of Sun Microsystems, Walt Disney, and Federal Express. Estrin clearly has an ability to sell a vision. She has won over investors to help her launch three new companies already. With Cisco experience, she is only enhancing her management skills, and proves that you don't have to start at a big business to make a splash at a leading company.

TIPS ON BECOMING A NEW PARADIGM LEADER

For young women who are starting out in business, or the millions of working women currently employed but aspiring to be great leaders themselves, it's difficult to find advice one can actually use. Here are ten tips to become a new paradigm leader in your own right:

1: *Be confident and take risks.*

To get noticed by the powers that be, young executives need to be confident and to take risks. Try something unexpected, like a challenging offbeat assignment, or a route that others believe to be a dead end. Have faith that your ideas can help you overcome obstacles that might deter colleagues. It's important to stand out by taking a back route just like Darla Moore, who made a name for herself in the dreary world of bankruptcy lending.

2:   Anticipate changes in the marketplace.

In an age where change is not incremental, and emerging businesses on the Internet are out to destroy established corporations, one can't afford to sit on the sidelines. Connecting with customers and being flexible as an executive are key aspects to developing new ideas for businesses. Customers are a resource in this endeavor. No matter how much travel is involved, there is no substitute for meeting face-to-face with clients and drawing out their ideas like Ann Winblad does every day while overseeing Hummer Winblad Venture Partners.

3:   Use traditional feminine qualities like empathy, collaboration, and cooperation.

Just as power suits with shoulder pads no longer spell success for women, playing up female talents, once considered a disadvantage, is no longer taboo. In fact, management gurus like Tom Peters and Robert Cooper increasingly advise executives to adopt female characteristics. Coordinating, supporting, and nurturing employees are the new directives for managers. The classic female view that one strengthens oneself by empowering others is finding greater acceptance and is emerging as a valuable leadership quality for gleaning better results from employees. Business theorist Robert Naisbitt wrote, "No longer is a manager a barking boss who is a know-it all. . . . We have to think about the manager as teacher, as mentor, as resource developer of human potential."[5] As Marilyn Carlson Nelson of Carlson Companies has found, women have natural abilities to cooperate with those around them who are an asset in today's team-oriented workplace.

4:   Sell your own vision.

Towing the corporate mantra is passé in business. Women who come to the fore today have their own sense of vision for the companies they lead and the will to drive a strategy to meet those goals. Like Orit Gadiesh, one must be able to articulate a vision in a compelling way that persuades colleagues to say, "Sign me up."

5:   Reinvent the rules.

Whatever you do, don't follow the rules of your business. Like Meg Whitman, leaders who excel today are creating new industries by rewriting their job descriptions every second of the day. Whitman was no technology expert, but she has proven she has the skills to make an Internet business soar. On-line auctions barely existed before she came along and built eBay into a household name through her marketing savvy and compelling message to consumers. Prizing innovation and breaking into new markets are par for the course.

6:   Stay focused on achieving your goals.

New paradigm leaders like Rebecca Mark share an ability to identify and hone in on opportunities that others simply do not see, then excel by navigating uncharted territory with a clear focus on achievement. Look globally for opportunities in countries far afield in high-risk economies. For instance, Mark saw a chance to wildly increase energy company Enron's fortunes by launching a risky but potentially high-return project in India, the world's second most populous country. The project fell victim to sabotage and international politics, but Mark kept her eyes on the prize, maintaining contact with key individuals to get the project back on track, and even expand it.

7:   Maximize high touch in an era of high tech.

Put time and energy into building partnerships by relating to managers, colleagues, and customers in a personal way. Often, just saying thank you for thoughtful advice or a business opportunity is enough to leave a lasting impression. An ability to produce good work and to connect with people has helped Shelly Lazarus define her remarkable career in advertising. That mixture has helped her win new business, and is a prescription for all young leaders in the making.

8:   *Turn challenge into opportunity.*

Tackling an unprofitable division takes a strong stomach, but new paradigm leaders like Patricia Russo know that the key to success is taking bold action and winning the cooperation of employees. Some of the best opportunities for advancement are those in which others have failed. Taking those chances can be a ticket to the top.

9:   *Obsess about customer preferences.*

In the Information Age, knowing your customer has a whole new meaning. One must get to know customers well enough to think like them. And luring new customers has an entirely different meaning. Patricia Fili-Krushel went against conventional wisdom in the television business to appeal to a mass audience rather than targeting a niche age group and revamping an outdated genre with her hit show *Who Wants to Be a Millionaire.* She revitalized ABC as a result. Rising executives have to adopt a similarly open attitude to attract new customers.

10:   *Fight back with courage under fire.*

Any bold idea is bound to encounter stiff opposition, but standing up to opponents is a necessary skill for new paradigm leaders. When she took over Ingram Industries after her husband's death, Martha Ingram had the strength to take on powerful rivals and take courageous and counterintuitive steps to run her business. She not only unseated his number two, but took a different route from her husband by splitting up the distribution conglomerate. She even took a unit of the company public. For young women rising through the ranks, this vital skill for overcoming resistance is vital to success.

STEPPING INTO THE MILLENNIUM

With all these new paradigm leaders around us, there is no doubt that the women rising today represent a new approach to leadership that is sure to gain many more converts in the new millennium. Gaining stature in companies and leading in their own way, these women are seeing their new brand of leadership validated in the most sincere way: imitation. Women will increasingly come to lay down the rules for how to manage corporations in this new age as the skills and characteristics they possess are best suited for today's world. Although many women still complain that their biggest deterrent in rising to the top stems from their gender, the prominent female executives in this book have been able to draw on their strengths as women to excel. And they are role models not just for women but for men, too.

By exploring the leadership qualities of some of the best female business leaders in the country, and drawing on lessons learned, this book is intended to offer some tools and strategies for readers to apply in their own search for success at work and career satisfaction. There is no substitute for experience, and the women featured here provide that knowledge and hard-won advice. With their insights in mind, just imagine what you can do.

NOTES

CHAPTER 1

1. U.S. Department of Labor, Women's Bureau, *1993 Handbook on Woman Workers: Trends and Issues* (Washington, D.C.: U.S. Department of Labor, 1993), pp. 32, 98.

2. Susan Faludi, *Backlash: The Undeclared War Against American Women* (New York: Anchor Books Doubleday, 1991), p. 367.

3. Peter Krauss, ed., *The Book of Leadership Wisdom* (New York: John Wiley & Sons, 1998), p. 448.

4. James Champy, *Reengineering Management: The Mandate for New Leadership* (New York: HarperBusiness, 1995), p. 21.

CHAPTER 2

1. *Forbes*, 18 February 1991, p. 67.

2. *Consultants News*, June 1999, Kennedy Information LLC, Fitzwilliam, New Hampshire, p. 6.

3. *Fortune*, 15 January 1996, p. 74.

4. *Fortune*, "The 50 Most Powerful Women in American Business," 25 October 1999, p. 106.

5. *Consulting*, June/July 1999, p. 18.

6. Betty Lehan Harragan, *Games Mother Never Taught You* (New York: Warner Books, 1977), p. 43.

7.   Sally Helgesen, *The Female Advantage* (New York: Currency, Doubleday, 1990), p. 225.

8.   *Management Consultancy*, 2 June 1999, p. 40.

9.   Ibid.

10. *Los Angeles Times*, 26 October 1999, p. C1.

11. *Fortune*, "The 50 Most Powerful Women in American Business," 12 October 1998, p. 83.

12. PriceWaterhouse Coopers LLP, *Money Tree Report*, Fourth Quarter 1998 and Full Year Results, p. 1.

13. Helgesen, *The Female Advantage*, p. 235.

14. *San Francisco Chronicle*, 23 July 1998, p. D3.

15. *Wired*, September 1996, p. 145.

16. Ibid., p. 210.

CHAPTER 3

1.   *USA Today*, 5 February 1999, p. A1.

2.   *New York Times*, 10 May 1999, p. C1.

3.   American Association of University Women, *Shortchanging Girls, Shortchanging America* (Washington, D.C.: American Association of University Women, 1991), Executive Summary, p. 7.

4.   Dr. Sally Morgan Reis, *Work Left Undone: Choices and Compromises of Talented Females* (Mansfield Center, Conn.: Creative Learning Press, 1998), p. 38.

5.   Kate White, *Why Good Girls Don't Get Ahead, but Gutsy Girls Do* (New York: Warner Books, 1995), pp. 5–6.

6.   Sally Helgesen, *The Female Advantage* (New York: Currency, Doubleday, 1990), p. 39.

7.   Marcus Buckingham and Curt Coffman, *First, Break All the Rules: What the World's Greatest Managers Do Differently* (New York: Simon & Schuster, 1999), p. 11.

8. *New York Times,* 25 July 1997, p. D1.

9. *Washington Post,* 13 May 1997, p. D1.

10. *New York Times,* 25 July 1997, p. D1.

11. *USA Today,* 9 August 1993, p. 2B.

12. *Forbes,* 30 August 1993, p. 40.

13. Buckingham and Coffman, *First, Break All the Rules,* p. 177.

14. *Forbes,* 12 October 1998, p. 328.

15. *Forbes,* 22 February 1999, pp. 116–17.

16. *Time,* 23 September 1996, p. 69.

17. *Wall Street Journal,* 19 April 1999, p. B1.

CHAPTER 4

1. *Fortune,* 8 September 1997, p. 62.

2. *Executive Female,* May 1991, p. 37.

3. *Fortune,* 12 October 1998, p. 84, and 25 October 1999, p. 106.

4. Virginia Valian, *Why So Slow? The Advancement of Women* (Cambridge, Mass.: MIT Press, 1999), pp. 191–92.

5. Connie Bruck, *The Predators' Ball: The Inside Story of Drexel Burnham and the Rise of the Junk Bond Raiders* (New York: Pelican Books, 1989), p. 99.

6. *Fortune,* 8 September 1997, p. 63.

7. *Fortune,* 12 October 1998, p. 83, and 25 October 1999, p. 106.

8. *New York Times,* 27 June 1999, p. B1.

9. Ibid.

10. *The Independent* (London), 23 June 1999, p. B4.

11. *Forbes,* 18 May 1998, p. 146.

12. Sally Helgesen, *The Female Advantage* (New York: Currency, Doubleday, 1990), p. 244.

13. *Wall Street Journal*, 5 February 1999, p. A6.

14. Dr. Sally Morgan Reis, *Work Left Undone: Choices and Compromises of Talented Females* (Mansfield Center, Conn.: Creative Learning Press, 1998), pp. 37–38.

CHAPTER 5

1. *Fortune*, 12 October 1998, p. 83, and 25 October 1999, p. 105.

2. Ibid.

3. Marcus Buckingham and Curt Coffman, *First, Break All the Rules: What the World's Greatest Managers Do Differently* (New York: Simon & Schuster, 1999), p. 112.

4. *Fortune*, 24 May 1999, p. 153.

5. *Houston Chronicle*, 30 May 1999, p. A1.

6. *Cleveland Plain Dealer*, 28 February 1999, p. 1G.

7. *American Demographics Journal*, July 1999, p. 30.

8. *New York Times*, 19 February 1997, p. D1.

9. *Forbes*, 25 October 1993, p. 194.

10. Ibid.

11. *BusinessWeek*, 17 August 1998, p. 52.

CHAPTER 6

1. *Fortune*, 12 October 1998, p. 86, and 25 October 1999, p. 105.

2. Noel M. Tichy with Eli Cohen, *The Leadership Engine: How Winning Companies Build Leaders at Every Level* (New York: HarperBusiness, 1997), p. 239.

3. *Orlando Sentinel*, 22 March 1995, p. B1.

4. *Chicago Tribune*, 6 June 1995, p. B1.

5. *National Post*, 6 January 1999, p. C13.

6.   *Business Communications Review*, January 1992, p. 22.

7.   *Business Communications Review*, January 1993, p. 32.

8.   *Business Communications Review*, January 1995, p. 25.

9.   *International Herald Tribune*, 24 July 1999, Finance, p. 9.

10. *Forbes*, 12 January 1998, p. 168.

11. *Forbes*, 10 January 2000, p. 136.

CHAPTER 7

1.   James Champy, *Reengineering Management* (New York: HarperBusiness, 1995), p. 76.

2.   Thomas Petzinger, Jr., *The New Pioneers* (New York: Simon & Schuster, 1999), p. 78.

3.   Dr. Jean Baker Miller, *Toward a New Psychology of Women* (Boston: Beacon Press, 1986), p. 43.

4.   *MacUser*, October 1997, p. 24.

5.   *San Francisco Examiner*, 21 September 1997, p. B9.

6.   *New York Times*, 14 November 1999, p. 36.

7.   *Forbes*, 20 March 2000, p. 168.

8.   *New York Times*, 14 November 1999, p. 36.

9.   Ibid.

10. *Fortune*, 1 March 1999, pp. 140–48.

11. Robert H. Reid, *Architects of the Web* (New York: John Wiley & Sons, 1997), p. 102.

CHAPTER 8

1.   *BusinessWeek*, 29 September 1997, p. 65.

2.   *Fortune*, 29 September 1997, p. 175.

3.   *Los Angeles Times*, 7 March 2000, p. C1.

4.   *Black Enterprise*, June 1997, p. 86.

5.   *Forbes*, 21 October 1992, p. 254.

CHAPTER 9

1.   *Seattle Post-Intelligencer*, 3 January 2000, p. E1.

2.   *BusinessWeek*, 8 November 1999, p. 130.

3.   *Investor's Business Daily*, 2 January 1997, p. A1.

4.   *Forbes*, 30 December 1996, p. 104.

5.   Robert Naisbitt and Patricia Aburdene, *Megatrends* (New York: Warner Books, 1984), pp. 60–61.

INDEX